McDonnell Douglas Douglas DC-9

By Terry Waddington

Great
AIRLINERS
SERIES

Volume Four

AUTHOR'S NOTES

The author and publisher acknowledge that the DC-9 was originally designed and built by Douglas Aircraft Company which was subsequently merged into McDonnell Douglas Corporation (MDC). After the merger, the new corporation continued to create new versions of the DC-9. In 1997, MDC was absorbed into the Boeing Company. However, for historical accuracy, the titles Douglas or McDonnell Douglas DC-9 have been retained throughout this book as the companies responsible for all relevant major design changes where applicable.

© 1998 by Terry Waddington
All rights reserved.
ISBN 0-9626730-9-9
First Edition June 1998
Printed and bound in Hong Kong

All information contained in this volume is accurate at the time of publication.

Series Editor: Jon Proctor

Book and cover design by Randy Wilhelm, Keokee Company, Sandpoint, Idaho
Copy Editors: Fred Chan and Billie Jean Plaster

Front cover photo courtesy of McDonnell Douglas Corporation
Title page photo courtesy of Roy Lock
Back cover photos courtesy of McDonnell Douglas Corporation
Inside back cover photo courtesy of McDonnell Douglas Corporation

Unless otherwise indicated, non-captioned photos are courtesy of McDonnell Douglas Corporation

The Great Airliners series:

TABLE OF CONTENTS

APPENDICES

ACKNOWLEDGMENTS

Though "I was there" almost from the start of the DC-9 program, I could not have recalled all that went on without the memories and insights of many others who worked on the "Compact Jet." Once again, my good friend Harry Gann was in the lead in assisting me in searching through the historical files. The writer is indebted to many other former fellow Douglas employees who were closely associated with the DC-9 and contributed information and other forms of help. These included Bob Archer, Jim Burton, John Burton, Bob Goforth, George Goumas, Jerry Kingsley, Bill Loesche, Herb Mailander, Gerry Markgraf, Mike Machat, Brian Parkinson, the late Paul Patten, John Rapillo, Jeff Richards and Roger Schaufele.

Credit should also be given to the company photographers, in particular the late Dewey Smith who, over the years, produced many striking air-to-air photographs. I wish to thank the Douglas Products Division for the generous help I received from Jim Kline, Eric Macklin, Pat McGinnis and Don Hanson.

My fellow slide collectors again allow me to present a colorful array of interesting and unusual paint schemes worn by DC-9s. These friends of many years include Andy Absher, Avimage, Jeff Burch, Eddy Gual, Malcolm Gualt, Martin Hornlimman, Paul Huxford, Clay Jansson, Peter Keating, Eric Legendre, Roy Lock, Jean Magendie, Malcolm Nason, Hans Oehninger, Mike Rathke, Harry Sievers, Bob Smith, Brian Stainer, Martin Stamm, Gary Vincent, John Wegg, Udo Weisse, and Tim Williams. In addition, many people that I have associated with at the annual and regional Airliners International conventions were the source of many slides. My sincere apologies to you if your name was omitted.

Jon Proctor has again been my guide and friend in getting this project brought to conclusion in a timely and painless manner and helped me chase down numerous details that I couldn't find elsewhere. My particular thanks go to Victor Archer for his superb color profiles of DC-9 projects.

Somehow, the new title "Boeing DC-9" does not sound right, so in view of the recent merger and the sad demise of the McDonnell Douglas name, I respectfully dedicate this book to all the people who helped to make the DC-9 Series a successful program.

Royalties from this book will be donated to charities in recognition of my long-time friend and fellow ex-"Dougloid" John Collins, whom I can never adequately repay.

Terry Waddington
Roseburg, Oregon

4

INTRODUCTION

Commencing in the 1930s, Douglas Aircraft Company became one of the most influential developers of modern day air transport, starting with the famous DC-1 through DC-3 series. Wartime gave Douglas the opportunity to develop the C-54 transport, which became the DC-4 and went on to sire a series of larger, faster four-engine transports culminating in the DC-7C.

Although the company looked fleetingly at the next natural progression, the turbine propeller-driven aircraft, the rapid advancement of pure jet engine development convinced Donald Douglas, Sr. and his experienced design team to forego the intermediate plateau and move directly into developing jet airliners.

The tough decision to proceed alone on the DC-8 program in 1956 almost bankrupted the firm, and costly development programs delayed a return to corporate profitability for an extended period of time. But, in the end, the Douglas tradition of "getting it right" has paid off with over half the production run of 556 aircraft still in service more than 30 years later.

In spite of the company's reputation for building sound economic aircraft, Mr. Douglas had to endure "betting the company" a second time, unique in the annals of the aviation industry, when it launched the DC-9 program without any firm commitments in 1963. In this case, Douglas had seen the need for a short-range jet capable of making multiple stops without refueling and with much lower operating costs than the piston-powered aircraft then serving this market.

The program was so outstanding from the outset that eventually its own success forced the company to merge in order to survive. Several diverse factors brought this about and, unfortunately the most critical were outside of the company's control. But an ensuing merger with the McDonnell Aircraft Corporation rescued the DC-9 program which developed into a still continuing production run of more than 2,250 aircraft.

In 1955, while addressing an audience in San Francisco, Donald Douglas, Sr. stated:

Donald Douglas, Sr. and grandson Jamie try out the DC-9. (via Bob Goforth)

"I have great faith in aviation and in the future .... the airplane will come into its own. It will transport most everyone and everything from every place to everywhere."

Mr. Douglas didn't say so, but perhaps he had the DC-9 Family in mind.

Chapter I
EARLY DESIGNS

The proposed twin-engine DC-9 of 1947

As the end of World War II approached, Douglas, in parallel with most of the aircraft industry, began to think about new programs to keep the company busy in the forthcoming years. The demand for military aircraft was expected to drop off drastically as, aside from Winston Churchill, few foresaw the specter of what became known as the "Cold War" in the immediate postwar years. The heavy usage of transport aircraft, such as the Douglas C-47, C-54 and, latterly, the Lockheed C-69 Constellation during the war had amply demonstrated that travel by air and movement of priority cargo, both on domestic and intercontinental routes, were the future means of transportation.

Douglas believed that the biggest near-term requirement was to find a successor to the DC-3/C-47, which was marginally economical, and had begun design studies for its eventual replacement. Initially, the studies centered on the concept that became known as the DC-8 Skybus. A twin-engine, 48 seater, it was powered by two Allison V-1710-125 piston engines which were to drive contra-rotating propellers located at the rear end of the fuselage. (See Great Airliners Series Vol. 2 for further details).

Meanwhile, Consolidated Vultee designed and flew a more conventional looking aircraft, the unpressurized, low-wing Model 110, fitted with a tricycle undercarriage. Designed to carry 30 passengers, it first flew on July 8, 1946. The type never entered production but was the forerunner of what became the 40-seat Convair 240 series, the first production twin-engine airliner to be pressurized. It first flew on March 16, 1947, and initially entered service with American Airlines on June 1, 1948. The Glenn L. Martin Company had also entered the competition with its unpressurized Martin 2-0-2 that made its maiden flight in November 1946 and entered service with Northwest Airlines in September 1947. However, it did not compete well due to the lack of pressurization, poor performance and structural problems, so was subsequently re-designed and became the Martin 4-0-4, entering service with TWA on October 5, 1951.

A belated attempt to recover the situation was undertaken in July 1947 when Douglas proposal TS1119, labeled DC-9, was presented to the airlines as a DC-3 replacement. This design was similar in layout and size to the

6

CV-240, though it carried only 28 passengers versus 40 on the Convair. Powered by two 1,400 hp Wright R-1820 or two Pratt & Whitney R-2180, 1,600 hp engines, it was designed to cruise at 250 mph at 11,000 feet. Its 790-U.S. gallon (USG) fuel capacity, stored in the inner wing sections, would have given it a range of 1,510 miles with full reserves at its Maximum Takeoff Weight (MTOW) of 30,000 pounds. An additional 550 USG in the outer wing tanks extended the range to 2,460 miles with a 4,740-pound payload. The aircraft required a 3,640-foot runway length. Pressurization and cabin cooling were offered as optional extras. But with the Convair 240 and the Martin 2-0-2 already in service and carrying more passengers, it attracted little attention from potential customers and was soon discarded.

TS1119 Specifications

Wing Span	.101 ft
Overall length	.75 ft 8 in
Overall height	.25 ft 4 in
Fuselage diameter	.9 ft 8 in
MTOW	.30,000 lb
MLW	.29,000 lb
Empty Weight	.19,594 lb
Capacity	.28 Passengers & Cargo
Payload	.7,000 lb

Douglas essentially abandoned the DC-3 replacement competition and elected to concentrate most of its energy on the bigger market potential offered by developing the DC-4/6/7 family. However, a program was initiated to modify existing DC-3s to meet the new airworthiness requirements promulgated by U.S. Civil Aviation Administration. This resulted in the Super DC-3 which, in spite of an intensive marketing effort, found little interest from the commercial airlines.

The Turboprop is Considered

The DC-9 designation re-appeared in the mid-1950s when a turbo-prop powered aircraft, similar to the Lockheed 188 Electra layout was being considered. In addition, the U.S. Navy was looking for a long-range patrol aircraft in a similar configuration. It featured the now familiar double-bubble fuselage cross section to give adequate headroom in the baggage holds. However, this program was abandoned when design efforts were concentrated on a simultaneously running four-engine jetliner project that was to become the DC-8. Comparison of contemporary artist's sketches of this proposal with the initial DC-8 project of 1953 would suggest that the fuselage design was essentially common to both studies.

With the launch of the company-funded DC-8 program on June 7, 1955, development studies on most other commercial airliner projects were reduced to a minimum effort. Donald Douglas, Sr. was virtually "betting the company" and thus had little capital available to develop a new aircraft for the growing short-to-medium-range market. The medium-to-long-haul market was being served by large fleets of DC-6Bs, DC-7s and various models of the Lockheed Constellation while the Convair, Martin and Douglas DC-3 propliners handled the shorter routes. A small advance design team did continue to explore new aircraft development to keep abreast of a rapidly growing demand for more advanced aircraft for these burgeoning markets. Douglas had to do this because the competition was improving the standards of air transportation at a breathtaking pace. To put things in perspective, it is worth recalling some of the notable advances that were taking place in the 1950s.

The British company, de Havilland Aircraft, had started the movement when it first flew the Comet I, a medium-range, 36-seat jet airliner designed to serve the African and Asian routes (via the Middle East), on July 27, 1949. It was followed by Vickers Armstrong initiating production of the Viscount four-engine turboprop airliner with an order for 20 aircraft from British European Airways (BEA) in August 1950. Just a over a year later, in October 1951, the French government asked its national aircraft manufacturing companies to make proposals for a medium-range jetliner capable of serving the French possessions in North and West Africa nonstop from Paris. Meanwhile, Vickers had begun to breach the North American market when Trans-Canada Airlines (TCA) ordered 15 Viscounts in November 1952. The American market was penetrated by the Viscount in June 1954 when Capital Airlines placed its initial order.

By the time the DC-8 was formally launched, on June 7, 1955, the Sud Aviation Caravelle had already flown two weeks earlier on May 28. In Russia, the first Tu-104 completed its maiden flight on June 17 and subsequently inaugurated service on September 15, 1956. American Airlines kicked off Lockheed's 188 Electra program with an order for 35 aircraft just three days after the DC-8 announcement, and Capital became the first U.S. airline to operate turbine-powered aircraft with Viscount service between Washington D.C. and New York City on July 26, 1955.

The 1953 DC-9 four-engine turboprop proposal was in parallel with the original DC-8 program, utilizing the same fuselage.

Over the next two years, the idea of serving short-range markets with jet aircraft developed rapidly, particularly in Europe. Air France launched the Caravelle program in early 1956 with an order for 12 aircraft and a British company, Hunting Aviation, revealed designs for a twin-engine jetliner, with aft-mounted engines and a tail configuration similar to the Caravelle, intended for operation from small airfields. Shortly afterwards, in May 1956, British European Airways (BEA), so as not to be left behind the Caravelle in the European arena, ordered the Comet IVB, an advanced, stretched version of the original ill-fated Comet.

The only other active jet transport in this class during the era was the East German-built Vereinegung Volkseigener Betriebe (VEB) BB-152, a four-engine type intended to seat 72 passengers. It first flew on December 4, 1958, but crashed shortly thereafter and development was curtailed.

The Mini-DC-8

In August 1956, at the request of Pan Am's Latin American Division, Douglas engineers proposed a scaled-down DC-8 powered by either Pratt & Whitney J-52 (JT3D) or J-79 engines. Initially known as Project 2000, and later called the DC-9, it was also shown to Swissair and Scandinavian Airlines (SAS) and other European airlines along with Japan Air Lines (JAL) and American Airlines. The engine selected centered on the Pratt & Whitney JT4A-5, but a new power plant, the JT8A-2 was offered to JAL, UAT and United Air Lines. A new entrant appeared in the competition when BEA placed an order for 24 deHavilland Trident I tri-jets on February 24, 1958, even though the size of the aircraft had not been finalized. In June 1959, Douglas announced targeted deliveries in 1961 for its DC-9.

Short-to-medium-range market competition heated up in 1959. Eastern Air Lines (EAL) introduced the 188 Electra into commercial service on January 12 between New York-Idlewild and Miami, just ahead of American which was suffering the effects of a strike at the time. In May Air

France inaugurated Caravelle services. Meanwhile, Boeing had begun designing a 50- to 60-seat twin-jet airliner designated the 727, but was also studying three- and four-engine airliners for the medium-range market.

In June, yet another power plant was being considered; this time it was the Pratt & Whitney JTF10A-1 "fan" engine which had a static thrust of 8,259 pounds and a fuel-burn rate 10 percent less than the JT3D power plant. A study using this engine was shown to European and American carriers shortly afterwards and, for a while, Northwest Orient Airlines took a strong interest in this version. The objective of the design was to replace the DC-6B, which was used as the yardstick for performance and size requirements.

The new DC-9 project, Model 2067, was made public on June 15, 1959, in a letter sent by Donald Douglas, Jr. to the presidents of 40 airlines, offering certificated deliveries in early 1963, provided that a minimum commitment for 75 to 100 aircraft was received. It featured the cockpit section of the DC-8 and utilized the same constant fuselage upper lobe cross-section (132-inch diameter) of the original 1953 DC-8 proposal because it was intended that the same Douglas-designed "Palomar" integrated seats would be installed. (Production DC-8 fuselage diameters were later increased to 147 inches.)

However, as sectors would not be as long as an average DC-8 flight, the seat pitch was reduced from 40 to 38 inches. Spacing of the fuselage frames and windows was adjusted accordingly. Sixty-eight first-class passengers would be accommodated in four-abreast seats, whereas 96 coach-class passengers would be seated five abreast. Entry was via a forward door with a manually operated integral airstair for rapid turnaround at intermediate stops. A rear entry required "roll-up" ramps to be used at major airports. The interior of the cabin measured 71 feet long, 124 inches wide and 81 inches high.

Though the DC-9 resembled a scaled down DC-8 in general design, there were some significant changes, particularly to the wing. The 30-degree

Artist's impression of the 1959 version of the DC-9 also identified as Model 2067.

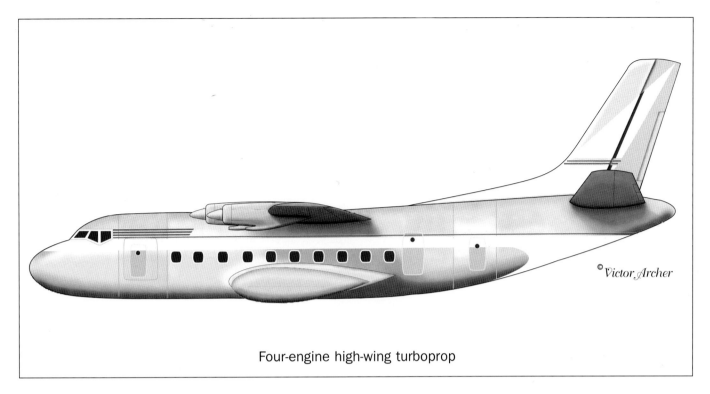

Four-engine high-wing turboprop

wing sweep-back and basic airfoil section were similar to the DC-8 with some modifications in cross section at the root and outer panels to reduce drag. The biggest change was the addition of full-span leading-edge slats which activated in conjunction with the flaps, allowing the DC-9 to operate from smaller airfields than the DC-6. Another aerodynamic difference was that the engine pylons were attached to the underside of the wing only. Aside from cockpit commonality to reduce manufacturing costs, regulations at that time mandated that any aircraft over an MTOW of 80,000 pounds operate with a three-man crew. Many of the systems had components common to the DC-8.

The Model 2067 would have a 120,000-pound MTOW, giving it a range of 2,325 statute miles in an all first-class configuration. Takeoff distance at sea level on a standard day was 6,030 feet. Cruise speeds were similar to the DC-8. Because the design had a high Maximum Landing Weight (MLW), the aircraft could stop at an intermediate point and fly another 730-mile sector, carrying full reserves and payload, without refueling. Break-even costs were calculated to be at a 66-percent load factor over a 500-mile sector and 48.5 percent over a 1,000-mile trip. The estimated price for the DC-9 was around $3 million. However, the major airlines around the world were still absorbing the cost of new DC-8s, 707s, Caravelles and Electras. Also, large fleets of comparatively new DC-6s and DC-7s had been relegated to the routes for which the proposed DC-9 was intended, so little serious interest was forthcoming.

In November 1960 Boeing launched the three-engine 727-100 and on December 5 announced that contracts had been signed with United Air Lines and Eastern Air Lines for 40 aircraft each. Both the 727 and DC-9 had similar payload/range performance, but the three-engine Boeing offered better seat/mile costs. Douglas could not afford to go ahead without firm orders, so the 2067 project was quietly dropped shortly afterwards.

DC-3 Replacement

As mentioned earlier, one portion of the market that continued to attract Douglas was a turboprop aircraft to replace the DC-3 and early Martins over short sectors. A small group of engineers continued to produce studies of an aircraft capable of being operated as a combination passenger freighter.

In March 1957 the company released details of Project 1940, a four-engine, high-wing aircraft powered by either four Lycoming T55s or Rolls-Royce Dart 510 engines. Designed to carry 60 passengers seated six abreast at the standard 40-inch pitch, it could be rapidly converted to a mixed-passenger-freight configuration capable of carrying 18 passengers and 10,000 pounds of cargo. The forward portion of the cabin floor was strengthened and fitted with cargo tie-downs. Seats in this area were designed to fold and be removed for stowage in main-deck luggage compartments. A movable partition could be positioned in 40-inch increments to separate cargo from the passengers who would board via a left-rear cabin door. Cargo loading was through a 48-inch-by-60-inch upward opening door on the forward right side; provision was made for a larger 75-inch-by-60-inch door if needed.

A second all-cargo version, designated Project 1940A, featured rear-loading doors with the sill located so that a truck bed 50 inches high could be backed up to it to facilitate loading. The cargo compartment had a floor width of 116 inches, height of 98 inches and length of 220 inches. Both versions had a nose wheel capable of castering 360 degrees to allow easy maneuvering in tight areas. The cargo version could be fitted with skis on all three wheels; the wheels would protrude below the skis for operational flexibility.

To achieve the required short-field performance, the wing was fitted with full span 15-percent chord leading-edge slats and full-span, double-slotted 40-percent chord trailing-edge flaps. The wing span was 102.5 feet with a 1,300 square-foot wing area. The 92.5-foot fuselage had a maximum diameter of 152 inches and the tail was 36.8 feet high. Design MTOW was 65,500 pounds with an MLW of 59,100 pounds, allowing multiple short sectors to be flown without refueling.

Fuel capacity was 4,000 gallons. The Model 1940 required a field length of 2,300 feet for takeoff and 3,000 feet for a maximum-weight landing with a 50-degree-flap setting. It could carry a 15,000-pound payload over 550 miles or 10,000 pounds over 1,075 miles.

This effort, considered secondary to the "Mini-DC-8" project, was intended to be a fall-back in the event that the jet's program was canceled. It would have been re-designated as the DC-9 if produced. If both projects had come to fruition, it would have been identified as the DC-10. However, the project did not go forward because, again, it was believed that the future lay in jet-powered transports.

Chapter II

MODEL 2086

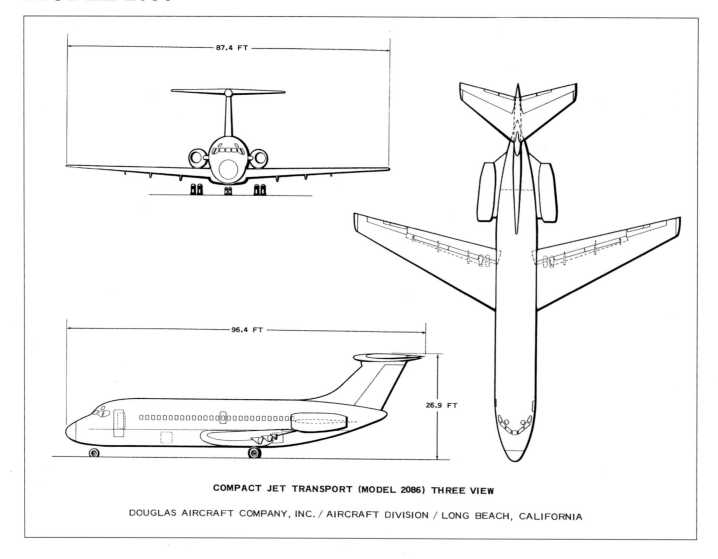

COMPACT JET TRANSPORT (MODEL 2086) THREE VIEW

DOUGLAS AIRCRAFT COMPANY, INC. / AIRCRAFT DIVISION / LONG BEACH, CALIFORNIA

The Caravelle Interlude

In a major effort to penetrate the American market with its Caravelle, Sud Aviation decided to offer a General Electric (GE) CJ805-23B-powered version as an alternative to the Rolls-Royce Avon. A single aircraft was purchased by GE on January 7, 1960, and converted to the newer power plants.

It made good sense when Douglas and Sud signed a cooperative agreement on February 10, 1960. The four-engine DC-9 project had failed to attract support and the initial DC-8 sales surge slowed down as airlines absorbed re-equipment costs, so Douglas needed to find additional work with minimal development investments. The terms called for Douglas to be responsible for sales and technical support of the Caravelle in areas outside Europe or any French-speaking regions worldwide. The arrangement also stipulated that should demand for the Caravelle exceed Sud's manufacturing capacity of approximately eight aircraft per month, a separate production line would be set up at Long Beach.

United Air Lines became the first and only North American carrier to operate the Caravelle, signing a contract for 20 firm plus 20 options on February 26. Douglas managed to sign a letter of intent with TWA in February 1961 for 20 Caravelles. However, TWA later canceled its

Douglas-financed order in June 1962 and purchased a fleet of Boeing 727s to be more competitive with Eastern and American.

The small Douglas advance design team continued to look at new layouts and market requirements, its primary target being the replacement of the Convairs and Martins on 300- to 500-mile stage lengths. Two separate approaches were explored in parallel. One team pursued a conventional design with a pylon-mounted engine beneath each wing while the second group worked on a rear-engined, T-tail design. This approach allowed the horizontal surfaces to act as an end plate, thus allowing a shorter vertical stabilizer. Both projects were designed to the same parameters of size, weight, range and payload with two engine choices being considered, either Pratt & Whitney 10,000-pound static thrust JTF10A-2 turbofans or Rolls-Royce RB163-2 "Spey" engines which developed 10,400 pounds of thrust. At the time, the JTF10A engine was being developed for the military TFX program, later known as the F-111A. A preliminary test engine was flown beneath a North American B-45 bomber mounted in a pod attached to the bomb-bay roof.

In the final review of the two designs by Don Douglas, Sr., both proposals met the specification regardless of the engine selected. Mr. Douglas was not very keen on the T-tail concept but became persuaded by the argument that passenger appeal would be greatly enhanced by the

Boeing investigated rear-mounted engine layouts during its early 737 design phase. Shown in model form is a 1965 study which included six-abreast seating and would have met the 70,000-pound MTOW rule for a two-man cockpit. (Boeing Archives via Brian Baum)

The "loser" proposal in the final DC-9 competition looks like a twin-engine version of the Model 2067, but the wing planform has changed significantly. (Courtesy of John Burton)

quieter cabin resulting from aft-mounted engines. In addition, there were several aerodynamic advantages to the T-tail approach that were confirmed by wind tunnel tests.

ENGINE LOCATION	AFT (T-tail)	WING (Low-tail)
Gross wing area (Sq.Ft)	1,001	1,100
Max Lift Coefficient	3.00	2.71
Efficient High Speed Cruise (Mach)	0.80/0.82	0.74/0.76
Nacelle/Wing Interference Drag	None	Severe

A large, wing-mounted nacelle eliminated part of the wing flap, increasing approach speeds and created unpredicted drag which increased with the Mach Number rise. The close-in engines would also minimize any yaw tendency when one engine was shut down.

Enter the BAC 1-11

United introduced the Caravelle into U.S. domestic service on Bastille Day, July 14, 1961. However, it was not the first Caravelle service to operate in the United States. That distinction went to Brazil's flag carrier, VARIG, with a multi-stop service to New York from Rio de Janeiro commencing on October 2, 1959.

In England, the Hunting 107 design was developing rapidly. Hunting had been merged into the British Aircraft Corporation during February 1960, and the design renamed BAC 107. A significant design change was the relocation of the horizontal stabilizer to the top of the fin. The project continued to grow and, in March 1961, the BAC 1-11 was announced, followed shortly afterwards by an initial order for 10 aircraft from British United Airways. Success for the One-Eleven in the U.S. market came on October 20, 1961, with an order from Braniff for six plus six options.

Also in October 1961, Douglas announced that it was showing airlines a study for a small short-range airliner designed to operate over sectors of between 300 and 500 miles, but was able to fly stage lengths of up to 1,000 miles as well. The aircraft was identified as the Project 2086. Soon the Douglas-Sud relationship cooled and was amicably terminated. There were several reasons for the breakup. Douglas engineers believed that a number of design changes were required to make the Caravelle more acceptable to American customers.

The general feeling was that the aircraft was a match of older technology with jet engines, and Sud appeared reluctant to listen to the Douglas improvement suggestions. The minimal cargo capacity, unusual window shape and the lack of use of Skydrol in the hydraulic systems were cited as major reasons. In addition, there were concerns among some potential buyers over Sud's ability to maintain its delivery schedules. At the time, France was continually in political turmoil and national strikes were frequent events. More importantly, American Airlines and Trans-Canada executives told Douglas salesmen that they would prefer to see a totally new design to their own specifications.

There have been many suggestions that Douglas used the Caravelle to develop the DC-9. However, a quick comparison of the projected Model 2086 with the Caravelle should dispel that notion. The most important difference was that the two aircraft varied considerably in takeoff weight even though both were capable of carrying 77 coach-class passengers at a similar comfort level. The Caravelle's 110,000-pound MTOW dictated a three-man cockpit crew under U.S. Federal Air Regulations, whereas the Model 2086 at 69,000 pounds MTOW was well below the maximum 80,000-pound limit for a two-man crew.

The Caravelle could carry a payload of 17,420 pounds over a distance of 1,475 miles, while the Model 2086 was intended to carry a 16,000-pound (77 passengers and luggage) payload over 500 miles or fly 1,100 miles with just 56 first-class passengers and luggage (11,480 pounds). A contemporary Douglas market research study had shown that 55 percent of all U.S. domestic passengers flew an average sector of less than 400 miles and 80 percent flew less than 1,000 miles; this was the market that Douglas was aiming for. In addition, the Caravelle was generally larger in size, as shown in the following table.

	Caravelle 6R	Model 2086
Span	112 ft 6 in	84 ft 7 in
Length	105 ft	95 ft 3 in
Height	28 ft 7 in	25 ft 8 in
Fuselage Diameter	10 ft 4 in	10 ft 8 in

The original Model 2086 was primarily targeted at Eastern, which had shown strong interest in an aircraft of this category, though it preferred that the MTOW not exceed 65,000 pounds and wanted engine starting capability with the use of internal power. EAL managers voiced other unique requirements, including the ability to profitably operate over 100-mile stage-lengths; 727s would be used for the 350-mile sectors.

The 2086 was designed to carry a maximum of 77 passengers in five-abreast seating (34-inch seat pitch), 56 in first-class, or a variety of mixed-class combinations. Initially, boarding was through a door with built-in stairs located just forward of the wing on the port (left) side. A unique feature was a 65-cubic foot external pull-out rack stowed in the belly adjacent to the entrance. Used to hold carry-on baggage, it could be operated by one person. Passengers would deposit their carry-on bags as they boarded, then pick them up when deplaning.

From the outset, the 2086 design was such that stretched versions would be a natural progression as improved engine thrusts became available. Fuel would initially be carried only in the outer wings, leaving the center section empty for future range extensions. The main design criteria for the project were to keep the aircraft systems as simple as possible to hold down maintenance costs, provide ease of maintenance accessibility and use proven aerodynamic experience in the wing design. No leading edge devices were envisioned to assist low-speed handling.

Donald Douglas, Jr., by then President of Douglas Aircraft, met with several major U.S. airline management teams during January 1962 and drew expressions of interest from both Eastern and American. In addition, prime prospects included Trans-Canada Airlines, Delta, National and Continental; Trans Australia (TAA) and Ansett also showed strong interest after a visit by a Douglas sales team. Douglas announced in late January that it would build a full-size fuselage mock-up for customer evaluation. By then, the engine choice had centered on the advanced Pratt & Whitney JTF10A-6 turbofan, now rated at 10,500 pounds static thrust, though the Spey engine was still an optional choice. Referred to in company literature as the "Compact Jet," the Model 2086's direct operating costs were estimated to be 1.2 cents per seat-mile for a 74-seat all-coach class flight of 550 miles, ranging up to 2.2 cents per seat-mile for a 100-mile segment.

By April 11, a mock-up was completed and shown to the airlines and press, which immediately began to compare it with the BAC 1-11. The only major external change to the 2086 to be seen on the mock-up was that the entry door had been relocated to the forward end of the passenger cabin. Douglas officials announced an estimated sales price of $3 million per aircraft, which would be designated DC-9, with a target delivery date of late 1964. Production would not proceed until firm orders for at least 125 aircraft had been received. This was understandable because cash flow from the DC-8 program was tapering off as sales slumped and Douglas was concurrently burdened by the pre-production costs of the newer DC-8 Series 61 and 62 models.

The market estimate was for about 400 aircraft in this category over the ensuing five years, most of it in the U.S. domestic market. Douglas acknowledged that it stood little chance of making deep penetrations into some overseas markets because of the proliferation of European types in this category, both jet and turboprop, already in service or committed to production. In addition, strong British and French influence still remained in many parts of the world. Prior to the press conference, 35 airline management teams had viewed the mock-up and received technical and performance briefings.

A trade press comparison with the One-Eleven was to be expected as the two aircraft were about to enter head-on competition for business from several North American carriers, particularly American and Trans-Canada, which had similar requirements for a new short-range jet airliner. The fuselage cross-sections, although different in shape, (Douglas stuck to the "double bubble" design while BAC chose the circular section), offered comparable standards in seating arrangements. However, the Douglas layout allowed three more inches of headroom in the cabin and six more inches in the under-floor cargo compartment. Externally, the major dimensions were within a few feet of each other as can be seen below.

	Model 2086	BAC 1-11
Span:	87.4 ft	88.6 ft
Length:	96.4 ft	92.1 ft
Wing area:	925 sq ft	980 sq ft
Max Takeoff Wt:	69,000 lb	68,250 lb
Max Landing Wt:	65,800 lb	65,000 lb
Fuel Cap. (Imp Gals):	2,248	2,250
Takeoff Field Length:	5,020 ft	5,300 ft
Passengers:	55-77	56-70
Cargo Volume:	585 cu ft	500 cu ft

Mohawk Airlines announced an order for four BAC 1-11s on July 24, 1962. This created a great deal of furor because Mohawk, like all the other local service carriers, was a recipient of federal subsidies to provide air service to small communities. The Civil Aeronautics Bureau (later Board), (CAB) was concerned that the airline was operating at only a 48-percent load factor with smaller aircraft, hence the need for subsidy. Mohawk argued that using jets would reduce this dependence, but the idea of U.S. tax-payers supporting the purchase of foreign-built aircraft became a political hot potato.

In the early summer of 1962, American Airlines and Eastern entered into a series of exploratory talks to merge the two companies. Naturally, both airlines eased off on evaluation exercises for a short-haul jet until the outcome of the talks. This was quite a setback for Douglas as it urgently needed orders from several major carriers to launch the program. The CAB was eventually approached to evaluate and approve the American-Eastern merger, a lengthy process. American decided that merger or not, it would proceed with negotiations for 25 aircraft and, by August, was heavily engaged in discussions with Douglas and BAC again.

One major outcome of these renewed discussions was upgrading the Model 2086 into the Model 2086B. American was not satisfied with the takeoff performance of the JTF10 engine, so Pratt & Whitney offered a de-rated version of its new JT8D-1 engine (later identified as the JT8D-5), rated at 12,000 pounds thrust. This made sense because the JT8D-1 was being used as the engine in the new Boeing 727 tri-jet that American had ordered. The 2086B's overall length was increased from 96.4 feet to 100.3 feet via a substantial change to the rear fuselage and vertical stabilizer. The fin and rudder were now more swept back while the wing remained unchanged.

The JT8's added thrust level allowed the MTOW to increase to 77,000 pounds with an MLW of 73,350 pounds and a Zero Fuel Weight (ZFW) of 60,000 pounds. Because of the high allowable landing weight, the need for an emergency fuel dump system was eliminated. These improvements reduced the takeoff field length from 5,200 feet for the original 2086 proposal to 4,750 feet on the 2086B on an 86-degree (Fahrenheit) day with a full load. Cruise speed was increased from 530 mph to 560 mph. The weight-limited payload remained unchanged, though a number of interior configuration changes were proposed. The Palomar integrated seats were now replaced with a more conventional design, and the passenger service units were relocated above to the underside of the hat racks.

Trans-Canada also informed the two manufacturers that it was not satisfied with either the JTF10 or the RB163-2 engine takeoff performance.

At one point, the 14,000-pound JT8D-1 was considered, but the higher fuel burn rate would have taken the 2086 above the 80,000-pound MTOW criteria for pilot staffing. TCA was a "must win" case for Douglas. At a meeting in Montreal in August 1962, Douglas was informed that TCA was looking at both a two- and a three-type-fleet mix. If it chose only two, there would be a twin-jet plus DC-8 fleet, but if they elected to go with three types, the combination of 727s, DC-8s and Viscounts would require fewer additional DC-8s. The sales team had to convince TCA's management that the twin-jet should be a key component in its fleet plan.

Reginald "Reg" Ansett, chairman of Ansett Airlines, publicly stated that he would buy the Model 2086 provided that the MTOW was increased to 79,000 pounds but wanted it to be powered by Allison-built Rolls-Royce Spey engines. Trans Australia Airlines (TAA) also liked the aircraft, but preferred it to be somewhat lighter. This was significant because at that time, both carriers were required to operate identical services with similar equipment under Australian law. Both airlines saw the aircraft as a Viscount replacement. Additionally, several other airlines that had received presentations on the Model 2086B had indicated to Douglas "If you build it, we will buy it," though none rushed to place the deposits which the company so desperately needed.

During this period, Boeing's advance design team had also been quietly looking into the same small jet requirement, though not with the same urgency since it was heavily committed to the 727 and continued to improve the 707. Like Douglas, it considered several alternative designs including both a rear-engine twin-jet powered by the 727's Pratt & Whitney JT8D-1, and a proposal featuring an underwing engine location. It utilized the same six abreast-seating fuselage cross-section, carrying a maximum of 85 passengers, with an overall length of only 86 feet. The wing plan appeared to incorporate a scaled down 727 layout. Both designs were made public in November 1964 when the project was labeled as the 737 which was formally launched on February 19, 1965 with

an order from Lufthansa for the under wing-engine version featuring a two-man cockpit.

Tension Mounts

As the year end approached, pressure increased on Donald Douglas, Jr. to make a launch decision. Several North American airlines told Douglas that they were hesitant to place orders until a firm decision was made, and would not wait much longer before signing with BAC. American Airlines, which had a long and close relationship with the company dating back to the DC-2, was pushing Douglas to make a launch decision. It was known that American was leaning toward the One-Eleven, mainly because it was already in production and BAC was willing to offer a much improved version tailored to American's specifications.

In an effort to assist in making the launch decision, Douglas market researchers were continually refining their forecasts and identifying the best marketing opportunities. To give an idea of the potential market, the following table shows the inventory that was targeted for replacement in early 1963:

DC-4	310
Convair 240/340/440	416
Martin 4-0-4	104
Viscount	421
Total.	**1,251**

In addition, replacement of many DC-6s, DC-7s, Constellations and Electras were seen as long-term potential for a stretched airplane. Even without factoring in traffic growth, there was a substantial market large enough for two to three competitors to share.

The "Douglas-Sud" Caravelle demonstrator, N4209E, at Los Angeles in August 1960. (Bob Archer)

The Model 2086 mock-up in its revised configuration. Note the original airstair installation and pull-out bin for carry-on baggage just forward of the wing root.

Difficult Times

Some additional pressure on Douglas came in October 1962 when a second local service carrier, Bonanza Air Lines, applied for CAB approval to purchase BAC 1-11s. But this event paled when, in late December, Douglas suffered a totally unexpected crushing financial blow. President Kennedy announced that the government had decided to cancel the Douglas Skybolt program, a loss of $300 million in current business. Though the company still had a backlog of $800 million and assets of $270 million, it was in need of an additional $100 million cash flow to launch the DC-9.

More than 5,000 people employed on the program were laid off by the end of January 1963, and Douglas stock plummeted. It was at this point that James S. McDonnell bought a significant block of Douglas stock. He met with Donald Douglas, Sr. and his son to propose a merger which they quickly rejected. In return, they asked Mr. McDonnell if he would be interested in funding and building the DC-9 wing as part of a unique risk/profit-sharing endeavor, but he declined.

In an effort to solve the funding problem, Douglas management had quietly embarked on a novel approach. It began negotiations with a number of potential suppliers whereby the sub-contractors would fund the development of their own piece of the aircraft and receive a pro-rated share of the profits. It amounted to "share the risk, share the gain." Rumors were circulating in the press that American had given Douglas a letter of intent which was dependent on the company declaring its intent to launch

the DC-9 within 30 days. Delta was also known to strongly favor the design and to be considering a purchase of 20 aircraft.

To the north, a major three-way battle had developed to win a potential order for up to 50 aircraft from Trans-Canada as a Viscount replacement. A distant fourth contender was the de Havilland Trident. Aside from negotiations with the airline, there was strong infighting within the government. In addition to the One-Eleven, the third aircraft being considered was the Caravelle. French-Canadian politicians naturally favored it, hoping for a second production line to be set up in Quebec. BAC offered to have a large part of the One-Eleven built at Canadair in Montreal and Douglas reached agreement with de Havilland Canada (deHC) to build part of the aircraft in the old Avro Canada plant at Malton.

The Douglas/deHC deal was an astute move because aerospace employment had taken a plunge in Toronto when the Avro Arrow program was abruptly canceled in 1959. At the time, deHC was part of the British-owned Hawker Siddeley Group, providing an immediate negative reaction in the United Kingdom to this agreement. Representations to the British Government to intercede were put forth, but no action was taken.

As a state-owned airline, much political pressure was being placed on TCA's board and senior management. President Grant McGregor and many of his senior staff threatened to resign en mass unless the airline was left to make its own the decision based purely on engineering and economic evaluations of each contender.

It was estimated that Australia's two airlines would need nine aircraft each, and a potential government purchase of five more was envisioned. Meanwhile, Douglas downsized its requirement from a minimum of 125 orders to 70. Also on the positive side, it was generally forecast that the total market worldwide for this category of aircraft would be around 1,000 units over the next decade; Douglas officials predicted that their company would capture 40 percent of the market.

Political Implications

Domestic politics also entered the arena. As part of its overall marketing strategy, Douglas naturally pitched its DC-9 design to the United States Air Force, primarily in the Aeromedical Evacuation (Med-Evac) role. In addition a convertible transport was offered with a large cargo door and strengthened floor for Military Airlift Command's LOGAIR role.

Meanwhile, C. R. Smith, president of American Airlines, wrote to Secretary of Defense Robert S. McNamara to point out that he would soon be in the difficult position of having to go abroad for a new aircraft if Douglas failed to achieve sufficient orders to guarantee a viable program. In turn, this would have a negative effect on the U.S. balance of payments. This was, of course, a veiled request for the government to buy some DC-9s to launch the program. Interestingly, Smith had previously instructed his evaluation team to arrive at a recommendation of aircraft type "without regard to the politics of U.S.-built versus foreign engines," as he would do the worrying about that problem. Douglas followed this up with briefings to various government departments, stressing the employment and export of U.S. gold reserves situations.

Another timely move was the creation of Douglas Finance Corporation (DFC) in February 1963, intended to help smaller airlines finance new aircraft and assist foreign airlines with the negotiation of loans from the U.S. Export-Import Bank. Though initially intended to help with DC-8 sales, it could also be used by airlines wanting to purchase DC-9s.

At the end of February, the CAB denied approval for Bonanza Air Lines to purchase the BAC 1-11, stating that such a purchase would prompt the carrier to seek larger subsidies. Bonanza was already receiving a government guarantee to help buy Fairchild F-27 turboprop airliners. Concurrently, the CAB was under pressure from Congress to reduce the $70 million annual subsidy being paid to the 13 local service airlines.

Douglas unveiled a second version of the DC-9 in late March. This design activated the center fuel tank, adding almost 9,000 pounds of additional fuel. The MTOW increased to 83,000 pounds and the range extended to over 1,000 miles with a 17,800-pound payload.

A rear ventral stairway was offered as an optional extra in the new version. By now, the carry-on stowage bin had been eliminated and the baggage compartment extended. Seating configurations were amended to include to an all-economy load of 83 passengers as smaller seat pitches became more acceptable. This version was on offer to non-U.S. airlines only as it exceeded the 80,000-pound MTOW/2-man cockpit limit.

Another significant change to the basic design was introduced when the forward entry door was changed to a plug type which opened inwards before swinging open on a vertical hinge. The airstair was changed to a telescoping unit which stowed just below the door sill. It could be operated from either inside the aircraft or externally. This change allowed the aircraft to use the covered "jetways" at major airports yet be self-sufficient at smaller facilities.

The fiberglass tail cone was also redesigned so that it could be blown off by explosive bolts when an emergency exit in the rear pressure bulkhead was opened. (This capability was retained when the ventral stairs were installed.) Originally offered as an option, an auxiliary power unit was installed below the rear fuselage section to make the aircraft totally independent of external power sources.

The Go-ahead

"We have concluded after a careful study of the potential market for such an aircraft that sufficient orders will be obtained to make the DC-9 program financially successful for our company." This proclamation, by Donald Douglas, Sr. on April 8, 1963, finally made the program official, though no announcement of existing orders was made at the time. Mr. Douglas also revealed that the company had entered into a cost-sharing arrangement with suppliers located in 27 states and Canada. The first flight was scheduled for Spring 1965 with certification in February 1966, and 16 aircraft ready for immediate delivery shortly afterwards. To ensure that the tight schedule would be met, John C. Brizendine, the current DC-8 program manager, was appointed to head the program, reporting to Jackson R. McGowen, Vice President and General Manager of the Aircraft Division.

In fact, the launch was a calculated risk. Delta was the only U.S. airline which had publicly stated its intention to buy the aircraft. United was committed to its Boeing 727, Caravelle and Viscount fleets, while Western and Continental were in no hurry to buy anything. TWA and TCA had teams evaluating several different types while Eastern and American were waiting the merger outcome to be decided by the CAB. A few days later, supported by the Justice Department, the CAB finally denied the merger application.

In effect, recent Douglas history appeared to have repeated itself. The company had launched a new airliner, without orders, to compete with a similar aircraft that was expected to enter service well ahead of it. The same scenario had occurred with the DC-8 versus Boeing 707 competition in June 1955. But, as with the earlier situation, the initial delivery gap would unexpectedly close substantially. Douglas took the calculated gamble with the full knowledge that an order from American was not guaranteed. The DC-9 price tag was set at $3.1 million, versus the BAC 1-11's $2.5 million price for the basic aircraft. However, import duties and required design changes to the One-Eleven and its engines eventually raised the U.S. price to around $3 million.

The original DC-9 cabin mock-up.

A new departure for Douglas was the sub-contracting of many items to reduce start-up costs. These components ranged from seats to air-conditioning units which traditionally had been built "in-house." All items put out for bid were based on 125 ship sets, then considered the break-even number. The day after the launch announcement, Douglas released its first DC-9 shop orders.

A decision was made to assemble DC-9s on the same production line as the DC-8 to take advantage of a skilled labor pool being underutilized at the time. The construction techniques were very similar for the two types in spite of their size difference. DC-8 production was ticking over at a rate of about 2.5 aircraft per month, well below the maximum capacity of two per week. Based on market forecasts, it appeared that DC-9 production would average around two-to-three per week.

The Canadian Deal

The need to win an order from Trans-Canada was considered critical to the future of the program. As mentioned earlier, Douglas signed a sub-contracting agreement with de Havilland Aircraft of Canada, Ltd. for the production of several major components in what initially appeared to be an offset agreement. This competition was probably one of the earliest situations in which this now common business practice was applied.

The deHC company at Downsview was working at a fairly high capacity in 1963. Beavers, Otters and Caribou were all in production. The Turbo Beaver was in the flight test stage and the first DHC-5 Buffalo short-field tactical transport was under construction, so there was little room for any DC-9 production at existing facilities.

A few miles away, one of three production bays in the old Avro plant at Malton Airport was being utilized for the overhaul of Avro CF-100 Canuck all-weather fighters; otherwise, the factory was empty. An agreement was reached with the Canadian government for deHC to take over the rest of the facility and set up a production line to build the DC-9 wings, tail stub, fin and rudder, and horizontal tail unit. The components would then be shipped via special rail cars to Long Beach for final assembly. It was calculated that the cost of transportation would be more than compensated for by the lower prevailing wage rates in Canada. Most of the materials used would be supplied from U.S. sources, especially the wing skins and forgings for the spar caps.

It took three years of negotiation with Canadian Customs to reach final agreement on import duties because material was being shipped in, processed and shipped out. One particular problem was the duty on wing spar caps. When the forgings arrived in Canada, they weighed several hundred pounds each. After machining, they were considerably lighter when exported as part of the finished wing. The argument was over what weight to tax. It got worse when these components were intended for TCA's aircraft since the components were in effect re-exported and then re-imported yet again!

The initial deHC contract was worth $65 million. Quickly, a small management team arrived from Long Beach and a number of staff were transferred from Downsview to Malton to organize production. An extensive sub-contract program for parts was created with many small machine shops throughout Ontario and Quebec. Fleet manufacturing in Fort Erie was also sub-contracted to supply some of the control surfaces. Initially, it was estimated that 2,000 sorely needed jobs would be created to handle production plus many more with the outside sub-contractors.

Other Participants

Seven other major U.S. suppliers were signed to a similar risk-sharing contract after a short but intensive bidding competition:

Garret-AiResearch	Environmental control systems
Rohr Corp.	Engine pods and thrust reversers
Sperry Phoenix Co.	Automatic flight control system
Westinghouse Electric	Electric power generating systems
Goodyear Tire	Wheels and brakes
Sunstrand Corp.	Constant speed drive
Pratt & Whitney	JT8D-5 engines

An additional 20 smaller sub-contractors entered into similar agreements. Part of the investment by each supplier would also be used as a contribution towards flight-testing and certification costs. Under the terms of the agreement, each supplier financed the engineering, tooling, qualification testing and work on components produced. Douglas purchased the goods under a fixed-price agreement, paying upon delivery of aircraft to customers. The associated companies were responsible for 45 percent of the development and production under Douglas control. Eventually, some 2,500 parts suppliers from 27 states would be involved.

First cabin interior for Air Canada.

Chapter IV
FIRST ORDERS

The first few DC-9s were built on the DC-8 assembly line. Production was later separated due to a large influx of orders.

A Slow Beginning

It was no real surprise when C. E. Woolman, president of Delta Air Lines, formally announced an order for 15 DC-9-11s plus 15 options on April 25, 1963. Initial deliveries were scheduled for February 1966. The order was placed by telephone after Delta's board of directors approved the deal.

The Delta order was significant in another way, too. There had been much discussion between the Air Line Pilots Association (ALPA), Delta pilots and management as to whether the new breed of twin jets should be crewed by three men or two, even though the aircraft met the current 80,000-pound rule. The Federal Aviation Administration (FAA) had been monitoring the Douglas and BAC designs closely and favored the reduced-crew complement. On June 7, 1963, an agreement was reached between ALPA and the airlines whose pilots were represented by the union to permit two-man DC-9 crews with a 75 hours-per-month flight time limitation. American Airlines pilots, represented by an independent union, had reached a similar unannounced agreement earlier. At the same time, the FAA stated that it planned to review a proposed rule that would abolish the 80,000-pound limit altogether and base the crew size on aircraft certification rather than weight.

However, the next order came only after an unnerving pause. On July 11, Bonanza Air Lines announced an order for three DC-9s plus three options, subject to CAB approval. In his letter to the Board seeking consent, Bonanza's chairman Edmund Converse cited the outflow of U.S. gold reserves situation that would have been eased. Also mentioned was that when he had asked for permission to order the One-Eleven, there was no alternative aircraft available. The proximity of the Douglas

plant to supply spares and the "DC" name were also quoted as reasons for choosing the DC-9.

The airline's net income had jumped substantially since its previous application, and this time the CAB gave its approval on March 30, 1964. The total price, including spares and training, was $11 million. The Department of Commerce guaranteed a $6.5 million loan from six lenders.

American Airlines was next to place an order, but it was for the BAC 1-11. Fifteen firm orders plus 15 options were finalized on July 17, with deliveries scheduled to commence in July 1965. To win this order, BAC had created the Dash 400 series. The earlier delivery schedule was quoted as the main reason for American's choice and, although it was deemed a setback for Douglas, the decision was not totally unexpected. Just one month later, the prototype One-Eleven made its maiden flight from Hurn on the evening of August 20.

Local Long Beach area politicians, led by California Governor Edmund G. "Pat" Brown, telegraphed the President to protest the actions of American, Braniff and Mohawk. However, it was to no avail; both the White House and the Congress refused to intervene.

Production Begins

A number of executives were present when milling commenced on the spar caps for the first DC-9 wing, on July 26, 1963, formally signifying the start of DC-9 production. The first five sets of spar caps were manufactured at Long Beach as the production contracts had yet to be placed in Canada.

Meanwhile, design and wind tunnel testing was proceeding at a rapid pace. No less than four different high-speed wind tunnels were used in

17

addition to DAC's own low-speed tunnel at Long Beach. More than 1,000 design engineers were assigned to the DC-9, with a goal to complete all drawings for release by March 1964.

Many development fixtures and individual laboratory samples were produced to proof-test components before release for production. Strong emphasis on reliability, maintainability and accessibility was fostered by Delta's engineering management, which worked very closely with Douglas to establish minimum acceptable requirements.

A 21-foot-long cockpit and fuselage assembly was placed in the large Long Beach factory water tank and subjected to a variety of loads to simulate those that would likely be experienced in daily operations. The pressurized fuselage section underwent 120,000 cycles to ensure a guaranteed 50,000 flights could be achieved without structural deterioration. Using experience gained from the DC-8 design, the use of titanium rip-stoppers was employed around skin cutouts and straps where the skin attached to the frames. The T-tail assembly, a new approach for Douglas, was fatigue tested to 360,000 cycles.

From the outset, heavy emphasis was placed on pilot input into the layout of the cockpit that was set up for a two-man crew plus observer. Paul Patten, an experienced test pilot, was assigned to head the cockpit engineering team. Some 100 pilots from airlines and government agencies were invited to make comments and provide input regarding the layout, as well as to assist in ergonomics testing.

The DC-9 cockpit mock-up. The panel is steel, and magnets on the fake instruments allow easy re-positioning to establish location parameters.

In order to minimize the forthcoming flight test program, a good portion of the preliminary work was carried out by "piggy-backing" some systems and components on production DC-8 test flights. By installing them alongside similar proven DC-8 systems, their accuracy and operational capability were easily analyzed. A new control wheel was also tested and eventually became standard on the DC-8-60 series in addition to the DC-9s.

To track work in progress, Douglas introduced the Electronic Data Processing System (EDP), to follow each engineering order as it progressed from the designer to the point of assembly via the tooling, manufacturing and purchasing processes. Almost 800 EDP stations throughout the factory delivered work orders and kept track of progress for managers. Overall progress monitoring was via a new computer program, Program Evaluation and Review Technique (PERT), that tracked some 9,000 activities on a bi-weekly basis to keep everything on schedule. Datafax machines provided a direct link between engineers at Long Beach and Malton for the transmission of drawings and other paperwork, unique in its day.

The First Military Proposals

By now, the U.S. Department of Defense was seriously considering the need for more efficient Med-Evac vehicles, staff transports and a convertible freighters for purchase with the Fiscal Year 1965 funding. Boeing, BAC, and Douglas continued to lobby for an aircraft order that was soon to become literally a life-saver. But Congress refused to budget for a replacement for the slower Convair C-131 versions (CV-240/340/440) and Douglas C-118s (DC-6) currently employed in these roles.

Douglas pressed the point that it could provide early delivery of an aircraft with four times the productivity of the C-131 in a more comfortable and quieter atmosphere for the patients. It featured a 119-inch-wide by 81-inch-high door with a built-in folding ramp for rapid loading and unloading of stretcher cases. Up to 30 litters could be carried plus one which could be environmentally separated for a patient requiring isolation care.

Taking advantage of the large door of the Med-Evac design, a convertible aircraft fitted with a cargo floor was proposed for the priority cargo mission. Another version was offered for the Special Air Mission

(SAM) role, essentially a standard DC-9-10 fitted with just 48 seats at a 41-inch pitch. Congress, however, was not yet ready to approve any funding required for a non-combat aircraft.

Stemming from this design effort, Douglas made it clear that a convertible version of the DC-9 would be available early in the development cycle. The company had learned from its DC-8 experience that a market for this type of aircraft existed. Company studies also showed that an executive DC-9 version could carry 15 people 3,300 miles by installing extra fuel tanks in the cargo hold.

The Breakthrough

The sales situation improved on November 22, 1963 when Canada's Prime Minister announced an order for six DC-9-14s on behalf of TCA. The airline's president had won his fight to make an independent re-equipment choice. The offer by Douglas of higher MTOWs for export versions of the DC-9 was further rewarded when KLM took out six unannounced options for Series 15s in early 1964.

Then, following an intense competition with BAC and Sud Aviation, Douglas won a vital order from Swissair for ten DC-9-15s plus two options on May 13, 1964. The choice was influenced by a number of factors. Douglas had managed to increase the MTOW by 17 percent and payload by 22 percent. Payload range jumped 40 percent over the initial offering and the slightly larger DC-9 had better seat-mile costs than the BAC 1-11. In addition Swissair knew that stretched versions were already on the drawing board and that SAS was leaning towards the DC-9. Perhaps emotionally, the long tradition of buying Douglas aircraft dating back to the DC-2 contributed to the decision as well. Swissair officials stated that the company felt there would be too many problems mixing the Caravelle 10B with its Caravelle 3 fleet.

Trans World Airlines finally put the DC-9 program on safe ground when a hard-fought $86.2 million contract for 20 firm orders plus 20 options was signed on July 20 by TWA's president, Charles Tillinghast. Hawaiian Airlines, expected to purchase the BAC 1-11, added to the tally with a $7.5 million two-aircraft order on November 16, and TCA increased its order by two in December.

Moving Forward

Assembly of the first wings commenced at Malton in January 1964. The main fuselage assembly began on March 6 at Long Beach, with the driving of the first rivet being ceremonially performed on the cockpit section by Jack McGowen and Donald Douglas, Jr.

On August 8, Douglas announced the formation of Douglas Aircraft Co. of Canada Ltd. (DACAN), with a small Ottawa-based staff. Initially it was to be a liaison between the Canadian government and industry to explore more production-sharing possibilities. This event would have a long-term impact on the Canadian economy just over a year later when Douglas reached agreement with deHC to buy out the Canadian company's share of the DC-9 program.

Flight Test Plan

To achieve the tight schedule that had been established, five aircraft were to be used in the flight test program. The first aircraft would be built in production jigs and later sold. It would be used for stability and control tests plus general design clean-up. Ship Two would be used for structural testing before joining the flight test program to measure air loads, a similar pattern to that carried out on the second DC-8. The third and fourth aircraft were scheduled to undertake specific FAA tests and also make demonstration flights. Ship Five's assignment was to handle function and reliability trials. In addition, the ambitious plan called for several aircraft to be delivered to customers for crew training before certification was approved.

The test schedule called for the initial flight of Ship One in March 1965, followed by Ship Two eight weeks later. The full five-aircraft test fleet was to be operational by July 1. To enable rapid delivery after certification, all were to have complete airline interiors except where space or access was needed for test equipment. Certification was expected after 1,000 hours of flight testing.

The Deep Stall Incident

A flying accident in the United Kingdom had a serious impact on the DC-9 design. On October 23, 1963, the prototype BAC 1-11 crashed while on a test flight. During a series of trials to explore the flight regime while approaching a stall, the aircraft was trimmed with a fully aft-located center of gravity (CG) and 8 degrees of flap setting. A deep stall condition resulted when the engine nacelles and fuselage blanked off the airflow over the horizontal tail surfaces. Despite all the efforts by the crew, the One-Eleven hit the ground in an almost flat attitude with little forward motion, killing all on board. BAC announced the cause almost immediately after the crash because not just Douglas, but Fokker and Boeing also were also working on T-tail configured aircraft designs at that time. BAC offered to work with the other manufacturers in investigating the problem, but only one meeting ever took place with Douglas and Boeing. Test pilots and aerodynamicists from each company met in Seattle in November 1963.

BAC engineers solved the problem by re-designing the mainplane leading edge and modifying the elevator control linkage. In addition, a device called a "stick-pusher" was installed to force the aircraft into a nose-down attitude if a critical angle of attack was approached. This became a British Civil Aviation Authority requirement for all future British-registered T-tail aircraft.

Douglas aerodynamicists, already investigating the deep-stall phenomena, immediately intensified wind tunnel testing. In October 1964, a solution was reached to prevent a similar occurrence with the DC-9. The re-design of the horizontal stabilizer and elevators entailed enlarging the surface area by 23.1 percent. This was achieved by increasing the span from 30.7 feet to 36.85 feet and the tip chord from 41.5 inches to 46.8 inches. The longer span put more of the enlarged surfaces outside the blanking effect of the nacelles and fuselage at high angles of attack.

These changes would give positive nose-down pitch control at angles of attack up to 50 degrees. In addition, a vortilon (wing fence) was added under each wing to delay the stall at up to a 30-degree angle of attack by restricting the spanwise flow of air. The vortilon also assisted in keeping the outer portion of the horizontal tail out of the disrupted airflow region at high angles of attack. Power augmentation was installed on the elevator control system. Rather than use a stick pusher, a stick shaker was installed which caused the control column to shake as the aircraft approached the stall regime, thus alerting the crew to the developing situation.

To maintain the DC-9's original first flight schedule, a modification program – entitled Project 2/28 for the February 28, 1965 completion target date – was given priority status. However, the re-designed horizontal stabilizer was built, tested and installed on the first aircraft by January 10, 1965, well ahead of schedule. Despite the BAC 1-11's unfortunate setback, Douglas didn't intend to be complacent.

The Canadian-built wings being joined to Ship One in November 1964.

Chapter V

MAIDEN FLIGHT

Ship One prepares to depart on its first flight. Note the dual wingtip pitot tubes.

The First DC-9-20 Project

Eastern Air Lines, United and Lufthansa all became the targets of strong sales efforts from Douglas, BAC and Boeing during the latter part of 1964. In November, Boeing, having decided that the time was right to offer a smaller jet, pitched its 737 design to complement the 707 and 727 series. Boeing initially offered an aircraft seating 86 with an MTOW of 79,000 pounds. BAC weighed in with the BAC 1-11-400 and Douglas tendered the DC-9-10. In fact, none of the aircraft first offered adequately met either of the U.S. carrier's requirements; all were too small.

Unfettered by the CAB's weight restrictions, Lufthansa, already an established Boeing operator, was offered a heavier aircraft by both American manufacturers. On February 21, 1965 it ordered 21 737-100s with an 85,000-pound MTOW specification, designed for a 2-man cockpit. Shortly afterwards, the FAA raised the weight restriction from 80,000 pounds to 90,000 pounds allowable takeoff weight with a two-man crew.

Boeing met the challenges of Eastern and United by increasing the MTOW to 93,000 pounds and stretching the fuselage by six feet, increasing the maximum seating to 115. Of course, the immediate penalty was to require a third crewman in the cockpit.

The JT8D engine had ample reserve power for a heavier version since the -5 was a de-rated power

plant. In early 1965, engineers simply stretched the DC-9's constant section fuselage by adding 76 inches forward of the wing and 38 inches aft. The MTOW was increased to the 90,000-pound limit and the Ramp Weight rose to 90,700 pounds, thus allowing 700 pounds of start-up and taxi fuel.

Fifteen additional passengers could be carried with no performance loss. A major design change was the addition of full-span leading edge slats to the wing to improve the takeoff performance, and a change to a

Ship One in a water soluble livery for a visit by Eastern officials in January 1965. A faked registration, appropriately N901E, was also applied.

The DC-9 roll-out reception in the DC-8 paint hangar.

Ship One N9DC (msn 45695) is followed by the almost complete Ship Two N3301L (msn 45696).

Known in-plant as "Mr. DC-9," John Brizendine gave a short speech emphasizing the airplane's simplicity and ease of maintenance. It would, for example, take only 55 minutes to change an engine. Landing gear struts were interchangeable and the fuel system was made up of 60-percent fewer parts than other types. The whole DC-9 concept was aimed at a 99-percent dispatch reliability, which meant minimizing technical delays in excess of 15 minutes. He also confirmed that freighter versions would be made available early in the program, and foresaw a market for 50 to 60 such aircraft.

The Orders Roll In

Shortly before the ceremonies, Ozark Airlines announced that it was negotiating for three firm plus three optional DC-9-10 orders, presaging an avalanche of orders that was to keep the expanded sales and contracts team very busy for the rest of the year. Not only were the salesmen busy signing DC-9 customers, but also by the end of 1964, thirteen airlines had signed up for the new DC-8-60 Series, and several customers were buying more DC-8 Jet Traders and Series 50s during the ensuing months.

The most significant deal was announced on February 25, 1965, when Eastern purchased 24 stretched DC-9s with an interim lease of 15 DC-9-10s, an $84-million package. Following a tradition that started with the DC-8, Eastern promptly called the new stretched version "DC-9B" in press releases. The early availability of the leased aircraft, plus DAC's willingness to carry a greater share of the initial funding of the order through DFC, had made the difference. This order put DC-9 "firm" orders ahead of the BAC 1-11 for the first time, 85 versus 76. With options, the DC-9 order book totaled 145. Though the Eastern order was for the longer Series 20, neither airline nor Douglas press announcements actually stated which version the contract was for, suggesting that both were confident that a further change to the two-man crew limitations was imminent, allowing an even bigger aircraft to be specified.

Maiden Flight

The Eastern proclamation came on the same day that Ship One – aptly registered N9DC – made its first flight after only two days of taxi trials. George Jansen, Chief Engineering Pilot, assisted by Paul Patten (also co-pilot on the DC-8 and DC-10 first flights) completed the maiden voyage. Flight test engineer Duncan Walker was watching the 10,000 pounds of test and monitoring equipment "down the back."

After a takeoff roll of 3,200 feet with a slight tail wind, the first flight lasted 2 hours, 13 minutes, reaching a programmed speed of 250 knots and 20,000-foot cruise altitude, ending at Edwards Air Force Base after a flawless flight. The MTOW was limited to 77,900 pounds for the initial trip, originally scheduled to last 1 hour and 45 minutes. All the aircraft systems were tested and the landing gear was cycled. The autopilot function was tried with no problems encountered.

Two additional flights were flown the following day. Patten was in the left seat for the second trip, expanding the flight envelope to 275 knots and 25,000 feet of altitude. On approach, the auto-pilot was coupled for an automatic landing from 9,000 feet. At 180 feet, the crew took over for a manual landing. On the third flight, each engine was shut down and air-started in turn. The DC-9 logged 6 hours and 13 minutes during the first three flights. After two weeks, 13 test flights had been accomplished

double-slotted flap design, a development that was to have far reaching benefits. The chord was extended forward of the front spar and the airfoil section modified slightly. Wing span was increased to 93.3 feet by extending the wing tips by two feet on each side, which provided space for additional fuel. The new design was identified as the DC-9-151 and later the Series 20 (not to be confused with the same designation re-introduced later for a different variation).

Roll-out

The first DC-9 was formally rolled out just 10 months after assembly began. Attendees were seated in the paint hangar when the large doors opened to reveal not one but two DC-9s being towed towards them. The first aircraft was brought into the building and, after the ceremonies, was made available for inspection by the guests. The tour guides were stewardesses representing the seven airlines that had announced orders to date.

Ship One in flight.

totaling over 24 hours. Turnarounds between flights had been reduced to 30 minutes and as many as eight observers were carried on some missions.

The aircraft began flying a steadily expanding pattern of tests, including stalls at various CG positions, amassing 50 hours of flight time by April 1. As the aircraft approached the stall, it had a tendency to drop a wing sharper than expected. Leading edge fences were installed and a stall strip was fitted along the leading edge close to the fuselage. Vortex generators located in front of the elevators were found to be unnecessary and removed. On one flight, the crew deliberately allowed the aircraft to enter a complete roll before recovery. Throughout these tests, the DC-9 displayed no longitudinal stability problems.

In common with the first DC-8 flights, a telescoping escape tunnel with a frangible cover was installed just aft of the DC-9 cockpit and a drag chute installed in the tail for stall/spin recovery. During drag chute deployment tests, the aircraft reacted as predicted, giving the crew quite a jolt as it opened. Instrument and night flights were soon introduced to the schedule that had already included single-engine performance and landings. So well was the test program proceeding that Douglas began to forecast that the certification program would be completed at least a month ahead of the already tight schedule.

A Busy Time

Meanwhile, a flurry of orders was received. During March alone, they came from Seattle-based West Coast Airlines (three Series 10s), followed by Ozark and KLM firming up their options. Continental Airlines launched the DC-9-15RC (Rapid Change) model with an order for 12 aircraft on the 16th. Initially, Continental's announcements and advertising dubbed the aircraft as the DC-9C. However, company president Bob Six had erred in his judgment for the potential air freight market and, once in service, these

The flight test crew, (L to R) Walker, Jansen and Patten talk to senior Douglas officials. Patten is flanked by Donald Douglas, Jr. and Sr.

aircraft rarely operated a revenue main-deck cargo flight. In later years, the variant was to become popular as an all-freighter in the American domestic overnight small package and air mail business.

The DC-9-15RC version had an upward opening cargo door installed on the port side. Measuring 81 inches by 119 inches, it allowed the carriage of up to twelve 54-inch by 88-inch pallets, each accommodating 180 cubic feet of cargo. To ensure maximum volume use, the hat racks were hinged in sections to fold down over the window belt. Other main deck and cargo hold space provided an additional 783 cubic feet of volume. In its mixed configuration mode, several passenger-pallet combinations were possible. When a mixed configuration was being utilized, removable cabin dividers

Ship Five in Delta colors with DC-9 titles for demonstration flights. Note the "sideways" Delta widget, later replaced by a vertical design.

shielded the passengers from the cargo areas. If the aircraft was operating as an all-freighter, restraining nets were installed behind the cockpit area to protect the crew in the event of a crash.

To permit rapid re-configuration, all the seats and galleys were palletized and could be removed in approximately 75 minutes. In an all-cargo state, the DC-9 could carry a 25,000-pound payload over 1,100 miles with full reserves. The operating concept was to fly passengers during the daytime, then convert to a freighter role at night. The aircraft was designed for a 90,700-pound MTOW using the 14,000-pound static thrust Pratt & Whitney JT8D-1 turbofan engine.

In mid-March, Swissair increased its order by two aircraft, and Saudi Arabian Airlines became the 12th customer with three firm Series 10 orders plus two options. Iberia also bought three Series 10s. Total orders reached 114 plus 15 leases and 102 options, valued at $432,745,000. Among 11 unannounced sales were two Series 10s for Standard Airways, the first U.S. supplemental airline to order small jetliners.

Reg Ansett then confirmed his decision to buy DC-9s on March 24, subject to government approval, signing up for two DC-9-20s plus four options. Earlier, while placing a $50,000 non-refundable deposit for each aircraft to reserve delivery positions, he took the liberty of also reserving matching positions for his competitor, Trans Australian Airlines (TAA)! This ploy was to ensure that TAA could have a common delivery schedule, thus meeting the Australian regulations. Douglas told both carriers that the reserved slots could be held only until March 31. The final "kicker" which persuaded Ansett was a Douglas guarantee to deliver two DC-9-20s to both carriers in time for the Christmas 1966 season. Douglas also agreed to fit low-pressure tires (100 psi) to allow operation into smaller airfields. On April 1, TAA signed an agreement with Douglas for three Series 20s plus 3 options.

The sales battle was a tough one. Boeing had offered a stretched version of the 737, the -200, with interim leases of 727-100s. BAC had tendered a new, as yet relatively elastic, stretched version, the previously unannounced BAC 1-11-500, for a March 1967 delivery with an interim lease of BAC 1-11-300s.

One problem was the subject of import duty. The Australian and U.K. governments had an existing trade agreement whereby Australian carriers purchasing aircraft from any other country than the U.K., when a comparable British-built aircraft was available, would pay a substantial import duty. This situation had arisen previously when Ansett and TAA had selected the 727 over the Trident; the import duty was charged at the insistence of the U.K. government. The airlines were eventually granted a waiver for the DC-9s by arguing that the stretched BAC 1-11 was not available when needed. The savings were about $300,000 per aircraft.

The Australian Department of Civil Aviation also had a ruling that a two-man crew was restricted to aircraft with less than 85,000 pounds MTOW. It was eventually agreed that a flight engineer would occupy the jump seat between the pilots, even though he could do virtually nothing to assist in the operation, for an interim test period after delivery of the first few aircraft. Eventually, the rules were changed to eliminate this requirement.

Losing the Big One

The last remaining major U.S. sales campaign was being hard fought in San Francisco and Chicago, United Air Lines' main bases. Though its headquarters were in Chicago, engineering management at the San Francisco maintenance base held considerable sway in aircraft evaluations. For quite some time, the DC-9 was considered front-runner in the three-way race but, on April 5, board chairman W. A. "Pat" Patterson announced that United would purchase 40 Boeing 737-200s with options for a further 30. In addition, an additional twenty-seven 727s were ordered.

To soften the blow at Douglas, United purchased four more DC-8-50s plus two options and launched the stretched DC-8 program with an order for five DC-8-61s plus two options. The total value of the transaction was $375 million, the largest single airliner purchase at that time.

Mr. Patterson stated that the twin-jet decision was based on a preference for the wider fuselage, spares commonality between the 727 and 737, and Boeing's offer of interim 727 leases. The lease agreement would save United an estimated $16 million in operating costs through the early phase-out of less efficient aircraft. What was not mentioned was the refusal of United's pilots to accept a 737 two-man crew.

Braniff inaugurated BAC 1-11-200 service in the United States on April 25, 1965, only two months after the DC-9's first flight. The One-Eleven had first entered service with British United Airways on April 9.

Chapter VI
THE SERIES 30

The prototype DC-9-31 N8916E (ln 48/msn 45733) appears with Douglas titles. Later turned over to Eastern, the aircraft accumulated more than 60,000 hours in the air. It was retired in 1991 and later broken up.

Two-Man Cockpit Breakthrough

April 21, 1965 was a pivotal day for American commercial aviation development in general and for the DC-9 program in particular. After a two-year deliberation plus many reviews with the manufacturers and pilot fraternity, the FAA announced the abolishment of a weight limit for two-man crew operations; henceforth, it would be based on design and certification criteria. However, the FAA reserved final judgment on each model pending flight testing. The new rule would now become a bitter dividing issue between some pilot groups and their employers.

From the outset, Douglas designed the DC-9 for operation by two pilots, believing that the FAA would eventually approve the staffing level at increased weights. However, as a fall back, consideration had been given to a three-man cockpit for domestic airlines and a two-man configuration for the unrestricted overseas customers. The detailed effort in concentrating on the crew ergonomics, positioning of instrumentation and more advanced technology had paid off.

Douglas moved quickly to offer a new model, stretching the basic fuselage by 14.9 feet, increased the seating to a maximum of 119 and raising the MTOW to 98,000 pounds. However, a more typical all-coach arrangement of 105 seats at a 34-inch seat pitch became the norm. The extension was gained by adding a 114-inch plug forward of the wing and 65 inches aft. To improve stability, the horizontal stabilizer was given 3 degrees of anhedral (negative dihedral). These changes put the DC-9 in direct contention with Boeing's 737-200 in terms of capacity and performance.

Priced at $3.4 million, the new version was identified as the DC-9 Series 31, initially powered by the Pratt & Whitney JT8D-1 engines rated at 14,000 pounds static thrust. Later, the power plant was replaced by the similarly rated JT8D-7 with higher turbine inlet temperature limits that improved cruise thrust by 10 percent at low altitudes and 6 percent at

higher elevations. The Series 20 wing was retained with some structural strengthening, thickening of skins and other improvements.

The first sale of the DC-9-31 came on April 28, 1965 when Allegheny Airlines announced a four-aircraft purchase of the "king-sized" version, plus four options dependent upon FAA approval of jet operations into noise-sensitive Washington National Airport.

On the same day, Eastern revised its firm order from Series 20s to Series 30s with the same interim lease. Douglas immediately initiated re-negotiations with Ansett and TAA to adopt the new model. By May 24, both airlines had amended their contracts to three firm and three options for Series 30s. Douglas then withdrew the DC-9-20 from its sales portfolio to concentrate on the larger aircraft.

Another consequence of the weight restriction removal was that the American operators purchasing Series 10 aircraft could now increase their certificated takeoff weights to either 85,000 pounds or 90,000 pounds. The DC-9 Series 10 through 14 models were structurally identical; higher weights applied to those fitted with center tank fuel capacity. Although initially approved to operate with the JT8D-5, all were cleared to change to either the JT8D-1 or JT8D-7 engines at a later date. Bonanza kept its first three aircraft at the 77,000-pound weight, the only airline to do so.

Flight Test Progress

After this flurry of activity, there was a short hiatus in announced orders. Meanwhile the production departments had rapidly expanded their output. Following its session in the mechanical test rig where the wing loading trials had been successfully undertaken, Ship Two – N3301L – completed its maiden flight on May 8. By then Ship One had accumulated more than 82 hours of flight time. The third aircraft, N3302L, flew one week later, on May 15.

When Ship Four took to the air on June 10, total fleet flight time had already exceeded 200 hours. To check out the de-icing system, leading edges of the wing and tail surfaces were painted red so that the formation of ice and its removal could readily be filmed. The fifth DC-9, N3303L, which joined the test fleet on July 2, was the first to be painted in airline colors. Fitted with a full passenger interior, it would be used for intensive route flying in the final qualifying tests.

By this time, the flight test department had increased total flight time to 400 hours and expanded the flight envelope to Mach 0.89 and 430 knots. Takeoffs at 90,000 pounds and landings at the maximum weight of 81,000 pounds had been accomplished and Ship One had amassed 200 hours. During stall tests, the pilots reported that the aircraft pitched down more violently with a full-aft CG than with a forward-located CG. A slight tendency to roll at some flap settings was cured by modifications to the vortilons.

The old meets the new. DC-9-14, N9684Z (ln 4/msn 45711; later CF-TLB with Air Canada) is seen with North Central DC-3 N21728 at a Minneapolis sales tour on December 17, 1965. The DC-3 had retired a year earlier after logging 83,032 hours in airline service.

The tests carried out to date indicated only a few areas that needed further attention. Ironically, the landing gear entered into noticeable vibration during smooth touchdowns that was less apparent in a more robust landing. The cause was eventually traced to the natural frequency of the gear and that of an unevenly worn tire matching at times around 100 knots. Mohawk had encountered similar problems when introducing the BAC 1-11. A temporary but inefficient fix was effected by adding 90-pound tungsten blocks on brackets ahead of each wheel. The first few aircraft to enter service were retrofitted with this arrangement but it was eventually eliminated by modifying the strut linkage.

When the Auxiliary Power Unit (APU) was initially installed, its exhaust was flush with the rear fuselage external skin. Under certain flight conditions, a vacuum created by the boundary-layer airflow across the exhaust would cause the APU to shut down. It was cured by extending the duct 5 inches into the airstream and accepting the small drag penalty. Aside from these issues, the flight test program remained ahead of schedule.

An item needing the most development work was the engine mounting structure. Unacceptable noise levels caused by unbalance in some of the engine rotors was noticeable in the rear of the cabin. After a protracted series of trials and the use of computer graphics, four individually tuned vibration dampers were installed on the engine-mounting structure to absorb the power plant vibrations. Extra thick insulation blankets were also applied in the rear cabin walls. Aircraft in service were fitted retroactively with the damper systems in 1967. However, the dampers, set to absorb the vibrations only over a limited frequency band, were not a complete solution.

This problem was finally resolved in early 1997 by a new damper developed at the request of Midwest Express Airlines. The system automatically adjusts to absorb noise throughout the entire frequency range, reducing the rear cabin noise by a dramatic 20 decibels. Northwest Airlines also announced that it was embarking on installing a new device called an Active Tuned Mass Absorber, developed by Barry Controls Aerospace, to eliminate the noise and vibration on NWA's fleet of 173 DC-9s as part of its "DC-9-2000" update program.

Sales Resume

On August 8, 1965, the official FAA flight testing phase commenced, following the formal design approval by the federal agency. The 500-hour milestone had been passed, and it was strongly predicted that certification would be achieved by the end of November, at least six weeks ahead of the original schedule.

North Central Airlines ordered five Series 10s plus five options on July 7, ammending it to 10 Series 30s shortly afterwards. Ozark then doubled its previous purchase to six firm and six options. Air Canada (formerly TCA) signed a Letter Of Intent (LOI) for ten Series 32s on July 23. The new -32 version differed from the -31 by virtue of increased weights. The MTOW was initially raised to 108,000 pounds; the landing weight remained unchanged, but the Zero Fuel Weight increased to 87,000 pounds. The aircraft could operate with either JT8D-1 or -7 engines. Minor strengthening and some changes in skin thickness were required to accommodate the new weight limits. Northeast Airlines signed for 10 firm Series 31s and eight options on August 10.

The first foreign trip by a DC-9 occurred between August 16 and 24, when a sales demonstration flight by the fifth aircraft was made to Mexico City. Seventeen demonstration flights were undertaken between several short-runway, high-elevation fields and Mexico City's main airport. The outcome was an order from Aeronaves de Mexico for nine Series 10s, although this was not confirmed until December 7.

Delta revised its contract on August 20 by reducing its buy of Series 10s to 14 and adding 16 DC-9-32s plus 12 options. Local service carrier Southern Airways bought three Series 10s plus three options on August 25.

Assembly Line Changes

By the end of August, total sales and leases were 201 firm plus 123 on option. All this success plus the boom in DC-8 sales soon caused the company to move DC-9 final assembly to a separate line. DC-8 final construction flowed through a single bay of the assembly building and the DC-9s occupied the other two bays on a U-shaped layout with nine positions on each leg.

At the rear of the building, four positions were established for the wing/fuselage mating operation. The fuselages were lowered onto the wings by overhead cranes and the empennage and landing gear added. After assembly, the airframe was taken outside for pressure testing and then brought around to the front of the building where it took up Position One.

Towards Certification

By early September 1965, four DC-9s were fully engaged in the FAA phases of certification. The fifth and sixth aircraft were not part of the tests, but they kept busy building up flight experience with a series of demonstration flights around the United States and Canada.

DC-9-14 N1061T (ln 7/msn 45714), first of a 20-aircraft order for TWA.

After a three-hour acceptance flight on September 18, Douglas formally handed over the first of Delta's aircraft for crew training on September 21, following the FAA's issuance of a provisional certificate. Initially, N3304L remained at Long Beach for training flights, then ferried to Atlanta on October 1 for additional crew instruction. In the last few days of November, Delta accepted two more DC-9s.

The Canadian Takeover

De Havilland-Canada was reluctant to invest any additional funding required for production line expansion nor did it want to purchase new fixtures required for the Series 30 wing. The larger version of the DC-9 was now in direct competition with the British parent company's deH Trident. In addition, deHC was embarking on its own Twin Otter production at Downsview.

Douglas could see no other solution to the Canadian problem but to bring the program in-house. On October 20 DACAN and deHC signed an agreement where Douglas would lease the DC-9 production areas of the Malton facility and take over full control of DC-9 component manufacture. The agreement was initially for five years with an option to extend for three additional five-year terms. The 2,400 deHC employees were offered employment at DACAN with all seniority and other traditional rights being recognized. The number of employees eventually rose to 4,000.

Douglas also bought out the Canadian company's $86 million investment to date. Although the Canadian takeover was considered necessary, it came at a bad time financially. Heavy investment in the DC-9 program plus expenditure on the DC-8-60 Series development was already stretching resources to the limit.

More Convertible Freighter Models

U.S. supplemental carrier Overseas National Airways, licensed to operate both passenger and cargo charters, launched a new version of the DC-9 with its order for six Series 32 Convertible Freighters (CF) on October 14. It featured a cargo door measuring 136 inches by 81 inches and had an initial MTOW of 108,000 pounds. Much of ONA's business was on behalf of the United States Air Force (USAF), and the DC-9-32CFs were intended to be used mainly for flights between domestic bases. Since

rapid interior conversion wasn't necessary, the seats were not palletized, but removed and stored when not required. To improve the range, a 580-gallon fuel tank was installed in the forward belly cargo area.

Yet another model was launched on November 3. Trans-Texas Airways became what would turn out to be the only customer to for the DC-9-15 Mixed Cargo (MC), with an order for five plus two standard Series 10s plus options for a further eight. Initially called the DC-9-15QC for Quick Change, it differed from the -15RC model in that the seats were not palletized but merely folded and pushed closely together to allow half-pallets to be carried near the cargo door. The floor panels were then flipped over to expose cargo roller tracks on the underside. Removable partitions hid cargo from the passengers who boarded via the aft ventral stairs.

Two other sales occurred that day. Air Canada formalized its previous LOI, raising its total Series 32 order by 10. In addition, two of the eight Series 10s were changed to Series 32s. Pacific Southwest Airlines (PSA) signed for one Series 30 plus two options to set up a DC-9 crew training program in conjunction with Douglas. Other airline crews were to be trained at PSA's San Diego base. However, this program was not a success and the DC-9, plus a second one purchased later, were sold after limited usage in passenger service. Ironically, PSA acquired four ex-Air Canada DC-9-32s many years later.

The DC-9 Series 5

Flush with success in the U.S. short-haul market, Douglas engineers proposed a new model in late 1955 with a 70,000-pound MTOW which was 10 feet shorter than the Series 10, reducing the seating by 15. Unfortunately, the JT8D-5 engine was greatly over-powered and its weight created Center of Gravity problems. In addition, the wing was probably too big. It was a concern because the Dutch-built Fokker F.28, just coming on-scene, was designed for just the kind of operations envisaged by Douglas to capture the market's lower end. Douglas decided that unless a more suitable engine became available, the project would not be viable. In addition to the Series 5 design efforts, even at this early stage, the advanced design group began looking at a stretched 160-seat version for shorter high-density routes. They believed that it could be powered by the existing JT8Ds but, by the time it would be needed, a high-bypass ratio

The DC-9 production line in May 1967. Note the four fuselage-wing join positions at the rear. The DC-8 final assembly line is to the left.

engine would be available. This was the forerunner of the DC-9-80 design effort which was launched as the DC-9-55 eleven years later, in 1977.

While Douglas engineers were looking at the DC-9-5, they also explored yet another variation. A study showed that by fitting the Series 30 wing – with all its aerodynamic improvements – to the Series 10 fuselage, it would create an aircraft capable of carrying an economic payload out of very short airstrips. Since it would be a marriage of two existing production sub-assemblies, the development costs were expected to be comparatively low. Designated the DC-9 Series 20, it elicited little interest from the airlines at the time and was temporarily shelved.

Although this model of the proposed DC-9-5 was built as a joke, it is close to scale size of the original design. (Courtesy of Jim Burton)

Standard Airways became the first supplemental carrier to order DC-9s. N490SA (ln 59/msn 45798), a DC-9-15, was sold to Ozark in 1968.

Top: Hawaiian Airlines DC-9-15 N901H (ln 20/msn 45717) in its original color scheme.
Center: Allegheny operated one DC-9-14 (N6140A; ln 42/msn 47049) for a year, prior to receiving its first Series 30s. The aircraft eventually migrated to Northwest as N948L.
Bottom: West Coast Airlines flew four DC-9-14s, including N9104 (ln 155/msn 47081) before merging into Air West in 1968.

Top: DC-9-14 CF-TLC (ln 6/msn 45712) in Air Canada's delivery scheme.
Second: DC-9-32 C-TFML (ln 431/msn 47350) in an early 1980 livery, displaying red fuselage titles. (C. Eleveld)
Third: DC-9-32 C-FTME (ln384/msn 47293) with revised titles and cheat lines in 1991. (Henry Tenby)
Bottom: DC-9-32 C-FTMK (ln 420/msn 47349) reflects AC's current markings. (via Eddy Gual)

The first DC-9 to be delivered was N3303L (ln 5/msn 45698), a Series 14, accepted by Delta Air Lines on December 4, 1965.

Certification

The FAA awarded the DC-9-10 a type certificate at Long Beach on November 23, 1965, just one day behind the BAC 1-11-400. It was presented to Donald Douglas, Sr. by Joseph H. Tippets, the FAA's western regional director, at a ceremony held on the flight line. Douglas had beaten its January 26, 1966 target by more than two months. This was particularly satisfying as the aircraft had also exceeded the manufacturer's performance guarantees by as much as 15 percent in many cases. The order book totaled 219 plus 142 options from 22 airlines. Four days later Ozark added three DC-9 Series 10s.

The five test-program aircraft had accumulated 1,280 flight hours. Four other DC-9s used for demonstration and crew training flights added another 650 hours of operating experience. During the 1,200 flights to date, only two were terminated and seven takeoffs delayed due to malfunctions. During the accelerated testing phase by a single aircraft, 55 flights totaling 151 hours were made in two weeks, averaging 10.8 hours utilization per day.

Throughout the flight test program, more than 2,000 stalls were initiated, covering all configurations, fore and aft CGs, low and high altitude, accelerated and non-accelerated, with idle to takeoff thrust at entry rates of up to 5 knots per second. During these tests the DC-9 reached angles of attack as high as 31.5 degrees and recovered from the ensuing stall without difficulty.

First Services

The first revenue service was actually flown on November 29 when a Delta DC-9 was substituted for another type on an Atlanta–Memphis service. Delta commenced regular DC-9 service to eight cities on December 14, the first flight being a roundtrip from Atlanta to Kansas City via Memphis, followed by Atlanta-to-Detroit service via Dayton and Columbus. By December 19, Delta had expanded services to 19 cities with four aircraft.

American Airlines received its first two BAC 1-11-400 Astrojets on December 22-23. Because of crew training, route proving and other preparations, its first BAC 1-11 service didn't take place until March 6, 1966, between New York's La Guardia Airport and Toronto.

The year ended with a rush of orders. Caribbean Atlantic Airways (Caribair), a San Juan, Puerto Rico-based airline, signed up for three Series 31s on November 14; Aeronaves firmed up its previously mentioned contract on November 30; and Eastern increased its backlog by three.

Although subsequently canceled, Trans Caribbean Airways reserved positions for two Series 30s. West Coast added a fourth Series 10 and Korean Air Lines bought its first Series 32 on December 28. But the biggest news of the month came from Alitalia, Italy's flag carrier.

Another Storm

Alitalia's board of directors announcement of an agreement to purchase 28 DC-9 Series 32s as a Vickers Viscount replacement unleashed a political uproar in Rome and London on December 17. A simultaneous statement revealed that Douglas had reached an agreement with AerFer, a subsidiary manufacturing company owned by the Italian state holding corporation Instituto per la Riconstruczione Industriali (IRI), for the production of DC-9 fuselage panels. IRI also owned 96.2 percent of Alitalia's stock. The airline's press release indicated that the board had reviewed other competing types, including the Trident and BAC 1-11 before making its decision.

The Mayor of Long Beach presents a commemorative plaque to Delta Chairman C. E. Woolman during handover of the first DC-9 to enter commercial service. Jack MacGowan and Donald Douglas, Sr. applaud.

One of the few DC-9-11s built, Bonanza's N945L (ln 14/msn 45728) was upgraded to a Series 14 in 1969 and sold to Itavia as I-TIGA. It is now with Airborne Express as N925AX.

Air California transitioned to jets with DC-9-14 N8961 (ln 23/msn 45842), shown wearing original colors in April 1968.

Germanair's DC-9-14 D-AMOR (ln 127/msn 45787) banks above Huntington Beach on its approach to Long Beach, California, in April 1969.

For some time, the Italian government had been trying to revitalize its flagging aircraft industry and talks with the British had dragged on at government levels for the previous 12 months. A proposal had been made whereby the Italians would co-produce a new version of the One-Eleven in partnership with BAC. When the purchase announcement was made, various Italian government departments, including representatives from Aer-Fer, were still working on their reports from a meeting held in London during November with officials of the British aircraft industry.

The British saw the announcement as a blow to establishing their economic presence in Europe as part of a commitment to join the Common Market. Another shock was that this was the biggest single DC-9 order to date, and comments were made to the effect that it was required before Douglas would agree to subcontracting work in Italy.

BAC stated that it had been unable to make any formal presentations to Alitalia's board as the airline had not provided the technical ground rules. An all-party delegation from the British Parliament went to Rome to put pressure on the Italian Cabinet to block the sale, leading to a major confrontation between opposing political parties in the Italian government.

However, it eventually emerged that the British had failed to clearly state for the record that co-production of the BAC 1-11 depended on Alitalia buying the aircraft.

TWA's first aircraft – N1051T – was used by Douglas in late November and early December for a nine-day tour of several eastern American cities and also paid a visit to Malton to show the aircraft to employees at de Havilland Canada. In addition to exhibiting the aircraft to officials at three military bases, it was also used to demonstrate its low external noise levels at Washington National Airport in anticipation of approval for Eastern and Delta to operate at the airport.

Bonanza Air Lines became the second airline to accept delivery of a DC-9 on December 21, but didn't place the aircraft into revenue service until March 1, 1966 after receiving its second aircraft. The first foreign carrier, Air Canada, accepted its first DC-9 on January 7, 1966, and received three more shortly before initiating scheduled service on April 6 between Montreal and Winnipeg as well as from Montreal to New York's La Guardia Airport.

SHIP ONE

After completion of the certification program, some additional development flying was continued on Ship One for several months, ending on April 30, 1966. Then it was stripped of all the test equipment and the cabin refurbished to full airline standards. On September 30, it was sold to Trans-Texas Airways as N1301T, having accumulated 579 hours and 629 landings with Douglas.

The aircraft remained with Trans-Texas – which changed its name to Texas International on April 1, 1969 – until the merger with Continental Airlines on October 31, 1982. At the time of the merger, N1301T had amassed 56,070 landings and 42,365 flight hours.

On May 13, 1983, the airplane was sold to Intercredit Corporation and immediately leased to Sunworld International Airways. By then, the hours totaled 43,375 and the landings 57,204. Sunworld leased the aircraft for just one year before returning it to Intercredit, which immediately leased it out to Emerald Airlines until May 1990, by which time it had accumulated 55,914 hours and 68,538 landings.

After being parked for several months, Ship One was leased to a small, privately owned Madrid-based charter airline, Air Sur, on January 29, 1991 wearing the temporary import registration EC-622. International Lease Finance Corporation (ILFC), acquired the aircraft with the lease in place, on April 18, 1991. Shortly afterwards, it received full Spanish airworthiness approval with the registration EC-FCQ on April 30, 1991.

ILFC re-possessed the aircraft on July 24, 1991. Upon return to the United States it was registered as N711LF and leased to Viscount Air Service for a few months.

After passing through several brokers' hands, Ship One was sold to Aircraft Support Group Inc. in May 1992. Title was transferred to International Aircraft Support Group in July 1992. The aircraft was then ferried to Sherman, Texas, and reduced to spares. It had reached 58,420 hours and 71,064 landings.

Ship One in "Pamper Jet" markings with Trans-Texas Airlines (TTA) at San Antonio in May 1967. (Author's Collection)

TTA was renamed Texas International in April 1969, leading to new colors. (Chuck Stewart)

Still wearing N1301T, the aircraft migrated to SunWorld in 1983. (Thomas Livesey)

Texas-based Emerald Air then operated Ship One on casino charters for about 18 months. (Jerry Stanick)

Ship One in temporary Spanish markings EC-622 and ex-Emerald colors, operated by Spanish carrier Air Sur. (Author's Collection)

Air Sur only used Ship One three months before it was re-possessed by ILFC. It appears in full colors with Spanish registration EC-FCQ. (P. De La Cruz)

MDC re-acquired the airplane from ILFC and sold it to IASG. Ship One was finally reduced to spares in 1992. (Author's Collection)

Top: In 1985, Emerald Air operated Ship Five (msn 45698) for Resorts International. (Ray Leader)
Above: Emerald also wet leased the aircraft to short-lived Air Puerto Rico in 1986. (Nigel Chalcroft)
Below: Royale Airlines was yet another U.S. operator in 1988. (Author's Collection)
Bottom: As N931EA it served the re-born Braniff in the winter of 1991-92. (Author's Collection)

For many years Spanish charter airline Spantax used the markings shown on DC-9-14 EC-CGZ (ln 8/msn 45699). (Author's Collection)

In 1983, Spantax leased DC-9-32 EC-DTI (ln 735/msn 47639) for three months from GPA, in revised colors (Author's Collection)

Regional carrier Tourraine Air Transporte (TAT) was the first French airline to operate DC-9s, leasing OH-LYG (DC-9-14; ln 37/msn 45730) from Finnair in 1982. (Christian Volpati)

Still flying with Midwest Express as N500ME, N85AS (ln 4/msn 45711) served All Star after periods with Air Canada, BMA and Finnair. (Ray Leader)

DC-9-15, N2892Q (ln 46/msn 45841) of Best Airlines was originally delivered to Ozark as N972Z. (Ray Leader)

Well-traveled DC-9-14, N949L (ln 33/msn 45844) ended its days with Eagle Airlines. (Author's Collection)

DC-9-15, N1068T (ln 114/msn 45782) retained its original registration when sold by TWA to Great American Airways in 1979. (John Wegg)

Skybus leased DC-9-15 N2892Q (ln 46/msn 45841) from Best Airlines for just three months in 1986. (Paul Brissette)

Milwaukee, Wisconsin-based Midwest Express has made only minor changes to its livery. DC-9-14 N700ME (ln 2/msn 45696) appears in the company's original scheme, which was later updated (see title page photo). (Norbert Raith)

Formerly KLM's PH-DNC, DC-9-15 N31UA (ln 27/msn 45720) later served with Guatemalan airline Aeroquestal for three years. (Author's Collection)

Air Margarita's DC-9-14, YV-830C (ln 8/msn 45699) has served 10 airlines during its long life, and currently flies for Mexican carrier Allegro as XA-SPA. (Author's Collection)

Air Panama leased DC-9-15 HP-505, (ln 15/msn 45786) from MDC in 1969. (Author's Collection)

Colombian airline Intercontinental is a medium-sized operator of DC-9s. HK-2865X (ln 55/msn 45722) was the first Series 15 delivered, in August 1986. (Jerry Stanick)

Acquired later, Series 14 HK-3859X (ln 54/msn 45738) wears Intercontinental's updated colors. (via Eddy Gual)

After a long career with several U.S. airlines, DC-9-14 YV-852C (ln 32/msn 45745) served with LASER in 1994-95. (via Eddy Gual).

Latvian carrier Baltic International's DC-9-15RC, YL-BAA (ln 173/msn 47016), was formerly with Continental, Hughes Airwest, Republic and Northwest. (Mike Axe)

via Eddy Gual

I-TIAN (ln 97/msn 47010), a DC-9-15RC in the colorful markings of Unifly Express (above). Sold to Fortune in the early 1990s, it acquired a modified livery before acquiring a blue and green scheme (below). The aircraft now flies for Air One (bottom).

Author's Collection

Dariö Cocco

Author's Collection)

Ex-Continental DC-9-15RC, N66AF (ln 170/msn 47152) of Air Florida also served with Air Canada and Emerald Airlines in later years. (Bruce Drum)

Built for Trans-Texas Airways, Air National operated DC-9-15MC N1305T (ln 194/ msn 47055) in 1982-84. (Gary Vincent)

Originally delivered to Aeronaves de Mexico as XA-SOA, DC-9-15 XA-RNQ (ln 15/msn 47059) now flies for Aero California, serving the Baja region. (Author)

XA-TIM (ln/msn 84/45778), a DC-9-14 of Mexican carrier Aviacsa, started work with TWA as N1064T. It later served with Midway, Air National and Great American. (Author's Collection)

Cyprus Airways leased DC-9-15 N54648 (ln 55/msn 45733) from MDC in 1975-76. (Author's Collection)

DC-9-15RC N29AF (ln 79/msn 45826) was leased to Cayman Airways by Air Florida during the winter of 1977-78. It currently operates for the U.S. Department of Energy. (Author's Collection)

DC-9-15RC N50AF (ln 97/msn 47010) served Emerald Airlines in the early '80s. (Author's Collection)

Converted from a DC-9-15RC to a -15F, N566PC (ln 242/msn 45828) of Emery WorldWide was originally N8918 with Continental. (via Eddy Gual)

XA-SMI (ln 102/msn 47011) of Aerocaribe was originally Continental's third DC-9-15RC. (via Eddy Gual)

DC-9-15F XA-TDV (ln 228/msn 47156) was leased by Mexicargo during the winter of 1996-97. (via Eddy Gual)

Originally with Delta as N3303L, Series 10 XA-SPA (ln 5/msn 45698) currently operates for ABACO in Mexico. (via Eddy Gual)

Operator of a large DC-8 fleet, Kalitta also flew DC-9-15F N9353 – later reregistered N901CK (ln 201/msn 47154) – between 1984 and 1994. (via Eddy Gual)

Purolator was one of several airlines to operate ex-Continental DC-9-15RCs as freighters, including N72AF (ln 156/msn 47015), formerly N8907. (Author's Collection)

Yet another ex-Continental DC-9-15RC, N9352 (ln 201/msn 47154), served the small package delivery business with Roadway Global in February 1994. (via Eddy Gual)

Kitty Hawk DC-9-15F N564PC (ln 194/msn 47055). It started life as a N1305T, a -15MC with Trans-Texas in 1967. (Author's Collection)

USA Jet Airlines began cargo operations in 1994. DC-9-15F N198US (ln 184/msn 47046) was also originally delivered to Trans-Texas as a DC-9-15MC. (Author's Collection)

Chapter VIII

CONTINUED STRETCH

DC-9-41 prototype N8960U (ln 218/msn 47114) became SE-DBX with SAS.

The Diplomat Fiasco

Market research had shown that the availability of a flexible seating version of the DC-9 might be beneficial to several airlines for peak loads on short commuter flights. A proposal was initiated in early 1966 to configure the aircraft with six-abreast seating at a 34-inch seat pitch, giving the Series 10 a maximum seating arrangement of 102 versus the standard 90 seats. To meet emergency escape regulations, this version, known as the "Diplomat," required a second pair of overwing emergency exits, similar to the Series 30.

Low-backed, vinyl-covered bench seats were used, with folding arm rests which could convert each unit to a twin or triple arrangement. The idea was to increase capacity during peak hours by simply manipulating the different combinations of arm rests. As a triple, the seat width was reduced from 17.9 inches to 15.8 inches. During off-peak periods, the triple would serve as a double seat with folding table/arm rest pulled down from the seat back between the passengers, affording first-class seat widths. The aisles were reduced from 19 inches to 16 inches.

One ship set of production seats was manufactured by the Flightline Company of Burbank, California, for passenger acceptance testing on a Continental DC-9-15RC. Just one revenue sector was operated in the high-density layout. The passenger complaints were so vociferous that all were refunded their fares immediately and the tests discontinued; the Diplomat concept was quietly dropped. Whether the aircraft could have been evacuated in the then required 120 seconds with the narrow aisles was never tested.

The DC-9 Series 40

As part of an on-going improvement effort with the Series 30, a heavier aircraft identified as the Series 33 (also sometimes called the DC-9-30X) had been developed, though no airline placed an order for this version in an all-passenger configuration. It had an increased MTOW of 114,000 pounds, MLW of 102,000 pounds and a Zero Fuel Weight of 95,500 pounds. One small aerodynamic change was made by increasing the wing

incidence by 1.25 degrees to improve cruise performance. Minor structural beef-ups and a strengthened landing gear were incorporated, allowing increased fuel capacity and extend range with the usual payloads. The designated engines were JT8D-9s rated at 14,500 pounds of thrust. However, by taking advantage of these improvements, Douglas was able to respond to a request for a larger aircraft at these same weights.

The Series 40 was created by lengthening the existing plugs ahead of and aft of the wing by 38 inches each, allowing two seat rows to be added, bringing the total capacity to 115 in a 34-inch pitch layout.

Scandinavian Airlines System (SAS), one of the launch customers for the Caravelle, saw the need for an even larger airplane as its traffic grew. An extensive study was done involving all the current and projected versions of twin-jet airliners for its medium-range routes; the Boeing 727 was considered for longer routes.

For some time there had been a strong technical relationship between SAS and Swissair, particularly concerning the DC-8s. This influenced SAS's eventual selection of the new DC-9 Series 40. To simplify maintenance and reduce development costs, SAS elected to have the identical cockpit and engines that Swissair used. Douglas proposed deliveries three years earlier than either BAC or Sud Aviation could offer for a similarly sized aircraft.

SAS announced its intention to buy 10 DC-9 Series 40s plus options for 14 more on January 25, 1966. The agreement included the interim lease of six DC-9 Series 30s until the initial order was complete. In the end, only five aircraft were actually leased and subsequently passed on to Swissair.

Just one day ahead of the SAS announcement, Douglas registered its first German sale when charter airline Sudflug ordered two DC-9 Series 32s. Unfortunately, the under-capitalized airline only operated the DC-9 during the summer season of 1968 before being merged into Condor, which then sold both aircraft to Swissair.

By now, sales had reached 276 plus 135 options to 27 airlines. In early February 1967 Swissair revised its contract from 10 Series 10s to eight plus four Series 40s, to be more compatible with SAS. However, Swissair performance engineers determined that, under certain conditions, the

DC-9-32 SE-DBZ (ln 149/47094) was one of five leased by SAS from Swissair pending delivery of Series 41s.

DC-9-41 SE-DDT (ln 898/msn 47779) in a short-lived bare metal scheme, carrying the Douglas test registration N1002L.

aircraft would have to endure severe payload penalties from some of the secondary runways at Zurich. The decision was taken to revise the entire order yet again, reducing the Series 10s to five interim leases pending delivery of 12 Series 30s, including those previously leased by SAS. The resulting commonality suited all concerned and was approved by Swissair's board on July 6.

After operating DC-9-32 D-ACEB (ln 313/msn 47218) for just five months, Sudflug merged with Condor in 1968 and sold the aircraft to Swissair.

Services Expand

The next few months of 1967 were comparatively slow for sales signings, but deliveries were starting to flow. During February, Bonanza added one Series 10 and two Series 31s. Iberia, after initially ordering 15 Series 11s, upgraded the last 12 to Series 15s at the higher weights, leaving the first three as three Series 11s. In April Iberia amended its entire contract to 15 Series 32s.

Trans World Airlines received its first DC-9 on February 22, and initiated service on March 17 with a daily roundtrip serving New York, Cleveland, Indianapolis and Kansas City. Continental placed the DC-9 into service between Los Angeles and Tulsa (with intermediate stops) on April 10.

Hawaiian took its first aircraft on March 8, in time to inaugurate inter-island jet services on April 20, one week ahead of rival Aloha's BAC 1-11 introduction. To deliver Hawaiian's aircraft, two rubber 1,000-pound capacity fuel tanks were carried in the main cabin and connected to the main fuel system. These DC-9s were also the first to feature rear ventral staircases.

The Hawaiian market provided the first real head-to-head competition between the DC-9 and the One-Eleven over sectors varying from the 45-mile Hilo–Kamuela sector to a 216-mile route between Honolulu and Hilo. Many executives from airlines yet to make a twin-jet choice visited both airlines to watch the high-frequency operations. Hawaiian operated its aircraft with 90 seats since minimal galley space was required. To compete, Aloha was forced to reduce seat pitch from 34 inches to 32 inches, raising capacity to 84 seats from 79. Coincidentally, tourist air traffic to the Islands was on the increase, and the advent of jet operations by both airlines brought profitability, leading to the withdrawal of federal subsidies.

Prior to receiving its DC-9Cs, Continental leased four DC-9-14s, the first being handed over on March 4 and entering service on April 10 over the Dallas–Lubbock–El Paso and Dallas–Albuquerque routes.

Top: DC-9-14 N1054T (ln 25/msn 45735), seen at New York's LaGuardia Airport in 1977, reflects TWA's second jet livery, with hollow titles. (Jon Proctor)

Center: A former TDA aircraft, DC-9-41 N934L (ln 764/msn 47618) was inherited via the acquisition of Ozark. (Author's Collection)

Below: In 1995, TWA applied its new livery to DC-9-34 N927L (ln 934/msn 48123). (Author's Collection)

KLM became the first European carrier to initiate DC-9 service, on April 25, between Amsterdam, Geneva and Nice. The initial aircraft had been delivered on March 24, without the installation of extra tanks, making the trip across the Atlantic Ocean via Gander, the Azores and Lisbon.

The next airline to begin DC-9 service was Allegheny, using a leased Series 10 for one year starting in July 1966 to gain jet operating experience.

KLM had anticipated receipt of its first aircraft in January, but delivery schedules were starting to be impacted by many material shortages, particularly engines and galleys, due to the build up of military aircraft production required by the expanding Vietnam campaign. As this problem became more apparent, Douglas was forced to issue a letter to all its customers explaining the situation.

Increasing production rates on both the DC-8 and DC-9, plus the A-4 *Skyhawk,* led to substantial hiring of labor, requiring training schools to be set up. In addition, Douglas had to expand its production facilities by leasing the old Ryan Aeronautical Company facility in Torrance, California, and set up sub-assembly plants in Tennessee and Arkansas. Even so, Douglas had its best financial quarter ever, with profits coming

from both the military and commercial programs. This was the first profitable quarter since the first flight of the DC-8 in May 1958. With a strong backlog of both military and commercial orders, Douglas was able to write off the $100 million in DC-9 development costs and cancel its revolving bank loan, thus operating on cash flow alone.

An order for three Series 10s received from Brazilian carrier VASP on April 24 was later canceled. The first DC-9 for Eastern was delivered on April 25 and entered service on June 1. At the delivery ceremony, Eastern announced that it was adding a further 22 Series 30s to its existing order, raising its DC-9 fleet total to 64 including the leased Series 10s.

A busy June saw a large order from Delta for 12 Series 31s plus 12 options, followed by Alitalia, which added two DC-9-32F all-freighters to its contract, the first all-cargo DC-9s to be sold. Continental also converted four optioned DC9-15Cs (its own designation for the RC), to firm buy status on June 20, bringing its total to 19 aircraft. North Central Airlines firmed up five options. KLM contracted for five DC-9-32s and also became the first DC-9-33RC customer with an order for five. The convertible aircraft would be fitted with JT8D-9 engines rated at 14,500 pounds static

Right: Ozark DC-9-31 N985Z (ln 599/msn 47491) shows the large titles added in 1977.

Below: A DC-9-34 in revised colors (N928L; ln 954/msn 48124) banks over Lake Tahoe in June 1980. Both went to TWA in 1986.

Allegheny's DC-9-31 N972VJ (ln 142/msn 47052) was part of a canceled Bonanza Air Lines order.

Top: Continental leased DC-9-14 N8961 (ln 23/msn 45842) from DAC until the Series 15RCs arrived. It still flies for Midwest Express as N800ME.
Above: N655TX, an ex-Texas International DC-9-14 (ln 45/msn 45736) reflects Continental's second jet color scheme. (Paul Brissette)
Below: One of Continental's transitional merger schemes is represented by DC-9-32 N352TX (ln 349/msn 45791). (M. Vogel)
Bottom: A revised red tail marking is displayed by N543NY (ln 217/msn 45789), a former Swissair DC-9-32. (Paul Brissette)

New York Air was formed in 1980 to compete with the Eastern Air Shuttle. Its DC-9-32 N524TX (ln 637/msn 47539) poses in front of two other company jets at LaGuardia Airport in 1984. (Jon Proctor)

Above: When New York Air was merged into Continental, this temporary livery appeared on DC-9-31 N536TX (ln 213/msn 47113). (Paul Brissette)

Below: In addition to its current livery, the word "Lite" worn by DC-9-32 N33056 (ln 900/msn 47765) reflects the company's short-lived low-fare market division, since abandoned. (Author's Collection)

thrust, and the MTOW raised to 114,000 pounds. All ten KLM airplanes were fitted with 580-gallon fuel tanks in the forward cargo hold, adjacent to the front spar.

Category II Approval

A flight test team led by Cliff Stout, who later captained the first DC-10 flight, had been busy working with the FAA to get the DC-9 approved for Category II all-weather landings for some time. Three different systems – two Collins and a Sperry – were tested using Ship One, a TWA and a KLM aircraft. The Sperry autopilot was approved to work with all three systems for coupled approaches that allowed landings with ceilings as low as 100 feet and forward visibility of 1,200 feet. FAA approval was received on June 20, 1966. Yet another Collins version was approved a month later for Swissair.

This was just in time for Swissair's delayed service startup on August 19, with flights from Zurich to London via Basel. Milan and Munich services also started later in the day. The six-week delayed start was due to engine shortages at Douglas.

Enclosed Overhead Baggage Racks

With its inauguration of DC-9 services, Swissair also introduced enclosed overhead compartments to the industry. Before the airline requested Douglas to provide lockable meshed doors to restrain baggage, the use of overhead racks had been restricted to hats and coats. The idea soon caught on and many airlines quickly undertook similar retrofits.

The Series 30 Flies

DC-9 firm orders stood at 374 when the first Series 30 rolled out on July 11, 1967, including 233 for that variant. The 48th production aircraft (N8916E) appeared in Eastern's colors with Douglas titles emblazoned on its white crown skin.

The first flight took place on August 1, flown by H.C. Van Valkenburg and accompanied by George Jansen, another veteran Douglas test pilot. Two flight-test engineers monitored the test instrumentation and recording equipment. The flight lasted 3 hours, 27 minutes, one hour longer than planned, because no problems were encountered. Several landings and takeoffs were performed at Palmdale to check handling and braking characteristics. Within a week, the first Series 30 had flown almost 20 hours, mostly out of Palmdale, and expanded its flight envelope to the maximum. To expedite the certification program, two more aircraft destined for Eastern joined the flight schedule over the next few months. As testing expanded, it became obvious that some drag problems existed when the aircraft did not meet its expectations fuel-burn rates. A program was instituted to improve gap sealing around the retracted flaps. The problem was eliminated after much trial and error.

In August, AVENSA of Venezuela joined the ranks of announced DC-9 customers and became the first Latin American customer by ordering two Series 10s. The Export-Import Bank financed more than 75 percent of the $8 million price tag. These Series 10s were the first to incorporate JT8D-7 engines developing 14,000 pounds of thrust for hot and high airfields. Hawaiian also placed an order for two Series 30s for late 1967 delivery.

The first DC-9-31 delivered to North Central Airlines, N951NC (ln 143/msn 47067), was sold to Texas International in 1977 and joined ValuJet in 1995.

Northeast Airlines DC-9-31 N970NE (ln 107/msn 47053) reflects the company's colorful "Yellowbird" theme.

Problems

At the time of the Series 30's first flight, the order book stood as follows:

Aeronaves de Mexico	9	**North Central**	10
Air Canada	18	**Northeast**	10
Alitalia	28	**Overseas National**	3
Allegheny	4	**Pacific Southwest**	1
Ansett ANA	3	**SAS**	15
Bonanza	5	**Saudi Arabian**	3
Caribair	3	**Southern**	6
Continental	17	**Sudflug**	2
Delta	42	**Swissair**	12
Eastern	64	**Trans Australia**	3
Hawaiian	2	**Trans-Texas**	7
Iberia	15	**TWA**	20
KLM	16	**West Coast**	4
Korean	1	**Unannounced**	51
TOTAL			**374 (plus 120 Options)**

Buried among the unannounced total was an order for three DC-9-32s, identical to Air Canada's, received from Air Jamaica. In dollar terms, DC-9 sales now stood at $1.46 billion, or an average price of $3.8 million per aircraft. DC-8 sales had generated $2.6 billion plus some $167 million in spares revenues. But despite of these impressive numbers, financial problems were beginning to appear. In tandem with the expanding number of DC-9 models, more DC-8 variants were being offered due to the advent of the 60 Series and its freighter versions.

Shortages were becoming a bigger issue, and work carried out in locations other than the planned station was creating inefficient use of manpower. Douglas began losing money on each DC-9 delivered. Numerous aircraft without engines were parked outside on the ramps all around the assembly halls, and some press sources quoted the losses averaging as much as $500,000 per aircraft.

Left: DC-9-14, YV-C-AVR (ln 109/ msn 47060) of AVENSA later flew for USAir and Emerald.

Center: After a period with Estrellas del Aire as XA-SKA, it joined Allegro Airlines. (via Eddy Gual)

Bottom: The aircraft also operated Caribbean services for KLM in 1967. (Paul Huxford)

Series 30 Flight Testing

By mid-November 1967, over 80 percent of the Series 30 flight testing had been completed. Another aircraft joined the test fleet on October 8 and was used for checking out several systems. During 212 flights some 260 hours of testing had been achieved. The first aircraft concentrated on stability and control maneuvers and had explored the entire performance envelope.

On December 22, the FAA type certificate was awarded to the DC-9-30. The two test aircraft had logged 380 hours over 325 flights. Though approved for an MTOW of 98,000 pounds, some were made at 109,000 pounds, with landings at 105,000 pounds.

The maximum design altitude of 35,000 feet and airspeed of Mach 0.89 had been reached. Approval was given for both auto-coupled and manual flight director approaches under Category II conditions with the Collins F-109 flight director, Sperry SP-50A autopilot and an autothrottle system.

This was the first time that an aircraft had ever been granted approval for Category II operations as part of its basic type certification.

The Category II trials had been mainly flown "under the hood" to simulate instrument conditions, but the actual FAA acceptance flights were performed in the San Francisco area under real conditions with cloud bases of 100 feet and forward visibility of 1,200 feet.

Meanwhile, production rates accelerated towards a target of 16 per month; 11 DC-9s were delivered in November, in spite of mounting supplier shortage problems. Standard Airways' first aircraft was accepted on November 3. On December 29, Northeast became the second airline to take delivery of a Series 15, on an interim lease pending arrival of its Series 30s. Just one year after the initial delivery, 64 DC-9s had been delivered to 14 airlines plus two others remained in flight test operations. Fleet utilization was averaging 7.5 hours per day with few technical delays being experienced.

The first of three DC-9-32s for German charter carrier Atlantis, D-ADIS (ln 549/msn 47459) was sold to North Central as N942N.

Trans American Charter specializes in sports team charters with DC-9-32 N967ML (ln 619/msn 47514). (Author's Collection)

VH-CZA (ln 86/msn 47003) became both the first and last DC-9-31 to see service with Ansett, serving from March 1967 to September 1982. It appears in delivery colors (above), and its final livery (below), with "Farewell Australia" markings. (MDC/Bob Smith)

Top: Trans Australia Airlines DC-9-32 VH-TJJ (ln 87/msn 47007) in 1967, wearing delivery colors.
Above: DC-9-31 VH-TJM (ln 270/msn 47072) with its updated livery in 1977. (Martin Hornlimann)
Below: DC-9-31 VH-TJL (ln 152/msn 47009), wearing America's Cup decals, in the third scheme. (Bob Smith)
Bottom: In 1980, the airline was among the first to introduce exterior artwork. (via CAF)

AeroLloyd DC-9-32 D-ALLC (ln 778/msn 47672) later became N202ME with Midwest Express. (M. Roser)

Delivered to Alitalia, DC-9-32 I-DIZF (ln 615/msn 47519) later passed to its domestic subsidiary, Aero Mediterranea. It currently flies in Colombia as HK-3927X. (Dariö Cocco)

During the Winter of 1979-80, Air Malta leased DC-9-32 OE-LDC (ln 635/msn 47520) from Austrian Airlines. (Author's Collection)

Binter Canarias operates ex-Iberia DC-9-32 EC-BIR (ln 237/msn 47093) on its scheduled inter-island services. (Henry Tenby)

Macedonian Airlines leased DC-9-32 YU-AJJ (ln 688/msn 47567) from JAT. It is seen at Zurich in 1997. (Tom Singfield)

In October 1996, Tuninter leased DC-9-32 YU-AJL (ln 695/msn 47571) from JAT. (Avimage)

Ex-Eastern DC-9-31, N8927E (ln 130/msn 45864) spent three years in desert storage before being acquired by Air Train in 1994. The airline changed its name to Jet Train in January 1997. (Bob Shane)

One of four ex-Air Canada DC-9-32s intended for Altair, N901AK (ln 112/msn 45846) was never delivered and instead went on to serve with PSA and USAir. (Author's Collection)

American International leased former Martinair DC-9-33RC N94454 (ln 343/msn 47291) from Hawaiian in 1981. (Author's Collection)

A former Air Canada DC-9-32, N715CL (ln 160/msn 47020) is seen at Montreal in January 1982, wearing the colors of Columbia Air. When the start-up carrier was unable to begin operations, it instead migrated to PSA as N706PS. (Gary Vincent)

Express One DC-9-31, N931ML (ln 400/msn 47202), an ex-Ansett aircraft, also flew for Midway Airlines and American International Airways before going to ValuJet. (Norbert Raith)

Grand Airways DC-9-31 N977ML (ln 406/msn 47329) was one of many ex-Midway Airlines aircraft that were parked in the desert for several years. It is seen at Atlanta in November 1995. (Brian Gustafson)

Southern's DC-9-31 N89S (ln 486/msn47042) in original markings.

Above: The second of Pacific Southwest Airlines' two factory-delivered DC-9-31s, N982PS (ln 244/msn 47251) was leased to Ozark after one year in service. It is still with TWA.

Below: In 1983, PSA bought several DC-9-32s from Air Canada including N706PS (ln 126/msn 47020). (Thomas Livesey)

DC-9-31 N972NE (In 122/msn 47057) displays a Delta widget following the merger in 1972. It was later sold to Allegheny. (Author's Collection)

Cebu Pacific's DC-9-32, RP-C1504 (In 910/msn 47792) was one of a batch acquired from Garuda Indonesian Airways. It also flew with Merpati. (Author's Collection)

When CARIBAIR merged with Eastern in 1973, its DC-9-31 (In 108/msn 47098) became N8988E, and later YV-760C with AVENSA.

Since its first livery in 1979, Midway underwent four color scheme changes before bankruptcy closed the airline in 1991. Included are:
Top: DC-9-15 N1067T (ln 101/msn 45781).
Above: DC-9-32 N901ML (ln 220/msn 47104). (Paul Brissette)
Below: DC-9-32 N939ML (ln 100/msn 45710). (Author's Collection)
Bottom: Ex-Eastern DC-9-31 N8944E (ln 266/msn 47167). (D. Stewart)

HK-4084X (ln 407/msn 47330), a DC-9-31 of Aero Republica formerly belonged to Eastern Airlines. (Karsten Heiligtag)

Venezuela's ASERCA has become a sizable operator of DC-9s, including Series 31 YV-707C (ln 390/msn 47272). (Karsten Heiligtag)

Isla Airlines acquired ex-Eastern DC-9-31 YV-705C (ln 283/msn 45867) in December 1994. (Author's Collection)

XA-TCT (ln 348/msn 47274), a DC-9-32, was leased to SAM by MDC in 1972 for two years. (Author's Collection)

SARO, a Mexican local service carrier, leased DC-9-31 XA-SHW (ln 265/msn 47166) between 1993 and 1995. (via Eddy Gual)

Ex-Eastern DC-9-31 YV-817C (ln 375/msn 47036) at Caracas in 1993. (via Eddy Gual)

Zuliana DC-9-32 YV-459C (ln 633/msn 47548) previously flew with Ansett, American International and Midway Airlines. (Author's Collection)

DC-9-32 EC-BPF (ln 484/msn 47364) was one of several ex-Iberia DC-9s leased by Viva between 1990 and 1992. (Author's Collection)

Nigerian airline ADC currently operates former Eastern DC-9-31 N8962E as 5N-BBC (ln 344/msn 45871) on domestic services. (Via Bob Smith)

Leased from JAT for one year in 1987, Air Djibouti DC-9-32 YU-AJI (ln 687/msn 47563) retained its Yugoslavian registration. (via Eddy Gual)

South African airline Sun Air began operating ZS-NRB (ln 611/msn 47468) in 1995; the DC-9-31 originally belonged to East African as 5Y-ALR. (via Bob Smith)

ZAS leased DC-9-32 YU-AHJ (ln 466/msn 47239) from Inex-Adria in 1989 to operate charters between Aswan and Abu Simbel. (Author)

Nigerian carrier Zenith Air DC-9-31 5N-INZ (ln 482/msn 47402) was ex-Eastern N8986E and now flies with Northwest. (via Eddy Gual)

To make way for MD-80s, Sun Air handed over DC-9-31 ZS-NRD (ln 121/msn 47037) to new airline Zimbabwe Express in July 1997. (via Martin Hornlimman)

Nigerian airline Bellvue Airlines acquired DC-9-32 5N-BLV (ln 373/msn 47276), ex-N3340L of Delta, in June 1995. (A. Schultheiss)

TAT DC-9-41 OH-LNF (ln 747/msn 47614) was leased from Finnair in 1983. (Author's Collection)

DC-9-32 PK-GNS (ln 906/msn 47789) is one of several transferred to Merpati from Garuda in 1995. (via Bob Smith)

Broker AAS is unusual in applying its logo to aircraft awaiting resale. Ex-TAA DC-9-31 VH-TJU (ln 640/msn 47552) is en route to Airborne Express as N942AX. (Tim Williams)

Air Aruba's single DC-9-31 P4-MDD (ln 389/msn 47271) supplements a fleet of MD-80s. (via Eddy Gual)

Trinity Air Bahamas DC-9-32 N1288L (ln 577/msn 47443), originally with Delta, was sold to ValuJet. (via Eddy Gual)

Air Vanuatu leased DC-9-31 VH-CZD (ln 269/msn 47065) from Ansett for just two months in 1981. Later with the U.S. Navy, it is now owned by Airborne Express. (Martin Hornlimann)

Above: Independent Air Freighters actually owns DC-9-33F VH-IPF (ln 467/msn 47408), seen at Melbourne in March 1984 while on lease to Hertz. It was joined by ex-KLM DC-9-33RC. (Martin Hornlimann)

Below: It was joined by N941F (ln 311/msn 47193), photographed in 1993 prior to obtaining the registration VH-IPC. (Bob Shane)

Evergreen's DC-9-32F N935F (ln 296/msn 47220) was built for Alitalia as I-DIKF. It is shown in the lighter version of Evergreen's colors. (John Wegg)

DC-9-33RC, Z3-ARA (ln 624/msn 45730) was originally sold to Inex-Adria as YU-AHW. (Hans Oehninger)

Martinair leased DC-9-33RC, PH-MAX (ln 619/msn 47514) to Iranair in January 1976 for a one-month tour by the Shah of Iran's wife. (Author's Collection)

KLM sold three DC-9-15s to its daughter company, ALM, including PJ-DNA (ln 55/msn 45722) in 1968. It is currently in Colombia as HK-2865X. (Author's Collection)

Colorful DC-9-32 of ALM, PJ-SNA (ln 761/msn 47648) at Miami in February 1982. (Ray Leader)

Air Jamaica's DC-9-32, 6Y-JIJ (ln 735/msn 47639) was later modified to a convertible freighter and currently serves in the U.S. Navy. (Jeff Burch)

In winter 1981, Aviaco operated Finnair's ex-TDA DC-9-41 EC-DQT (ln 742/msn 47613) for six months. (ECMS)

Airborne Express has amassed a large fleet of DC-9s for its parcel service, including DC-9-41, N951AX (ln 759/msn 47616) which previously served with JAS. (via Bob Smith)

The Viking ship cheatline reveals the origin of Thai International's DC-9-41 HS-TGM (ln 555/msn 47395), leased from SAS in 1970-71. (Author's Collection)

The prototype Series 20, N8965U (ln 382/msn 47301) during its flight test program.

The Series 20 Re-emerges

SAS began looking for a replacement aircraft for its Convair 440 fleet in early 1966, needing some 15 aircraft. After reviewing several types, competition narrowed to the DC-9-10 versus the BAC 1-11-200, or possibly converting the Convairs to turboprops.

Douglas decided to offer its previously shelved DC-9 Series 20 configuration. The design married the Series 10 fuselage to the Series 30 wing. Its takeoff capability was further improved with upgraded JT8D-11 engines rated at 15,000 pounds static thrust. With a full space-limited payload of 19,200 pounds, the Series 20 could operate from 4,500-foot strips on an 84-degree day, permitting operations from all but one of SAS's domestic routes, Alta, Norway. The 98,000-pound MTOW gave it a range of 1,250 miles with a full payload.

Seating was a mixed-class arrangement for 80 passengers. An obvious advantage for Douglas was the commonality of spares, engines, cabin fixtures and cockpit. SAS awarded a contract for 10 firm plus 10 options for the DC-9 Series 21 in late summer although the announcement wasn't made public until December 19 after formal board approval. The Convairs were eventually relegated to Linjeflyg's Swedish domestic routes.

More Sales

KLM subsidiary Martinair, an Amsterdam-based DC-8 passenger charter and cargo operator, became the DC-9's thirty-second new customer on October 20, 1966, with an order for one DC-9 Series 32RC. Just a week later, on October 28, Delta exercised options for 12 more Series 30s. Including some unannounced contracts, DC-9 sales had now reached 400, with 53 delivered to 13 airlines. Although in service for less than one year, the fleet had exceeded 65,000 flying hours with only 2.5 flights per 100 incurring mechanical delays of more than 10 minutes.

Resplendent in Euro-white, DC-9-21 LN-RLL (ln 382/msn 47301) at Dusseldorf in 1986. (Author's Collection)

Martinair's DC-9-33RC PH-MAN (ln 343/msn 47291) shows off its original colors on a pre-delivery flight. It is currently with Airborne Express as N933AX.

Saudia was an early buyer of DC-9-14s, including HZ-AEA (ln 83/msn 47000), but later switched to Boeing 737-200s for short-range services.

Delta simplified its titles after the first few DC-9-32s were delivered. N3317L (ln 119/msn 47026) shows the single word "Delta" without "Air Lines." The carrier eventually operated 77 DC-9-32s. (via Eddy Gual)

West Coast Airlines announced an order for three Series 30s for 1968 delivery on November 15, just one day after initiating DC-9 services linking Seattle with Portland, San Francisco and the Tri-Cities of Pasco, Richland and Kennewick, Washington. Delta's 14th – and last – Series 14 was handed over on January 6, 1967, the 75th DC-9 to be delivered.

The 22nd anniversary of Saudi Arabian Airlines was celebrated with the delivery of its first DC-9 on January 23. A few days later, on January 26, Delta increased its buy with six more DC-9 firm orders and 12 options.

On the following day, Eastern accepted its first DC-9-31 for use on the Washington D.C.–New York Air Shuttle. Following the hand-over ceremony, negotiations were completed for five more Series 31s. The first 14 Series 30s, all fitted with 110 seats, were eventually assigned to the Shuttle, allowing its Constellations to be withdrawn except for back-up flights. The remainder of the DC-9 fleet was configured with 87-seat dual-class interiors.

Turkish Airlines (THY), the 33rd DC-9 customer, ordered two Series 30s on February 3. However, a Series 10, TC-JAA, had been leased from Douglas in August 1967 for five and a half years. Northeast then added four more aircraft to its planned DC-9 "Yellowbird" fleet, raising the total to 14. Coincidentally, Continental raised its DC-9C contract total to 10.

Things Go Sour

The total order book jumped to 431 when a major contract was signed with Air Canada on March 2, 1967. The Canadian airline announced the purchase of 24 jets from Douglas, including 17 DC-9-32s. But the production delivery schedule was now beginning to slip more noticeably as shortages accumulated. Only 16 DC-9s were delivered in the first quarter of 1967, down from 21 in the last quarter of 1966. The ramps

Top: Used by THY pending delivery of Series 32s, DC-9-15 TC-JAA (ln 35/msn 47048) was previously leased to Continental. It is currently operated by Intercontinental as HK-3827X.
Above: DC-9-32 TC-JAK (ln 636/msn 47397) in the 1970s livery. (Steve Miller)
Below: TC-JAG (ln 224/msn 47442) in an experimental scheme in February 1981. (Author's Collection)
Bottom: THY's last colors on TC-JAD (ln 527/msn 47488). (via Eddy Gual)

became littered with engineless aircraft containing incomplete interiors. Meanwhile, what had been forecast to be a successful fiscal year ending March 31, 1967, was turning into a huge deficit of more than $27.5 million.

Efforts were made to re-establish the revolving line of credit and to raise $50 million in equity capital, but the banks were unwilling to agree unless there were changes to senior management, which the Board was loath to accept. Donald Douglas, Sr., on the advice of some bankers, hired a New York firm, Lazard Brothers, to assist in finding a solution to

the problem. After a few weeks of investigation, Lazard concurred with the banks' viewpoint. The only alternative suggested was to seek a merger; the Douglas board eventually, but reluctantly, agreed.

Within a few weeks, merger proposals were received from Fairchild, General Dynamics, Martin-Marietta, McDonnell Aircraft, North American Aviation and Signal Oil & Gas.

After reviewing the offers, the Douglas board recommended the acceptance of McDonnell's offer to the shareholders. It included the purchase of 1.5 million new shares of Douglas stock for $68.7 million and, subject to Justice Department approval, a complete merger of the two companies. The formal announcement was made on January 13, 1967, with Justice Department approval following on April 26.

The new company, McDonnell Douglas Corporation (MDC) was officially formed on April 28. Its new board chairman was James S. McDonnell, with Donald Douglas, Sr. becoming Chairman Emeritus. Donald Douglas, Jr. gave up his president's title but remained a board member with the new company.

A revised master plan was devised with the goal of getting deliveries back on schedule by the summer of 1969. In the interim, delays could be expected and letters were sent to all customers explaining the situation. Part of the problem, apart from engine shortages, was the proliferation of models being offered. The complex engineering orders which followed complicated production scheduling more than previously anticipated.

To give some idea of the situation, prior to the merger, the 1967 production plan had called for delivery of 170 DC-9s comprising of 29 DC-9-10s, 114 DC-9-30s, 18 DC-9-15RCs, five DC-9-15MCs and four DC-9-30CFs. At the same time, 55 DC-8s, including 22 DC-8-61s, 15 DC-8-62s, seven DC-8-61Fs, five DC-8-50s, five DC-8-63s and one DC-8-62CF were scheduled for delivery. Further compounding the problem were the 24 customized versions being built for the first time during 1967!

The outlook for 1968 was similar, featuring an additional 10 newly tailored configurations plus new freighter versions of the DC-8-63. Meanwhile, a landmark was reached on April 13, 1967 when the 100th DC-9 was delivered to Eastern Air Lines (N9822E, Line Number 103). Northeast accepted its first two DC-9-31s on May 5 and started service between Boston and New York on May 15. Southern Airways decided to go for a coast-to-coast record when its first DC-9-15 flew from Long Beach to Charleston, N.C., in 4 hours, 13 minutes on May 9. Service commenced between Atlanta, Charleston and several other cities on June 15. On June 2, 1967, Allegheny order six additional DC-9-31s.

Automatic Landings

By May 24, over 200 fully automatic landings had been accomplished by Douglas test crews and line pilots. Led by Cliff Stout, the team flew the first Eastern DC-9 Series 30 under Category III conditions, amassing 80 hours of flying time during a nine-week period. "Cat III" permitted the DC-9 to land or take off with a runway visual range of 700 feet and no ceiling restriction. The prototype installation included a "head-up" display (HUD) that allowed to pilot to look ahead outside the cockpit and still see instrument readouts directly in his line of sight. This was the first time that the HUD had been installed in a commercial airliner.

Apart from company test pilots, the Air Line Pilots Association also assigned a four-man team to assist in the trials. Additionally, 25 other pilots, including several with no previous jet experience, landed the aircraft manually using the HUD system, achieving excellent touchdowns at low sink rates.

Iberia's livery was revised twice over the 19-year service life of its DC-9-30 fleet.
Top: Series 32 EC-BIG (ln 122/msn 47037) in the initial scheme.
Center: Iberia's global aspirations are reflected in the revised tail logo shown on Series 33RC EC-BYN (ln 675/msn 47565). (Author's Collection)
Bottom: Series 32, EC-BIO (ln 190/msn 47090) wears the final scheme. (Author's Collection)

Series 30 Starts European Services

Iberia became the first European DC-9 operator to take delivery of a Series 30 on June 29, 1967, just one day after the Spanish airline had celebrated its 40th Anniversary. EC-BIG was delivered to Madrid via Gander and the Azores. Service began in August.

Aeronaves de Mexico was the next to take initial delivery on July 6, putting the DC-9-15 into service on July 11 between Los Angeles and Mexico City with three en route stops. On July 20, Korean Air Lines flew its first DC-9 from Long Beach to Seoul, a 9,155-mile delivery flight.

In spite of the announcement of late delivery problems, orders from new customers continued to come in at a steady rate. The 33rd customer was Linea Aeropostal Venezolana (LAV), buying a single Series 10 on July 26. The price, including spares, was $4.4 million. Universal Airlines contracted four DC-9-32CFs plus two options on July 31 for 1969 delivery. This order was later canceled when Universal ceased operation.

Purdue Airlines, a new supplemental air carrier, signed a contract for a single DC-9-32 to be used on charter flights and also to provide aviation services to Purdue University. An order for a second was placed shortly afterwards. Martinair exercised its option for a second DC-9-32CF on August 3. North Central picked up the first of 10 Series 30s and began service on September 1 from its Minneapolis base.

Alitalia took delivery of its first Series 32 on August 17. KLM brought its DC-9 fleet total to 20 with an order for four Series 32s on September 29.

By now, DC-9 orders had reached 477, with 143 aircraft delivered; DC-8 contracts totaled 488. FAA certification of the DC-9-32CF followed the delivery of the first aircraft to Overseas National (ONA) on October 6. It was handed over in an all-passenger configuration, pending formal issuance of the type certificate that came on October 13.

Aeronaves de Mexico has seen a variety of color schemes while operating DC-9s:

Left: DC-9-15 XA-SOA (In 15/msn 47059) in the original delivery livery.

Below: XA-DEJ (In 717/msn 47594) DC-9-32 in bare metal with the shorter titles.

Center: To celebrate it's 50th anniversary, the scheme was revised, as seen on DC-9-15, XA-SOD (In 224/msn 47122). (Author)

Bottom: DC-9-32, XA-AMF (In 976/msn 48130) in the current markings. (Mike Rathke)

Two DC-9-32s were operated by Korean Air Lines, including HL-7201 (ln 135/msn 45827) which was sold to Hughes Airwest in 1973 as N9347.

Aeropostal has been a staunch user of DC-9s for many years in a spectrum of markings:
Above: DC-9-14 YV-C-AAA (ln 393/msn 47309) was later sold to Midwest Express.
Center: DC-9-32 YV-25C (ln 847/msn 47721) spent its entire life with Aeropostal. (Author's Collection)
Below: DC-9-15 YV-C-ANP (ln 83/msn 47000) in a short-lived color scheme. (Plane Fotos International)

Purdue Airlines ceased operations after operating DC-9-32s from 1969 until 1971. N393PA (ln 447/msn 47392 was sold to Inex-Adria as YU-AJB.

KLM's association with the DC-9 saw three different liveries.
Above: The initial colors are shown by DC-9-32 PH-DND (ln 198/msn 47102).
Center: DC-9-33RC PH-DNM (ln 280/msn 47191) features the white tail introduced in 1971. (Brian Stainer)
Bottom: DC-9-32 PH-MAX (ln 959/msn 48133) reflects KLM's ultimate markings in 1981. (A. Storti)

Another big order from Eastern – for 12 Series 30s – was announced on October 13 after it arranged a large financial package consisting of a $75 million revolving account plus an offering of $75 million in new stock. Later in the month, Alitalia announced that it had purchased eight more DC-9-30s, bringing its total to 40.

Series 40 First Flight

On schedule, the first DC-9-40 made its maiden flight from Long Beach on November 28, 1967, flown by Heimie Heimerdinger and W.L. "Bill" Ewert. Flight Test Engineer R.A. Capiola monitored the test equipment. Its JT8D-9 engines, rated at 14,500 pounds of thrust, launched the aircraft after a ground roll of only 3,500 feet at an MTOW of 95,000 pounds. The flight returned to Long Beach after 4 hours and 12 minutes of checking out its systems, flight characteristics and basic airworthiness. Following several more flights from Long Beach, the aircraft continued to fly the remainder of its test program from Edwards AFB.

200th Delivery

Just two years after the first scheduled DC-9 flight by Delta, the 200th DC-9 was flown away by Alitalia on November 30, 1967. It was the 195th to come off the line, but had been delayed by shortages. At this milestone, aggregate flying time by DC-9s had exceeded 380,800 hours, the average flight being only 45 minutes. Daily average utilization was 7 hours, 44 minutes per day, though individual airlines reported daily utilization of up to 10 hours, 45 minutes.

Delay rates were less than two per 100 departures by the fleet. Some 29 airlines were now using the DC-9 and the total order book stood at 486 plus the eight C-9As

Flower Bombings

The *R.M.S. Queen Mary* made its first trans-Atlantic crossing on June 1, 1936 and, as it approached New York, it was "bombed" with fresh flowers dropped from three Eastern Air Lines DC-3s led by Capt. Eddie Rickenbacker. In 1967, at the end of its illustrious career, the liner was purchased by the City of Long Beach, California, as a tourist attraction. This event led to one of the more publicized flights by the Series 40 during its test program, on December 8.

It was decided to re-enact the flower bombing event using the test aircraft. A load of fresh carnations and chrysanthemums were strewn over the ship from low altitude about 500 miles from Long Beach. This was achieved by using the ventral stairs, partially extended in low speed flight, and scattering the flowers in the slipstream. The crew for the flight were Chief Test Pilot Heimie Heimerdinger and Paul Patten. Heimerdinger was popular with the flight ramp mechanics and, as a joke, the name *Baron Von Ping Phabie* was inscribed under the cockpit window just for this flight as part of the unusual nose art applied for the occasion.

A rare photo of the DC-9 nose art applied for "flower-bombing" of *RMS Queen Mary*. Chief test pilot Heimie Heimerdinger and the Deputy Mayor of Long Beach prepare to load the "bombs."

N8960U salutes *RMS Queen Mary* off Baja, Mexico

Ex-SAS DC-9 Series 20s have operated with the following airlines:
Above: SE-DBO (ln 488/msn 47361) Nordic East. (Tommy Lakmaker)
Center: 125NK (ln 422/msn 47302) Spirit Airlines. (Avimage)
Bottom: N126NK (ln 432/msn 47303) ValuJet. (Karsten Heiligtag)

OY-KGE (In 441/msn 47305) was leased to Air Alpes for one year in 1981-82. (Christian Volpati)

Wearing the tail markings of Venus Airlines and Summer Express fuselage titles, DC-9-21 SX-BFS (In 441/msn 47305) flew for ValuJet after a long career with SAS. (Author's Collection)

Air Canada's first DC-9-14 (CF-TLB) served with many carriers, including Finnair as OH-LYC (In 4/msn 45711). (Brian Stainer)

This DC-9-32 (In 189/msn 47089) is one of the first ValuJet aircraft to reflect its company's name change. (Brian Gustafson)

Chapter X

MILITARY APPLICATIONS

USAF C-9A 67-22583 (ln 281/msn 47241). The red panel aft of the tail is a crash position locator.

The CX-2 Competition

B y late 1966, the Vietnam campaign had become a major conflict and the flow of sick and wounded casualties returning to the United States was rapidly increasing. Lockheed C-141 Starlifters brought the patients across the Pacific to West Coast military bases. Transportation on to Veteran's Administration and military hospitals was undertaken with C-131s and C-118s that made multiple stops to drop off their passengers. Douglas identified 432 potential airfields in the domestic aeromedical evacuation system network, when the need for a small, faster air ambulance capable of "fly-through" operations without ground facilities was considered critical.

In March 1967, the Pentagon issued a new Request for Proposal for an aircraft designated CX-2 for this mission, intending to announce a winner by July 1. In part, the urgency was accelerated after President Lyndon Johnson attended a med-evac presentation at Andrews AFB and toured the interior of a C-131. He was told that patients could be brought across the Pacific in 24 hours, but they would then wait at the U.S. terminals for several days before onward transportation to the specialist hospitals because of the inefficiency of the piston-powered transports. At the same time, the U.S. Air Force had finally been able to convince Secretary of

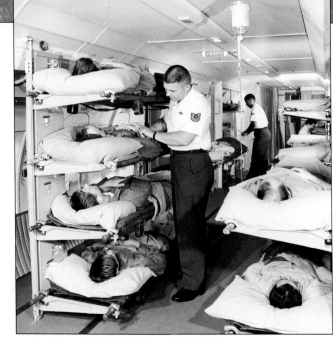

The C-9A has a 30- to 40-litter-patient capacity. Oxygen is provided in the service panels that support the litters, which swing up as hat racks when not in use.

Defense Robert MacNamara of the cost effectiveness of upgrading the service with jet transports.

The Douglas offer filled a requirement for an "off-the-shelf" aircraft capable of carrying 30 litter patients, up to 40 ambulatory patients or any combination of both. It also met the required conversion from an all-litter to all-ambulatory (or reverse) configuration in less than one hour. The litters and seats could be folded and stowed in the cargo bays, while the end stanchions and service panels were swung up and locked to the side walls to act as overhead utility racks.

The aircraft had to have an integral patient loading ramp 54 inches wide that could be fitted with weatherproof curtains when needed. Folded, it stored just inside the doorway; extended, it angled down at 19 degrees to facilitate wheelchairs and litter bearers. Other special requirements included self-start capability, a nurse's station that also controlled the medical systems, and separate refrigeration for food and medicine.

An isolation area, with its own air-conditioning system, for three contagious or intensive care patients was adjacent to the nurse's station. Avionics for military communications was included in addition to its standard commercial installation. The only significant changes to the basic DC-9 involved the oxygen and electrical systems. The oxygen system used liquid oxygen in lieu of the compressed gaseous oxygen used in commercial aircraft. In its proposal MDC also included the rear ventral stairs for ambulatory patient boarding. Normal medical staffing included two nurses and three aeromedical technicians.

The range specified was a minimum of 2,000 nautical miles, but 2,600 miles was preferable. The aircraft had to be capable of landing over a 50-foot high obstacle in 5,000 feet. An additional 1,780 gallons of fuel would be carried in tanks located in the cargo compartments, allowing it to make multiple stops without en route refueling. The engines selected were JT8D-9s; MTOW was 108,000 pounds.

MDC, particularly anxious to win this contract, took the precaution of reserving early delivery positions for February 1968. The USAF estimated that 13 aircraft were needed to replace the 16 C-131s and seven C-118s then in use. Funding for four aircraft was allocated in Fiscal Year (FY) 1967 and the USAF requested funding for an additional four in FY 1968.

On August 31, 1967, MDC was awarded a $28.7-million contract for eight aircraft – appropriately designated C-9A – with deliveries commencing in 1968. Eventually, this increased to a total of 21 aircraft delivered over several years; the final contract for eight aircraft being signed on August 4, 1970.

At the June 17, 1968 roll-out ceremony, the C-9A was formally named *Nightingale* in recognition of Florence Nightingale, an English nurse who went to the battlefields of Crimea in the 1870s to attend to the injured; she is credited as the founder of the military nursing profession.

The first C-9A was delivered to the 375th Aeromedical Airlift Wing at Scott AFB, Illinois, on August 12, 1968. The last delivery occurred in

Former Lt. Elsie Otte, the U.S. Army Air Force's first flight nurse, pours water from the Sea of Galilee to christen the C-9A *Nightingale*. (Author)

February 1973. Initially, the first eight were all based at Scott AFB, but others were later assigned to the 55th Aeromedical Airlift Squadron based in Germany and the 20th Aeromedical Airlift Squadron assigned to the Philippines. More recently, the latter C-9As have been re-deployed to the 20th Air Ambulance Squadron, 374th Air Wing at Yokota, Japan. Some C-9As are currently operated by the 73rd Aeromedical Airlift Squadron, an Air Force Reserve unit based at Scott AFB which provides additional crews to support the active duty crews.

The *Nightingale* service record has been remarkable. It has partaken in many historic events, such as returning the American hostages held in Iran to Germany in January 1981. A single aircraft has been converted to a VIP role, based in Belgium for use of the NATO Supreme Commander.

Other Proposals

While this competition was occurring, MDC offered two other military applications for the DC-9. The first was the Advanced Tactical Electronic Warfare System (ATEWS) version as a replacement for the Douglas EB-66 that was being used in Vietnam to jam radar emissions from North Vietnamese anti-aircraft defense systems during air strikes. The proposal was based on utilizing the Series 10 airframe and was identified as Project 3545. However, it was eventually abandoned when it was determined that the ATEWS lacked the capability to defend itself while over hostile territory.

The second unsolicited proposal was to build two special executive versions of the DC-9-30 for use by the White House on domestic travel missions. July 1967 and December 1967 deliveries were made possible by

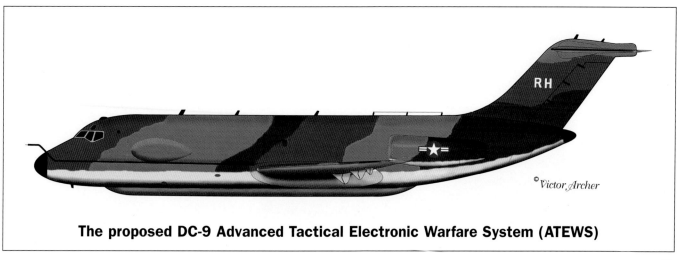

The proposed DC-9 Advanced Tactical Electronic Warfare System (ATEWS)

arranging with an airline to give up the slots in exchange for later delivery positions. The design featured a forward stateroom on the starboard side with an aisle running down the port side to give access to 40 seats at the rear of the aircraft. Ahead of the stateroom was a special communications center. However, it wasn't until December 24, 1973 that the Department of Defense finally ordered three VC-9Cs for the 89th Airlift Wing at Andrews AFB to be used by the President and senior government officials. The revised Request for Proposal had been issued less than five weeks previously. Deliveries occurred in 1975.

A little piece of aviation history was made on June 8, 1980 when a C-9A became the first U.S. military aircraft to be operated by an all-female crew of pilots, mechanic, flight nurses and medical technicians.

Above: VC-9C 73-1682 (ln 769/msn 47670), the second of three delivered to the 89th Airlift Wing at Andrews AFB for VIP use.

Below: Compared to many corporate jets, the VC-9C interior is relatively plain. Note the old style overhead racks used to simplify security checks.

U.S. Navy C-9B 159116 (ln 704/msn 47580) of VRC-30 based at North Island Naval Air Station (NAS), photographed over Mt. Shasta, California. (Harry Gann)

U.S. Navy C-9B

On April 19, 1972, the U.S. Navy (USN) announced the purchase of five DC-9-32CFs, to be designated C-9B for use as a logistics aircraft. It was nearly identical to the Air Force's C-9A, except for being fitted out as a convertible freighter. Powered by JT8D-15 engines with an MTOW of 110,000 pounds, it permitted an increased auxiliary belly fuel tankage of 2,250 gallons, enabling the aircraft to operate trans-Pacific flights via Hawaii, as a navigation lead ship for transiting fighter squadrons while carrying a 10,000-pound payload. To aid in overwater navigation, the C-9Bs were equipped with Omega and Inertial Navigation Systems (INS).

In all, 12 new C-9Bs, officially named *Skytrain II* after the Douglas C-47 of World War II, were bought for use by the U.S. Navy. Deliveries between May 1973 and March 1976 were shared between two regular squadrons, VR-1 and VR-2. A change of policy later resulted in four new USN Reserve squadrons being established with each being allocated two aircraft. The program's success prompted acquisition of used DC-9-32CFs, either through leases or direct purchase, and a fleet of 30 aircraft is now operated by some 12 Reserve units scattered around the United States.

The U.S. Navy, acting as purchasing agent, also contracted for a pair of new C-9Bs on behalf of the U.S. Marine Corps for use as staff transports. The Marine variants were delivered in early 1976 and both based at the Cherry Point, North Carolina, Marine Corps Air Station (MCAS).

In 1973, the Marines seriously considered the acquisition of a DC-9 Series 20 version that could be used as a command transport able to operate from advanced airstrips of shorter field length. This was superseded by the C-9B purchase.

Acting on behalf of the Kuwaiti Air Force, the USN also contracted for two C-9Bs that were delivered on October 15 and November 11, 1976. Prior to delivery, the aircraft carried USN Bureau Numbers 16049/50 respectively before being re-identified as KAF-320 and KAF-321.

KAF-320 was destroyed on the ground by the Iraqi forces on February 8, 1990, during the Gulf War.

One other foreign military service, the Italian Air Force (Aeronautica Militare Italiana), purchased a pair of new DC-9-32s for use as VIP transports. Sold directly to the Italian government and identical to those bought by Alitalia, the two were delivered in January and March 1974 and still serve with 306th Gruppo, 31st Stormo based at Rome's Ciampino Airport.

To date, the Venezuelan Air Force is the only other military organization to have operated a DC-9. It leased a DC-9-15 from Linea Aeropostal Venezolana between May 1977 and September 1981.

The Proposed Deck-landing C-9

The most interesting of the many proposals created by the MDC advanced design team was in 1972, a USN deck-landing version of the DC-9 Series 20. The Navy was seeking a replacement for the venerable Grumman C-1 *Trader* used for Carrier On-board Delivery (COD) missions, involving the delivery of high priority cargo and passengers to an aircraft carrier at sea. In addition, a tanker aircraft for air-to-air refueling was needed to replace the aging Douglas A3D *Skywarrior*. The proposed aircraft was referred to as the C-9 (COD), and deliveries were targeted for mid-1976. The competitor in this case, Grumman's C-2A *Greyhound*, which was already part of the Fleet inventory in small numbers.

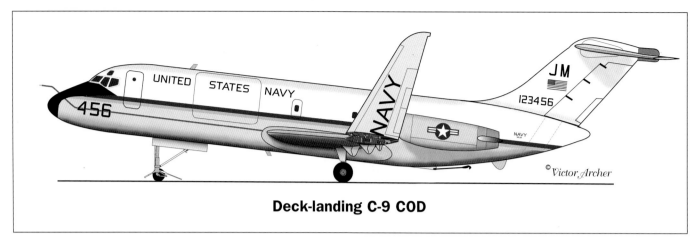

Deck-landing C-9 COD

The most noticeable exterior change was the re-positioning of the nose wheel 12 feet, 6 inches farther aft. The gear strut could also be extended by two feet to give the aircraft a 6-degree nose-up attitude for a catapult launch. (Several other aircraft types require this feature.) Local structural strengthening was required for both the retractable tail hook and the catapult hold-back attachments and heavier landing gear struts were substituted to absorb the deck-landing loads. A large tail bumper was also added.

Provisions were made for an in-flight refueling probe located below and ahead of the pilot's windscreen and the fitting of pylon attachment points some 12 feet inboard from each wing tip. These pylons were designed to carry a pod containing a standard USN "buddy" refueling package consisting of a pump and drum-mounted flexible hose with an attached drogue basket. An additional 780-gallon tank in the forward hold plus a second 1,000-gallon unit in the rear hold would have permitted the tanker to off-load more than twice the fuel volume of either the *Skywarrior* or the tanker version of the Grumman A-6 *Intruder*. An earlier study showed a single, retractable-drogue system installed under the rear fuselage, adjacent to the ventral stairs.

One other exterior change was the elimination of the heavy-thrust reversers, replaced by simple straight-exhaust cones. The thrust reversers were of no use because instant full power for a "bolter" (or "go-around") – due to a missed approach or the failure of the hook to engage the wires – was required. The aircraft would be stopped during deck landings by the arrestor hook only. The MTOW for shore-based operations was 110,000 pounds, but catapult limitations reduced on-board MTOW to 104,000 pounds. The carrier landing weight was restricted to 75,000 pounds, versus 93,400 pounds ashore. Overall COD modifications raised the empty weight 3,000 pounds; nearly half of the increase came from the stronger landing gear. The built-in airstairs were also removed to save weight, and replaced by a standard crew ladder. The engines were JT8D-9s.

The C-9 (COD) was intended to utilize the larger CVA-41 and CVA-59 aircraft carriers fitted with angled decks. As the aircraft would normally spend minimal time aboard the ships, a folding wing system was deemed to be unnecessary. A typical turnaround time for the C-9 (COD), from landing until being catapulted off, was intended to be 30 minutes. Because of the cargo door location, the C-9 could be parked with the tail overhanging the deck edge while safely off-loading and loading personnel and cargo.

The folding wing aspect was explored – the wing-fold point being between the elevators and flaps, and the wings folding 115 degrees. For deck parking, the folded span was 58.5 feet. A more complex change moved the hinge line inboard to give a folded span of just 47 feet and, with the nose gear strut extended to lower the tail, the aircraft could be taken down to the hangar deck on larger carriers.

The plan called for two production flight-test aircraft, an eight-month test program and an in-service date of less than three years from contract award. However, the winding down of the Vietnam campaign and the general reduction in the carrier fleet eventually eliminated the need for this intriguing development. Instead, belatedly, the Navy ordered a second batch of 39 upgraded C-2As in the mid-1980s.

In 1989, Hughes Aircraft proposed using a DC-9 platform for missile testing. The model shows an F-14 nose and a pylon-mounted air-to-air missile.

C-9B 160046 (ln 786/msn 47684) of the U.S. Marine Corps is operated by the Station Engineering Squadron at MCAS Cherry Point, North Carolina. (Harry Gann)

Delivered in March 1974, the Italian Air Force still operates this immaculate DC-9-32 MM62013 (ln 710/msn 47600). (Martin Stamm)

The Venezuelan Air Force (FAV) leased DC-9-15 YV-03C (ln 83/msn 47000) from LAV between 1977-85 and re-identified it as 0003, then YV-03. (Author's Collection)

Chapter XI

EXECUTIVE JETS

Probably the most glamorous of the executive jets, Playboy's DC-9-32 N950PB (ln 458/msn 47394) reverted to airline service and now flies for AeroMexico as XA-JEB.

The Black Bunny

From early on the DC-9 has been promoted as a suitable aircraft for conversion to a executive transport. The idea of using jets for corporate use was just beginning to catch on in the mid-1960s, although the Lockheed Jetstar and North American Sabreliner had been around in limited numbers for several years. Grumman's Gulfsteam I twin-turboprop was the most popular of the more modern aircraft, supplemented by a sprinkling of early Viscounts, the new Jet Commanders and deHavilland 125s. Numerous large corporations operated both propeller-driven and turboprop airliner conversions and a few F-27s.

The first large jet sold as a private conveyance was a de Havilland Comet 4C that was delivered to the Saudi Government in June 1962. BAC delivered a One-Eleven to a German company in January 1966. Two others were delivered to the United States later that year.

MDC sold its first executive DC-9 on July 9, 1967, when Playboy magazine publisher Hugh M. Hefner ordered a $4.5 million Series 30 for his own use. Extra fuel tanks carrying 1,780 gallons were installed in the belly, giving the 33-passenger aircraft trans-Atlantic capability. During night flights, the sofa-style seating could be transformed into 12 comfortable beds.

Designed by Daniel Czubak, the interior continued Playboy's black and white theme throughout. Its most famous feature was Hefner's private quarters with a 6-foot by 8-foot elliptical bed plus separate shower and toilet accommodations located at the rear of the aircraft. The main aisle curved its way throughout the cabin rather than in a normal straight run. To minimize sound, the cabin had a special insulation of nylon flocking installed in the ceilings and sidewalls. This later proved to be a problem as a heavy touchdown would result in a "snow shower" of insulation flakes throughout the cabin. A change in materials eliminated the problem. The aircraft was registered N950PB and delivered on

Playmates from Playboy's Los Angeles mansion pose on the forward airstair in its extended position. The airstair is controlled from the opened panel on the forward lower fuselage, and can also be operated from a switch within the cabin.

February 24, 1969. In its all-black finish and the white bunny logo on the tail, the aircraft was an attention-getter wherever it appeared.

A long delay in service start-up was caused by the requirement for a non-airline interior. Originally, AiResearch of Los Angeles had contracted to design and install the custom furnishings but, after some differences of opinion with the customer, the work was completed by Pacific Airmotive Corporation at Burbank. The interior itself added over $1,000,000 to the basic aircraft price. N950PB entered service in early 1970.

The aircraft was maintained and operated by Purdue Airlines, which also had an agreement to charter it out when not needed by Hefner. Ozark Airlines took over the operating agreement after Purdue's demise.

The first executive DC-9 Series 15 was N228Z (ln 285/msn 47151) for Tracy Investments (above). It currently operates as VR-CKO (top). (via Eddy Gual/MDC)

The Black Bunny was under-utilized, amassing only 1,341 hours as an executive jet. Unfortunately Playboy Enterprises hit a bad patch financially in 1976 and Omni Aircraft Sales Inc., an aircraft brokerage house, bought the airplane for just over $4 million. It was converted for regular airline passenger use and currently flies as XA-JEB for AeroMexico.

Other Exec DC-9s

The only other DC-9 to be sold new for corporate use was a Series 15 acquired by Tracinda Investment Corporation as N228Z and delivered on April 22, 1968. It entered service after the interior was installed by Pacific Airmotive Corporation. Since then, it has been through the hands of several owners but still flies in an private configuration.

A more traditional executive interior was fitted, with a forward lounge for 14 passengers, a state room for six, plus a secretary's office for four. Auxiliary 1,760-gallon tanks give it a flying endurance of more than eight hours.

The Los Angeles Dodgers professional baseball team ordered a Series 30 in 1967 to replace its Lockheed 188 Electra, but later canceled in favor of a used Boeing 720B.

Line Number 34, which had been originally leased to Swissair pending delivery of Series 30s, was the only other executive jet to be sold directly by MDC. Registered N60FM, it went to Forbes Magazine in 1974. Since then the aircraft has changed hands at least eight times, but still serves as a corporate transport.

However, DC-9s have become quite common as business jets. The Series 30s are popular with professional sports teams, such as the Seattle Seahawks football team and Minnesota (later Dallas) North Stars ice hockey team. This trend is an outgrowth of the chartering of aircraft from both scheduled and supplemental carriers on a seasonal basis, with the aircraft being reconfigured to give ample space for the players, their equipment and staff.

In the early 1990s, El Mirage, Harrahs and the Golden Nugget casinos all used DC-9s to bring "high-rollers" to their tables. The Bank of Mexico acquired two ex-Continental DC-9-15RCs for use in transferring bullion as well as for staff travel, while country and western singer Kenny Rogers owns a DC-9 for extensive travel on tour with his entourage.

The FAA was an early user of DC-9s both for staff transport and the checking of navigational aids on the airways. It bought an ex-Swissair Series 10 in August 1968 and flew it until June 1994 when the twin-jet was transferred to the U.S. Department of Justice and is now used to transfer inmates between federal prisons throughout the United States.

More recently, NASA based a DC-9-30 at its Lewis Research Center. One other government entity to use the DC-9 is the United Nations which frequently charters aircraft from a Geneva-based company.

Forbes Magazine's DC-9-15 N60FM (ln 34/msn 45731). (Author's Collection)

Sports team private aircraft include:
Above: DC-9-32 N800DM (ln 621/msn 47466) of the Dallas Mavericks. (Author's Collection)

Below: The Florida Marlins' DC-9-31, N947ML (ln 619/msn 47514). (via Eddy Gual)

DC-9s used to carry high-rollers include:
Above: DC-9-10 N711SW (ln 62/msn 45740). (R. E. Garrard)

Below: DC-9-32CF, N934F (ln 246/msn 47148). (Author's Collection)

Banco de Mexico's corporate DC-9-15RC XA-BDM (ln 180/msn 47088). (Brian Stainer)

Above: Previously leased to Swissair, DC-9-14 N29 (ln 41/msn 45732) was bought by the FAA in 1968.

Below: The agency changed from its traditional colors of red/white in early 1980. The U.S. Department of Corrections now uses it to transport prisoners. (both Chuck Stewart)

Above: After the break-up of East African, Kenya Airways kept DC-9-32 5X-UVY (ln 612/msn 47478) as 5Y-BBR. (Author's Collection)

Below: Spirit Airlines operated the aircraft as N942ML. Recently it was sold to NASA as N650UG. (via Eddy Gual)

The United Nations frequently charters commercial airliners. Swiss company Aeroleasing provided DC-9-14 HB-IEF (ln 7/msn 45702) in 1990. (Author's Collection)

The U.S. Post Office leases a large fleet to move mail, including DC-9-15F N563PC (ln 194/msn 47055) which was operated by Emery in 1989. (via Eddy Gual)

Air West's triple-delivery aircraft pose in June 1969.

Recovery

The first 1968 order came from Hawaiian Airlines on January 2, for a third DC-9-30 to be delivered in early 1969. This statement, signifying a more normal time span between contract and acceptance, was a clear indication that deliveries were getting back on track. By the end of the first quarter, aircraft were being handed over to customers less than four weeks after roll-out, compared to a two-month gap just a year earlier.

Aero Transporti Italiani (ATI) then ordered the first four of an eventual total of 12 DC-9-32s, identical to those of its parent company. On February 14, local service carriers Bonanza, West Coast and Pacific announced their intention to merge, subject to CAB approval. The resulting carrier, Air West, planned to standardize on two jet types, the DC-9 and Boeing 727 plus F-27s. At the time, Bonanza and Air West both operated DC-9-10s with a combined total of five Series 30s on order. Pacific was about to receive 737s, however it was decided to cancel the Boeing contract and purchase an additional 11 DC-9-31s, bringing the order to 16 Series 30s.

The Series 40 Enters Service

By early February the Series 40 flight test program was well ahead of schedule. On 120 flights it had explored the entire design flight envelope during 140 flying hours. Part of the schedule included using two different power settings, the JT8D-9's 14,500-pound thrust and the 15,000-pound

thrust setting of the JT8D-11 power plant. The improvement was achieved by slightly reducing the by-pass ratio and increasing the compressor ratio through some modifications to the fan cooling and combustion chambers.

On February 27 the DC-9 Series 40 was awarded its type certificate for operation, at an MTOW of 110,000 pounds and an MLW of 102,000 pounds. Two days later, the first aircraft for SAS was delivered to Stockholm via Winnipeg, Montreal, Goose Bay and Keflavik. It entered service on March 12. The flight-test aircraft was refurbished and repainted before being delivered on May 23.

All-Freighters Delivered

The next notable delivery was on May 13, 1968, when the first all-freighter DC-9-32F for Alitalia left Los Angeles International Airport, bound for Rome. As an all-freighter, the type could carry a 40,000-pound payload on eight full-size and two half-size pallets. This delivery triggered the ordering of three more freighter versions, two for SAS and one for Swissair; all were delivered in the second half of 1969. SAS also increased its Series 40 order to 16 with a contract for six on June 28.

North Central Airlines added five more Series 30s to its backlog on July 15. Since introducing the DC-9, the carrier had increased its traffic by 35 percent. Similarly, Allegheny exercised its options for six Series 30s on July 17, with deliveries commencing in June 1969; two additional options remained for acceptance in 1970.

Alitalia used only two basic liveries on its DC-9-32s:
Above: I-DIKG (In 305/msn 47221; an all-freighter version). (Author's Collection)
Below: I-DIKA (In 136/msn 47038). (Author's Collection)

Among the steady stream of deliveries, Martinair's first DC-9-32RC was accepted on July 25; it became the first of that type to enter service. Three more Series 30s were added to Air Canada's order on August 15. The 37th airline to purchase DC-9s was Garuda Indonesian Airways, with an order for two Series 32s on October 2. These aircraft were fitted with life rafts (carried in the cabin ceilings) for inter-island services. The Garuda purchase brought DC-9 sales to 556 (with 382 delivered), matching the total DC-8 production.

Looking at Another Stretch

During the summer of 1968, presentations were made to several airlines showing yet another stretch. Eastern, Allegheny and Hawaiian all expressed continuing interest in the concept. Tentatively identified as the Series 50, it extended the Series 40 fuselage by approximately 136 inches, bringing the aircraft in direct competition with the Boeing 727-100. It was proposed that the Series 50 be re-engined with the Pratt & Whitney JT3Ds used on the DC-8.

Potential customers soon pointed out that the JT3D was an old technology engine, unacceptable for the next decade. At the time, no other suitable power plant in the 20,000- to 25,000-pound thrust range existed, and the project was eventually shelved. One other approach was considered to widen the fuselage to a six-abreast configuration, but this was abandoned due to both weight and cost considerations.

The Hot Rod Flies

After a takeoff run of only 2,700 feet, the first DC-9 Series 21 made its first flight on September 18 with Harry Van Valkenburg and Jim McCabe at the controls. It was airborne for three hours before returning to Long Beach.

The Series 21, at its MTOW of 98,000 pounds, required 1,000 feet less than either the Series 30 or 40 for its minimum field-length requirements. After logging a total of 142 hours in just 85 test flights, the Series 21 received its type certificate on November 25. The second Series 21 was also used briefly in the test program, then delivered to SAS on December 11, 1968, entering service almost immediately.

The prototype aircraft was delivered in March 1969, having been retained by MDC for some additional test flying to develop the HUD system. This time, two different units were installed, an MDC-developed unit on the left side and an Elliot Automation system on the right. The testing was done as part of the development of the systems for use on the DC-9 as well as the DC-10 that had recently entered production. It was also intended as a retro-fit item on the DC-8. Based at Long Beach, the aircraft made a total of over 100 approaches at several California airfields during nine flights. Pilots from 18 airlines and the FAA took turns making approaches using the systems.

While the Series 21 flight test program was being completed, design engineers were looking at developing a light-weight version identified as the Series 22. This was in response to a similar light-weight version of the 737 that Boeing was proposing as a short-field aircraft. The project stemmed from requests by TDA and All Nippon Airways for a design to replace the YS-11 on feeder routes. The requirement was to operate from a 4,000-foot strip with 60 passengers. To achieve this, the DC-9 proposal included removal of components such as galleys and oxygen systems plus the addition of nose wheel braking. The project was put on hold in view of the general downturn in airline traffic, but re-emerged in 1974.

The Third Anniversary

Three years after the type's service entry, 416 DC-9s had been delivered, logging in excess of one million flight hours and more than 428 million miles. Two aircraft had already topped the 9,000-hour mark and the fleet average delay rate had dropped to 1.6 percent.

During 1968, twenty-two DC-9-10s that had been leased to Swissair, Continental and Eastern were returned to the company for disposal. Some were put out on further interim leases while others were sold outright. The prices at the time ranged between $2.3 million and $2.8 million.

Air California, Cyprus Airways, Dominicana, Germanair and THY were typical of the smaller airlines that moved into the jet era via these aircraft. Germanair operated one ex-Swissair DC-9-15, D-AMOR, appropriately christened the "Lovebird," for six months starting in April. The charter airline had placed an unannounced order for two DC-9-30s in early 1969, and the first one flew in October 1969, wearing Germanair's colors and registered N1796U. However, the airline canceled at the last moment due to its merger with Bavaria Flug which already operated a fleet of BAC 1-11s. The new DC-9 was repainted and sold to Atlantis. This was the only DC-9 transaction that fell through at such a late stage.

Hams for Planes

In March 1969, after a campaign lasting three years, Inex-Adria and Jugoslav Aerotransport (JAT) jointly announced that they had selected the DC-9 to replace their piston-engine fleets. A major hurdle facing the manufacturers was the lack of hard currency earnings by the Yugoslavs to pay for the aircraft. Almost all international aircraft sales transactions are carried out in U.S. currency, so BAC had offered a straight barter system of aircraft for Yugoslav goods and produce. However, since trade with the United Kingdom was already well established, it would not create the new export markets that the Yugoslav government was anxious to achieve, and the offer was rejected.

John C. Wallace, an MDC salesman charged with developing new markets, seized on the idea and developed his own approach. He suggested that MDC would make its best efforts to find buyers for Yugoslav products in the United States but not commit to taking any of the goods in straight trade. The good faith offer by MDC was worth $9 million, some 25 percent of the total purchase price for seven aircraft. He then promised that MDC would provide an experienced buyer to arrange contacts with American importers. The aircraft would be paid for in U.S. dollars in the normal way, via loans arranged by the Export-Import Bank and MDC Finance Corporation.

The initial sales were two DC-9-32s to Inex-Adria and five similar aircraft to JAT, though only the Inex-Adria sale was made public at the time of its first delivery on April 25. This speedy hand-over was made possible when Alitalia agreed to reschedule a delivery to a later date, thus enabling MDC to deliver the first aircraft within a few weeks. Inex-Adria was owned by the Slovenia, by far the wealthiest and most "westernized"

Aero Transporti Italiani (ATI) is the domestic arm of Alitalia.
Above: DC-9-32 I-ATIA (ln 520/msn 47431) appears in original markings.

Below: More recently, Alitalia's basic design has been adopted, as represented by DC-9-32, I-ATIK (ln 613/msn 47477). (A. Storti)

DC-9-32 YU-AHN (ln 591/msn 47470) was part of the original "Hams for planes" deal.

YU-AJK (ln 689/msn 47568) shows the markings introduced in 1990. (Hans Oehninger)

of the Yugoslav states. Its aircraft would be used almost entirely on western Europe charter flights to bring tourists to the region, thus earning the needed hard currency.

At the same time, another DC-9-32 about to be delivered to Alitalia was instead handed over to JAT on a one-year interim lease. The aircraft, already in Alitalia's colors, was flown to Burbank and repainted, then delivered on April 15, 1969, just a few days after the first indication that negotiations were in hand. It operated for one year still wearing an Italian registration. Though MDC arranged it, the company did not make any formal announcement of the transaction that was between the two airlines. As a side agreement, MDC offered to buy a token batch of canned hams worth about $40,000

for use in the company cafeterias, in addition to some small machine tools and other related items. Surprisingly, the story of the unusual agreement didn't reach the press until March 1970 when the formal announcement of the JAT sale was finally made.

The long delay was because of the efforts required to complete financing and find buyers for Yugoslav products. Special exemption for the sale of U.S. technology to Eastern bloc countries also required the President's approval. When the story was revealed, the press had a field day with this "Hams for Planes" story.

The successful program was considerably expanded over the ensuing years to cover other contracts, and a special department was set up just to

ONA was one of the few cargo airlines to apply names to its fleet. DC-9-32CF N931F (ln 172/msn 47040) was sold to Evergreen, then Airborne Express.

deal with similar agreements. MDC and many of its suppliers have continued to buy the hams, and this innovative approach led to many additional sales of MDC-built aircraft to Yugoslavia, including DC-10s and MD-80s.

The 500th DC-9 was delivered to Allegheny – its 19th – with suitable ceremonies on May 27. Delay rates continued to improve and one U.S. airline achieved a dispatch on-time rate of 99.2 percent from its 57-aircraft fleet. Hawaiian's short-haul, high-frequency operations achieved a 99.6-percent dispatch reliability. SAS brought its Series 40 total to 24 with an order for eight aircraft on July 1.

Rocket-Assisted Takeoff

The idea of boosting heavily laden aircraft into the air using auxiliary rocket systems was not new, having been used by the U.S. military for years. However, civilian use had been mainly limited to a few propliners operating out of hot and high airfields such as Mexico City. At Addis Ababa, Ethiopia, DC-3s, DC-6s and Convair twins used the system regularly.

The Overseas National Airways (ONA) fleet of four DC-9-32CFs encountered some reduced payload situations during the summer months because of single-engine climb restrictions they faced when operating out of 5,000-foot elevation military bases. To overcome this problem, an ONA pilot suggested that the DC-9s be equipped with four Aerojet-General 15KS-1000-A1 rocket engines to provide instant thrust when needed.

DeVore Aviation Service was awarded a contract to develop the installation for ONA. The mounting structure, a welded steel assembly, was designed and installed by Fairchild-Hiller Aircraft. Two engines were mounted on each side under the fuselage in modified wing-fillet fairings. To retain the fairing's lines, the exhaust openings were covered with fabric that was blown off by the exhaust when the engines were fired. The fuel was a solid propellant. Ignition was provided by an electric current activated by a switch in the cockpit. The rocket motors added 700 pounds to the aircraft's weight and would run for just 15 seconds. However, their availability for use at the high-elevation airports allowed a payload increase of 8,400 pounds.

Exit velocity of the rocket exhaust exceeded Mach 4.0, but adjacent skin temperatures did not exceed 150 degrees Fahrenheit. Certification testing was conducted from the Atlantic City, New Jersey, National Aviation Facilities Test Center and was completed in May 1969. Trials confirmed that the rockets improved the payload/range by 35 percent. Depreciated rocket fuel costs were only $6 per flight hour, based on a 1,000-flight hour limitation.

Another Stretch?

MDC engineers re-visited the proposed DC-9 Series 50 yet again in May 1969. This time the power plants being considered were JT8D-15s rated at 15,000 pounds thrust. Although talks were held with several airlines, no further progress was made in launching the aircraft.

A quiet spell set in for DC-9 orders as salesmen concentrated their efforts on marketing the DC-10. Manufacturing was also tapering off, and by September the production rate had dropped to 1.43 DC-9s per week. Just 22 were delivered in the third quarter compared with 41 aircraft in the first three months and 37 in the second, bringing total deliveries for the first nine months to 100.

Production of the first DC-10 was just beginning, so plans were made to relocate the DC-9 final assembly lines. As part of the reorganization, the A-4 *Skyhawk* production line was transferred to Palmdale. In the past, all A-4 major sub-assemblies were built at Long Beach then trucked to Palmdale for final assembly and flight test.

The entire DC-9 production moved into a building that was already in use for DC-9 fuselage sub-assemblies, freeing up a major portion of the high-ceiling structure for DC-10 final assembly. DC-8 production remained in place, alongside the DC-10 line. Many years later, this process was to repeat itself when the MD-80 production line moved out of the same building to make way for MD-11s. DC-10 assembly was then condensed onto the old DC-8 line.

Air West DC-9-14 N9102 (ln 65/msn 45795) first flew with West Coast Airlines. (Author)

Originally ordered by West Coast, Air West DC-9-31 N9331 (ln 320/msn 47263) outlived three airlines to fly for Northwest today.

After Howard Hughes bought Air West, the fleet was repainted in this eye-catching scheme, seen on DC-9-31, N9332 (ln 329/msn 47264), which also migrated to Northwest. (Author)

During its long career with Garuda, the DC-9-32 fleet operated in the three schemes portrayed by:

Top: PK-GJE (ln 542/msn 47385).

Above: PK-GNN (ln 826/ msn 47722). (Author's Collection)

Below: PK-GNW (ln 911/msn 47793). (Author's Collection)

THY's DC-9-32 TC-JAE (ln 528/msn 47489) was leased to Kibris Türk Hava Yollari between 1979 and 1981. (Author's Collection)

The DC-9-51 prototype (In 757/msn 47654), went to Swissair as HB-ISK on completion of the test program. It later flew for Hawaiian as N669HA.

Business As Usual

In November 1969, two ex-Swissair DC-9-15s were allocated for lease to East African Airways (EAA) to replace three Comet 4s that were being sold to Danair in the United Kingdom. The first aircraft was painted and registered; however, the lease was abruptly terminated in January 1970. EAA, a consortium of the governments of Kenya, Tanzania and Uganda, then purchased three DC-9-30s on May 19, 1970. A short-term lease of other Comets from Danair allowed time for DC-9 crew training and the establishment of a new maintenance organization. There were a few unsold "white tails" on the production line, so MDC was able to offer delivery in November and December 1970.

Martinair added a fourth DC-9-32RC to start the year and JAT ordered three more Series 30s on June 30. Atlantis added a third Series 30 on June 23, for delivery in April 1971. Austrian Airlines ordered eight Series 30 aircraft with deliveries spread between 1971 and 1972. Two previously unannounced aircraft were delivered to THY in August and another was purchased for delivery in 1971.

Low-Pressure Tires

In a belated effort to compete with the Fokker F.28 and at the same time dispose of a few returned DC-9-10s languishing at Long Beach, MDC proposed modifying several aircraft for TAA to replace its Fokker F.27

Austrian Airlines OE-LDA, DC-9-32 (In 629/msn 47521) was sold to Texas International as N521TX, then became N16521 with Continental.

Swissair's short- to medium-range fleet included DC-9s for some 20 years before introduction of MD-80s. DC-9-32 HB-IFZ (ln 605/msn 47479) and DC-9-51 HB-ISO (ln 790/msn 47658) display original markings. (MDC/Jon Proctor Collection)

turboprop fleet. Low-pressure tires were required for operation at smaller airstrips. Working with Dunlop of Australia, a new tire was developed and certified in early 1971.

TAA decided not to proceed with the offer, but in November 1972 the DC-9-32, equipped with JT8D-7 engines, was approved by the Australian authorities to operate with the 100-psi low-pressure tire. Measuring 42 inches in diameter by 15 inches wide, it allowed the aircraft to operate at a 100,000-pound MTOW from strips that had previously imposed payload restrictions. If the aircraft was powered by JT8D-15s, it could operate at its 114,000-pound maximum weight. In 1975, TAA and Dunlop further improved the tire, lowering the pressure to just 86 psi. It was successfully demonstrated in December of that year when the airline uplifted a number of stranded rail passengers from a small Australian airfield.

The problem of disposing of the used Series 10s was alleviated on September 30, 1970, when Finnair agreed to purchase eight aircraft to replace its fleet of Convairs and DC-3s. The fleet received a number of systems and interior changes to meet Finnair's cold weather operations, including enlarged storage capacity for heavy winter coats.

On December 3, the 600th DC-9 was handed over to Swissair, a Series 32 registered HB-IDR. Accepting the aircraft for Swissair was Harry Liljeblad, the airline's representative based at Long Beach for most of his working life.

The first sizable order for 1971 came on April 2, when Iberia ordered a total of 11 DC-9s including four Rapid Change models. By the end of September sales were in a slump, and the backlog had fallen to just 43 aircraft including six more Series 32s for JAT. Firm bookings totaled 677 plus three options.

Design Improvements

In an effort to boost flagging sales, the interiors design group embarked on an effort to upgrade the cabin features and a new mockup was built. It featured redesigned enclosed overhead racks, new sidewalls and fluorescent lighting controlled by a dimmer switch. Improvements were made to takeoff and landing performance to remain competitive with the Boeing 737 that was undergoing similar efforts.

Part of the testing included improved stopping performance on runways covered with standing water. A "squeegee" device was located ahead of the main gear wheels which eliminated hydroplaning. To assist in the braking improvement, better anti-skid units were developed. Other changes included increases in engine thrust and the introduction of "smokeless" burner cans. Deflectors fitted to the nose wheel and main landing gear were also offered as an option for gravel runway operations.

Airline Innovations

Airlines often take it upon themselves to improve some aircraft items that are then adopted by many other operators. A significant development created by Air Canada's engineers during 1971 illustrates this point. The original DC-9 thrust reverser design placed the blast-deflector "buckets" in the vertical position when deployed. Unfortunately, this directed the jet blast forward, creating some re-ingestion of exhaust gasses that contained residue and debris lifted by the blast, thus causing damage to blades and vanes. Air Canada's engineers designed a modification which rotated the bucket positioning away from the fuselage at an angle of 17 degrees, thus directing the exhaust gasses clear of the intakes. The modification saved the airline approximately $500,000 per year in fuel and maintenance costs.

Many other airlines were quick to purchase modification kits and MDC incorporated the change on all future aircraft.

The Series 50

By April 1972, DC-9 sales had reached the following levels:

Series 10	137
Series 20	10
Series 30	489
Series 40	24
C-9A	21
Total	**681**

It was time to launch yet another version, the Series 50. Again, this was undertaken with no confirmed orders, although several were in negotiation. On July 5, 1972, the MDC board of directors approved production of essentially the same configuration that had been examined in 1971. A 76-inch forward fuselage plug plus a 57-inch extension aft of the wing brought the high density seating capacity to 135 with a 30-inch pitch or 125 at 34 inches between rows. The engines, Pratt & Whitney JT8D-15s rated at 15,500 pounds thrust, were installed in

Above: Toa Domestic's first DC-9 was Series 31 N9331 (In 320/msn 47263), leased from Air West.

Below: DC-9-41s were delivered in a new scheme as worn by JA8426 (In 727/msn 47606).

Bottom: In April 1988 TDA was renamed Japan Air Service (JAS). DC-9-41 JA8428 (In 736/msn 47612). (Author's Collection)

Purchased new by Aeropostal, DC-9-51 YV-22C (ln 841/ msn 47703) appears at Caracas in the airline's current livery. (Karsten Heiligtag)

Wearing test registration N1343U, this DC-9-32 (ln 684/msn 47570) was sold to Pan Adria in 1973 as YU-AJF. A year later, the carrier merged with Inex-Adria. (Author's Collection)

nacelles treated with new acoustic linings, enabling the aircraft to still met the FAR 36 Part 2 noise requirements. With a 114,000-pound MTOW, the Series 50 had a range of about 900 miles with a 30,000-pound payload. The maximum landing weight was 104,000 pounds. If powered by the JT8D-11, it was restricted to 108,000 pounds MTOW.

As usual, a conservative launch approach was taken, with a minimum of 20 orders required. The asking price was $6.1 million in 1974 dollars. By year's end, no firm orders had been announced for the Series 50. Swissair and several other airlines were also talking to MDC and Airbus Industries about large wide-body twin-jets for their next purchase, evaluating all three types for the same market requirement.

Total DC-9 firm orders had crept to 707, including an Allegheny agreement to acquire four DC-9-32s in August 1972, bringing its fleet to 33. North Central also continued its fleet expansion with orders for three more aircraft.

On January 30, 1973, SAS announced an order for 16 Series 40s plus four options to replace its Caravelle fleet. On the following day, Japan's Toa Domestic Airlines (TDA) also contracted for 14 Series 40s for use on domestic routes. In the interim, a one-year lease of two DC-9 Series 30s was arranged with Air West on July 26, to give TDA some DC-9 operating experience.

The Japanese Civil Aeronautics Board (JCAB), was reluctant to allow TDA to start operations immediately. There was some doubt as to whether the airline had enough qualified manpower to maintain the large new fleet. TDA approached Japan Air Lines (JAL) for assistance, but that carrier

had no experience with the type. Then Air West offered to supply 10 licensed engineers to help support the operation. The JCAB eventually gave its approval on April 28, but restricted the TDA to an initial purchase of eight DC-9s and allowed six options that were quickly picked up for delivery immediately after the eighth aircraft was received. The airline took delivery of the two Series 30s as planned, inaugurating service in early September.

A ready market for used DC-9-10s continued to flourish as Continental sold off 10 of its Series 15RCs to the renamed Hughes Airwest for $2.1 million each. (Howard Hughes bought Air West in April 1970.) AeroMexico ordered six new Series 30s in early February.

Aviaco ordered six DC-9-32s in March to replace its Convair 440s followed by Texas International adding two Series 30s. Garuda also picked up three DC-9-30s for 1974 delivery. On May 16, a third Yugoslav airline, Zagreb-based Pan Adria, took delivery of a Series 32 for charter operations. However, the airline remained in existence for less than a year before merging with Inex-Adria.

Noise Reduction

With external noise reduction becoming an important issue, MDC and Pratt & Whitney in 1972 embarked on a program to make the DC-9's JT8Ds quieter. In April, the two companies, assisted by Rohr Industries which built the nacelles, brought the aircraft within the FAR 35 Part 2 regulations by modifying the inlet areas and thickening up the tail pipe linings. The weight penalty was 200 pounds. Production line modifications were incorporated in late 1973. Kits were made available for retrofitting existing DC-9s at a cost of $170,000 per aircraft. This program, plus similar ones from other manufacturers, were initiated under the aegis of the FAA.

Swissair Launches the Series 50

Swissair's purchase of 10 Series 50s plus two unannounced options on July 6, 1973, had a major impact on another decision that MDC had been contemplating – the launching of the DC-10 Twin. Swissair chose the smaller aircraft because it was better suited for high-density short-haul routes. In addition to its lower purchase price, seat-mile costs were predicted to be about 50 percent below that of either of the wide-body twins.

The JT8D-15 engine was by then up-rated to 16,000 pounds of thrust, raising the Series 50's MTOW to 120,000 pounds. Swissair also opted for 1,760-gallon fuel tanks in the belly pits; the MLW was increased to 110,000 pounds. A new "wide-body look" cabin interior, developed by Heath Techna in conjunction with MDC, was also introduced. Design and development costs of the Series 50 were less than $5 million.

The DC-10 Twin decision was deferred. Simultaneously, Jackson McGowen announced his retirement, and John Brizendine succeeded him as president of the Douglas Aircraft Company, a division of McDonnell Douglas Corporation.

Shortly after the Swissair order, Austrian Airlines also contracted for two Series 50s in layouts identical to the Swissair aircraft. Efforts were made to sell Series 50s to Air Canada and Hughes Airwest. The Air Canada campaign failed, but the Hughes Airwest effort translated into a subsequent order from successor Republic Airlines.

Spanish charter airline Spantax ordered two Series 50s, but the agreement was canceled later due to a lack of financing. The 700th DC-9 delivered, a C-9B for the U.S. Navy, was handed over on July 26, leaving a backlog of just 61 aircraft.

By the end of September, MDC had sold over $3 billion worth of DC-9s in sales totaling 768 aircraft. Among all the usual statistics released in the quarterly statement was a notable comment that DC-9s had now flown in excess of 3 billion miles and the average sector length was 291 miles. The original MDC view of the market requirement was truly substantiated.

The Re-fan Program

While FAA-managed efforts to make quieter existing engines by concentrating on the exhaust areas were proceeding, NASA pursued re-fanning the engines, increasing the by-pass ratio and adding acoustic material to the nacelles. It was a more expensive approach but also offered additional fuel economies. The larger fan diameters caused major problems with the underwing installations on the 737 and the 727's buried center rear engine. The DC-9's dilemma was having a heavier engine at the rear, thus affecting the Center of Gravity.

On July 5, 1973, NASA, MDC and Pratt & Whitney agreed to a cost-sharing contract to develop and flight test two re-fanned JT8D engines installed in a DC-9-30. The accord called for flight testing to start in early 1975. A similar agreement was reached with Boeing to install an engine on a 727 for testing on the ground and resolving airframe interface problems.

Six engines were to be modified by Pratt & Whitney under a $14.6-million contract issued by NASA. The intent was to develop a modification kit for existing engines to increase the by-pass ratio, thus reducing noise and improving the fuel-burn rate. The weight penalty was estimated to cause a 1-to-2-percent reduction in range that would be offset by re-certifying the aircraft at slightly higher takeoff weights.

The modified engine, based on a JT8D-9, was re-designated JT8D-109 and rated at 16,500 pounds thrust. The two front fans, 40.5 inches in diameter, were replaced with a single 49.2-inch diameter fan. A fourth stage compressor was added and the by-pass ratio increased from 1.05 to 2.03. These changes resulted in a nacelle 9 inches wider and 5 feet longer than the original. The bare engine weight increased from 3,218 pounds to 3,788 pounds. To avoid deep-stall problems created by the larger nacelles, engine pylon lengths were reduced from 16.7 inches to 8.05 inches in order to bring the engine as close to the fuselage as possible. A titanium lining was installed in the inlet and exhaust areas to absorb noise. The estimated cost per aircraft for the rework was $1 million.

An aircraft scheduled for delivery to Allegheny Airlines was initially considered for the flight test program because it had been used during the earlier FAA-sponsored noise suppression trials, but another DC-9 Series 30, registered N54638, was allocated instead. While the engines were being fitted, parameters – including specific fuel consumption and high-

The difference in engine size is shown on DC-9 Refan N54638 (In 741/msn 47649). Converted back to a Series 31, it was sold as YU-AJR to Inex-Adria and destroyed in a midair collision with a BEA Trident 3B in September 1976.

altitude performance – were established in wind tunnel tests at NASA's Lewis Research Center at Cleveland, Ohio.

The first flight of the DC-9 Refan took place on January 9, 1975 under the command of John Lane with A. P. Johnson in the right seat. The 3-hour, 19-minute flight plan included basic engine and airframe checks plus shutting down and air-starting each engine. A few approaches to measure noise were made at Yuma, Arizona, where the company had established a flight-test center for the DC-10. The entire 90-hour test program was flown from Yuma over a three-month period in conjunction with a team from NASA and Pratt & Whitney. The aircraft weighed 2,500 pounds more than the standard DC-9-30, but part of this penalty was offset by reduced fuel consumption.

On completion of the trials in March 1975, the aircraft was re-fitted with JT8D-9s and sold to Inex-Adria on February 28,1976. It had logged 81 hours, 20 minutes during 49 test flights.

The DC-9 Series 60

Evaluation of the JT8D-109 was timely as MDC considered an even longer version of the DC-9 tentatively known as the Series 60. In late 1973, studies were underway to stretch the aircraft by another 6.25 feet, and raise the maximum seating capacity to 155, versus 139 in the Series 50. This required installation of additional emergency evacuation exits. The MTOW would be raised to 123,000 pounds with an empty weight of 60,000 pounds. Design range was planned for 1,350 nautical miles.

A development of the JT8D-109 (identified as the JT8D-117) was considered, rated at 18,000 pounds of thrust; the JT8D-17 was also being looked at. However, MDC was in no hurry as there were several proposals for "10-ton" (20,000-pound) thrust engines on the drawing boards at Rolls-Royce, General Electric and Pratt & Whitney. These were expected to have a 25-percent reduction in specific fuel consumption over current DC-9 power plants while meeting the newly proposed FAR 36 Part 3 noise regulations.

Meanwhile, MDC stopped allocating numbers to "paper" airplanes and referred to all as DC-9Xs until the projects were formally presented to the airlines.

Series 50 Into Production

The 1973 annual report issued in March 1974 was upbeat with its announcement that DC-9 production would increase to one per week after only 23 were delivered in 1973. Part of the increased output would come from the DC-9-30s for AeroMexico, all being delivered during that year. Deliveries of the Series 40 to TDA commenced on March 13, 1974. A new customer, ALM, ordered three Series 30s on April 1. Previously, ALM had leased Series 10s from KLM, its major shareholder, and also from Avensa.

Development of the new Series 50 began to pay off when Hawaiian ordered four of the 139-seat variants on April 29. Delivery was scheduled for Fall 1975. At the time, assembly of the first Series 50 was starting with construction of the cockpit at the Santa Monica plant of the MD Astronautics Division.

Aviaco accepted its first Series 32 on June 17 followed by a second aircraft later in the month. Allegheny expanded the Series 50 backlog by eight on June 18, opting for a 125-seat mixed-class configuration.

On June 17, the DC-9-50 order book got a significant boost with contracts for eight aircraft each from North Central and Austrian, bringing the order book to just over 800 aircraft; both carriers subsequently placed further orders. In the used aircraft market, Delta sold eight DC-9s to Ozark and five to Allegheny in July.

N920VJ (In 788/msn 47682) was one of eight DC-9-51s acquired by Allegheny. All were subsequently traded to Eastern for DC-9-31s.

Above: When Allegheny became USAir, only a simple title change was applied to its aircraft, as seen on DC-9-31 N938VJ (ln 943/msn 48119). (Air Pix Photo by M. Charles Pyles)

Known as the "deep rack" interior, this configuration allowed 4.4 cubic feet of storage space per passenger. (MDC via Jerry Kingsley)

USAir later adopted a bare metal livery for its fleet, as reflected by DC-9-31 N993VJ (ln 461/msn 47332). (Jon Proctor)

Experimental color schemes were applied to two DC-9-31s in early 1988.
Above: N966VJ (ln 556/msn 47420) poses at Port Columbus International Airport, Ohio. (Jim Thompson)
Below: N978VJ is seen at Hartsfield Atlanta International Airport. (Jerry Stanick)

The final livery worn under the USAir name appears on N920VJ (ln 1027/msn 48140), the same registration earlier applied to the DC-9-51 pictured on page 101. (E. H. Greenman)

Chapter XIV

FURTHER DEVELOPMENT

Finnair operated DC-9 -10s, -40s and -50s, including OH-LYN (ln 805/msn 47694). The carrier's markings changed very little over the DC-9 era.

More Design Studies Emerge

In August 1974, a change of management at American Airlines brought about a decision to re-evaluate retention of its BAC 1-11 fleet. MDC offered variations of an advanced Series 50, including stretched and re-engined combinations; most involved a more advanced wing design. For brochure purposes, the Series 60 designation was again used, although referred to as DC-9X in house. Mixed-class layouts ranged from 110 to 130 seats, with the most interest being directed towards the smaller capacity. The key to American's requirements was fuel efficiency; the effects of recent oil crises created by the OPEC cartel were still lingering.

Critical to the development of the new model was Pratt & Whitney's willingness to go ahead with an engine designated JT8D-158, an outgrowth of the previously flight-tested JT8D-109. MDC also looked at the 22,000-pound thrust General Electric/Snecma CFM56 as an alternative, particularly on the 160-seat version. However, the amount of fuselage structure re-work required to support the engine's main attachment points was a major stumbling block. In addition to CG problems, the new, heavier engine would also cost more than the Pratt & Whitney approach of re-working an existing engine core.

Another alternative was the Pratt & Whitney JT10 "10-ton" power plant still under development. Blocking the go-ahead on this variation was the fact that the existing JT8Ds were meeting current noise requirements and the comparatively high cost of the new engine types; $1 million to 1.5 million each versus $600,000 for existing models.

Yet another version of the DC-9X was being aimed at the Japanese airlines. Known as the DC-9SE (Special Edition), it was a Short Takeoff and Landing (STOL) design to replace the Nihon YS-11. Japan had 40 commercial airports with runways less than 4,000 feet long. Extending the runways had been abandoned because of the increasing value of land and the sometimes violent opposition from nearby residents. The DC-9SE, identical in size to the Series 40, featured an increased wing area, modifications to the flap and spoiler systems, and JT8D-17 engines. Nose wheel braking, previously developed for Eastern's Series 30 but not taken up, was also included.

The Series 50 Flies

By September 1974, the first Series 50 wing and fuselage had been mated, and the first flight scheduled for January. In the interim, two other Letters of Intent had been signed for the Series 50, by Finnair for six plus three options, and Egyptair for six. However, the Egyptian government refused to approve the second deal which included the interim lease of three DC-9-10s commencing in spring 1975, and the order was subsequently canceled. This loss was off-set by Garuda's order for three Series 30s plus three options, announced on October 23.

Just prior to roll-out of the first Series 50 on December 10 – well ahead of schedule – ALPA agreed that it could be flown by a two-man crew, subject to FAA certification. A 5-hour, 10-minute maiden flight was made on December 19, captained by H. H. "Nick" Knickerbocker. The aircraft, powered by JT8D-17s rated at 16,000 pounds of thrust, reached a maximum altitude of 35,000 feet, and a speed of 350 knots. Technical advances, such as automatic engine synchronization, improved autopilot, and air data systems were brought into use during the flawless flight. Unique to the Series 50 were aerodynamic strakes mounted below the cockpit to assist in lateral stability at low speeds and high angles of attack by stabilizing the vortex pattern.

A second Series 50 joined the test program on January 20, 1975; by mid-February both aircraft had accumulated 150 hours of testing, including maximum takeoff weights of 121,000 pounds. Most of the performance envelope had been explored and testing of the avionics and autopilot systems had begun. With 500 flight-test hours completed by June, the second aircraft was withdrawn in preparation for delivery to Swissair.

DC-9QSF

In February 1975, MDC teams were back in Japan offering the DC-9QSF (Quiet Short Field) to TDA, Southwest and All Nippon. This version featured the JT8D-209 engine and included two-foot wing tip extensions which allowed smaller ailerons to be moved outboard and the flaps enlarged. Additional ground spoilers and variable-camber Krueger flaps with a 4-percent leading-edge extension were introduced. The Krueger flaps, which replaced leading-edge slats, were flexible and conformed to the leading-edge profile when retracted.

The QSF was intended to operate from 3,200-foot runways, with a range of 1,000 nautical miles. The MTOW equaled the Series 40's 114,000 pounds, but the payload was decreased by 2,050 pounds. In addition, the same wing/engine combination was offered on a Series 50 fuselage albeit with a slight penalty in performance. Willing to commit to production with a combined order for 20 aircraft, MDC approached Mitsubishi, Kawasaki and Fuji Heavy Industries, to share in the development and production of the aircraft. All of the new components were offered to the Japanese industry for production as an offset program.

Shortly afterwards, MDC revealed that it was looking at stretching the Series 50 by one seat row and installing JT8D-209s, but this aroused little interest in the Japanese marketplace and was abandoned.

Meanwhile orders continued to trickle in. Aviaco added four Series 34s and SAS picked up two more Series 40s in July; then Inex-Adria ordered two Series 50s. In addition BWIA signed for four DC-9-51s to be delivered starting in June 1977. Cyprus Airways leased two of the used Series 10s still on the books, to replace BAC 1-11s that were destroyed by strafing aircraft at Nicosia during the Turkish invasion of Cyprus in 1974.

In July TDA undertook a series of short-field trials in adverse weather conditions with a DC-9-41 to test operations from 1,500 meters (4,900-foot) runways. To qualify, the aircraft – fully loaded – was required to reach an altitude of 150 feet before the runway end and land from the same height without use of thrust reversers.

With rotated thrust reversers and autobrakes loaned by MDC, the aircraft was halted in 3,000 feet, but without the reversers, it barely stopped on the runway. Grooved runway surfaces were introduced to further reduce braking distances, especially in wet conditions.

First Series 50 Delivered

Swissair took delivery of the first Series 50 on August 15, 1975, four days after type certification, and put it into service on August 24. It was a month late due to strikes at Long Beach earlier in the year. Hawaiian received its first Series 50 on September 10.

On September 28, Aviaco ordered four DC-9-34CFs. The original contract was for Series 34s, a 121,000-pound MTOW version powered by 16,000-pound thrust JT8D-17s, but just prior to signing, Aviaco switched its selection to DC-9-34CFs. This last-minute change had repercussions after delivery in 1976. During early service flights, Aviaco reported that the aircraft was not meeting range specifications on the critical Stockholm–Canary Islands routes. MDC resolved the problem by revising the fuel-management schedule. The aircraft's cruise attitude had been affected by the addition of the heavy cargo door in combination with the

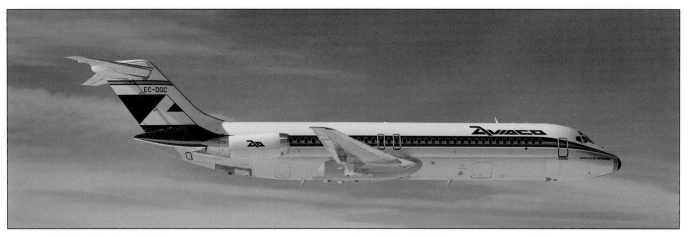

Iberia's domestic associate Aviaco launched the long-range DC-9-34. EC-DGC (ln 928/msn 48104) was one of four ordered.

Balair DC-9-33CF HB-IDN (ln 584/msn 47465) currently flies for Airborne Express as N932AX.

Hawaiian Air was another recipient of factory-delivered DC-9-51s, including N699HA (ln 879/msn 47763) shown in the current livery.

Alisarda DC-9-51, I-SMEI (ln 824/msn 47714) previously served with Hawaiian. (via Eddy Gual)

Meridiana's DC-9-51 I-SMEA (ln 820/msn 47713) served previously with Hawaiian Air and Alisarda. (Dariö Cocco)

Originally delivered to Inex-Adria as YU-AJT – but shown above with test registration N8709Q – Eurofly DC-9-51 I-FLYZ (below; ln 816/msn 47697) operates domestic services on behalf of Alitalia. (MDC/Martin Stamm)

Spanair operated a single DC-9-51 EC-246 (ln 783/msn 47656) on lease from GPA. (via Eddy Gual)

Ex-Hawaiian DC-9-51 N619HA became N920PJ (ln 791/msn 47677) prior to joining Sun Jet International in 1994. The carrier ceased operations in 1997. (Author's Collection)

Above: Muse Air, the first all non-smoking airline, operated DC-9-51s, including N670MC (ln 807/msn 47659), obtained from Swissair. The type supplemented a fleet of MD-80s. (Author's Collection)
Below: Muse Air changed its name to TranStar and adopted a new livery, seen on N672MC (ln 849/msn 47726). (via Eddy Gual)

The second National Airlines was a short-lived, scheduled carrier affiliated with Private Jet. It operated two DC-9-51s, including N919PJ (ln 851/msn 47663) in 1994. (Author's Collection)

Wearing temporary registration N8714Q, Austral DC-9-51 (In 891/msn 47773) was leased off the production line. It later became OH-LYW with Finnair.

North African Aviation existed for just a few months in 1988. It leased DC-9-51 SU-BKK (In 783/msn 47656) from GPA which later sold it to Alisarda. It is now with Meridiana as I-SMEE. (Martin Stamm)

modified wing angle-of-attack, leading to increased drag. Early in October, LAV ordered three Series 50s plus three Series 30s for $42 million. The DC-9 sales totals now reached 840 plus 26 options, of which 787 had been delivered by the end of October.

In October, Federal Express, operating its fledgling express parcel service with a fleet of Falcon 20s under an air taxi exemption, requested government approval to supplement these with five DC-9-15Fs. Although most government departments supported the application, it was heavily opposed by scheduled and supplemental airlines. A full CAB hearing held in December resulted in FedEx subsequently became a regular certificated cargo carrier, but the delay led the company to expand by adding bigger equipment.

Allegheny became the first U.S. mainland Series 50 operator on December 1. Flight attendant Bonnie Tinley took formal delivery of the initial aircraft, in Allegheny's new red and maroon paint scheme, on November 19.

Finnair's first DC-9-51, handed over on January 23, 1976, was the 800th DC-9 to be delivered in just over ten years. The entire DC-9 fleet had carried 714 million passengers, logging 12 million flying hours and four billion miles. The first order of the new year came from Balair, for a DC-9-34 on February 5.

QSF Developments

After re-appraisal of the DC-9QSF, MDC approached the Japanese airlines in the spring of 1976 with yet another proposal. The basic aircraft was unchanged, but a centerline landing gear had been added as an option. The tires were also changed to slightly larger diameter low-pressure (95 psi versus 130 psi) design, allowing operation from unimproved runway surfaces. New gear doors were required to accommodate the thicker tires. An auto-braking system was also added, incorporating improved anti-skid units developed for the Series 50. Another, more complex approach was explored to replace the main, twin-wheel landing gear with four-wheel bogies to spread the load, but landing gear stowage was a major problem.

Meanwhile, Pratt & Whitney bench-tested the JT8D-209, now rated at 18,000 pounds thrust, with a re-designed low-pressure section to improve specific fuel consumption over that of the JT8D-109.

Depressed Markets

The airline industry's over-capacity during the mid-1970s, caused by a worldwide recession, depressed aircraft sales and development. All the manufacturers offered aircraft for early delivery at attractive prices to tide the airlines over until the cyclic rebound expected between 1977 and 1978. The inability of the industry to absorb any more debt was illustrated by a press release from MDFC, stating that it was still owed $196.5 million from 26 foreign airlines and $208.9 million from 14 U.S. carriers.

In April TDA announced the purchase of rotated-thrust reverser kits plus autobrakes for three of its DC-9-40s. The aircraft would be used on scheduled flights into 1,800-meter (6,000-foot) fields until the 1,500-meter (5,000-foot) runways were grooved. The first aircraft was in service by mid-June operating out of three airfields, including Kadena which already had grooved runways.

Some good news for MDC came on June 22 when Eastern entered into a 14-year leasing agreement with MDC for nine DC-9-50s equipped with 1,000-gallon supplemental fuel tanks, delivering in 1977. This was part of an out-of-court settlement over a $35-million lawsuit arising from tardy deliveries of DC-9-30s in the late-1960s. The agreement included the return of nine Series 10s still on lease from MDC.

On July 5, SAS augmented its 52-aircraft fleet – plus two others previously ordered – with a commitment for two Series 41s plus five options for 1978-79 delivery. BWIA became a Series 50 customers on July 7 with an order for two plus one DC-9-34CF. Ozark also picked up an additional Series 30 in September.

Further Enhancements

Atlantic Aviation introduced two wide-body look interior modification kits for DC-9s in June. One package was a simple addition of strengthening to existing open racks and the addition of an upward opening door, while the second version was a completely new and enlarged overhead bin, revised sidewall panels sculpted outwards between the windows, new ceiling panels and indirect-wash lighting. HITCO, another interiors manufacturer, also introduced a similar series of modifications to update DC-9s at about the same time.

Its system could be purchased in four phases: closed baggage bins, new sidewall and ceiling lights, new sculpted ceiling panels

and, finally, new matching sidewall panels. The total cost per aircraft was $105,000.

One bright spot in July was the introduction of DC-9s into U.K. service by British Midland on July 27. The CAA had finally accepted that the Series 10 did not require a stick-pusher. However, when BMA acquired Series 30s with leading-edge slats, the CAA demanded incorporation of a similar device. TDA increased its fleet with a purchase of four more Series 40s on October 13, bringing the total sales to 865 with 829 delivered. When Balair took delivery of its Series 34 in November, the aircraft flew 3,727 miles nonstop from Montreal to Zurich, the longest recorded flight of a DC-9 on standard internal fuel.

In November, MDC introduced a Performance Improvement Package (PIP) for the DC-9. High fuel costs led the industry to look for ways of reducing fuel burn by any means possible. Some solutions were quite simple; reducing long-range cruise speeds from Mach 0.78 to Mach 0.76 lowered the fuel burn by 2 to 4 percent. Others options included tighter rigging tolerances between the spoiler and flap, reduction of slat-to-wing step and re-rigging the flaps to a full-up position.

The ASMR Joint Venture

For some time, MDC had been working in partnership with the French to develop the Dassault Mercure 2000, powered by two GE/Snecma CFM56 engines, with the projected named ASMR (Advanced Short- to Medium-Range). The work program expanded rapidly in November with the primary goal of replacing the Air France Caravelle fleet. French aerospace unions wanted the government to force Air France to purchase 10 unsold A300s, not an unreasonable request as Airbus sales were weak at the time. Interestingly, Air France had already announced that it preferred to add more Boeing 727-200s, supplemented by 737-200s.

Coincidentally, the Japanese airlines were losing interest in the DC-9QSF. TDA had upgraded the balance of its DC-9-40 fleet while All Nippon and JAL decided to remain standardized on Boeing products. These factors, together with a belated decision by the Japanese government to extend the runways, caused MDC to shelve the program.

Getting U.K. certification was a lengthy process, so BMA operated DC-9-14 OY-LYB (above: ln 6/msn 45712) on lease from Finnair. (Author's Collection) The airline eventually added DC-9-30s, including Series 31G-PKBD (ln 772/msn 47666). (Eric LeGendre)

Above: DC-9-51 N411EA (ln 861/msn 47732) reflects the last Eastern scheme. It is currently leased to TWA. (Author's Collection)
Below: Another ex-Eastern Series 50 now with TWA is N414EA (ln 864/msn 47746). (Bill Hough)

DC-9-34CF, 9Y-TFI (above; ln 872/msn 47752) and DC-9-51 9Y-TGP (below; ln 972/msn 48122) are representative of the two earlier BWIA color schemes. (Author's Collection/Keith Armes)

Above: Adria Aviopromet DC-9-51 YU-AJT (ln 816/msn 47697) shows the second of three title variations. (Author's Collection)

Below: DC-9-33RC YU-AHW (ln 624/msn 47530) in Adria's contemporary livery. (via Eddy Gual)

DC-9-51 HB-IST (ln 850/msn 47662) shows Swissair's updated colors. (Max Fankhauser)

Chapter XV

THE ULTIMATE DC-9

New Designs

MDC advanced design engineers continued to examine ways to extend the product line and, in late 1976, produced a wide spectrum of studies for future growth versions. The baseline was the DC-9 Series 50 with two common major changes, a 63-inch plug at each wing root plus a larger horizontal tail with a 40-inch increase in span. Also envisioned were heavier weights and a strengthened landing gear.

From this foundation, several separate projects developed, the first being yet another model known as the Series 60, featuring a 10-ton engine, again either the General Electric/Snecma CFM56 or Pratt & Whitney JT10D, and a completely new landing gear. The fuselage was lengthened by inserting a 209-inch plug ahead of the wing and a 57-inch plug aft, increasing the overall length to 155.6 feet. As a 180-seat aircraft, it was intended to be a Boeing 727-200 replacement candidate. It is worth noting that this project was in the same class as the ASMR, which may have also contributed to its early demise.

A second approach, based on the JT8D-209, featured a forward 95-inch plug that added three seat rows while maintaining CG limits. It was called the DC-9RS for "Refanned Stretch." From this design, three

alternatives were considered. The simplest, identified as the DC-9-17S, merely substituted the JT8D-17R engine for the JT8D-209. The -17R could automatically increase takeoff thrust by an additional 500 pounds if the opposite engine failed.

A parallel proposal – the same airframe – fitted with the JT8D-209s and a super-critical airfoil wing, became the DC-9SC. A long-term study, it was subsequently abandoned in view of the program's ultimate evolution.

The final approach to improving the Series 50 combined the JT8D-209 engines with a 133-inch forward fuselage plug and a 19-inch aft plug, giving a maximum capacity of 159 seats and overall length of 146.16 feet. The 2-foot wing tip extension previously proposed on the DC-9QSF was added. Identified initially as the DC-9 RSS (Refanned Super Stretch) then DC-9-55, this closely met the 155 single-class seating requirements that Swissair wanted: a larger and quieter aircraft seating 12 first-class and 125 economy-class – at 38-inch and 34-inch pitch respectively – that would replace the Series 50s.

In spite of the refinements to the engine core and nacelles, its 121,000-pound MTOW – requiring 16,000-pound thrust JT8D-17 engines – made the Series 50 unpopular with people living near airports, even though it met current noise regulations. The Series 55 had an MTOW of 136,000 pounds and a wing fuel capacity of 5,779 gallons. The much quieter JT8D-209s were rated at 18,000 pounds of thrust, but also had the reserve capability of 19,000 pounds for single-engine performance. With a range just over 1,700 nautical miles, it required a shorter field length than the Series 50; 8,175 feet versus 8,420 feet.

The design embodied many features common to the earlier DC-9s, but also included digital avionics and a Category III fail-safe digital automatic flight control system. The anticipated development costs of $110 million again induced MDC to approach potential suppliers, particularly the Japanese airframe manufacturers, to share the burden and profits. The sales target was 300 out of a forecast market of 1,200 aircraft in this size range.

By January 1977, Swissair was pushing for the DC-9-55 launch, but MDC was still involved with the joint venture 160- to 180-seat ASMR and undecided on which to launch first. Management saw no conflict between the two designs and offered the French a share in the DC-9-55 program as part of the joint venture. Meanwhile, Delta's decision to start replacing its DC-9s with Boeing 727-200s was announced on February 7, adding pressure on MDC management to introduce a larger DC-9 replacement.

The ASMR situation deteriorated in early March when the French became concerned that the DC-9-55 was too close in size and performance to the ASMR. They issued an ultimatum to MDC: make a decision between the two projects by March 31. MDC was concerned by the lack of any real interest in the ASMR from targeted launch customers but, more importantly, faced an in-house projection that the Series 55, with an anticipated return on investment of 18 percent, was much better than that forecast for the ASMR, even with a possible subsidy from the French government.

This quandary was compounded in late March 1977 by Pratt & Whitney's decision to proceed with the development of the JT8D-209; its initial marketing effort was aimed at the DC-9-55. Flight-testing of the engine had commenced on March 4, utilizing the second of two McDonnell Douglas YC-15 experimental four-engined STOL military jet transports. A month earlier, on February 16, the CFM56 had been air-tested on the first YC-15.

Continued Production

While the DC-9-55 efforts continued within the Sales and Engineering departments, production of existing models proceeded at a steady pace. Part of the ongoing development of the DC-9 improvement program was to prove that existing DC-9-30s powered by JT8D-9s could meet FAR 36 Part 3 noise requirements up to a maximum takeoff weight of 105,000 pounds. This was demonstrated to the FAA at Yuma, Arizona, in a joint MDC-Eastern Air Lines program in March; the results exactly matched the limits of acceptability.

In April 1977, MDC again resurrected its short-field DC-9-22 for TDA, which had suffered several non-fatal YS-11 incidents in a short time period

and urgently needed an interim replacement that could be delivered within two years. The Series 22 featured the same cockpit as the -41, but with low-pressure tires, a modified spoiler system and the auto-brakes designed for the DC-9QSF. The MTOW was reduced from 98,000 pounds to 90,000 pounds and the landing weight was limited to 84,000 pounds – versus 93,400 pounds for the Series 21. Passenger capacity was 95 with a 29-inch seat pitch. The aft ventral stairs were removed, saving 500 pounds and improving CG limits that in turn permitted lower approach and stall speeds. Engines were either the JT8D-15 or JT8D-17. The need for the DC-9QSF was now considered to be for the mid-1980s.

Ghana Airways joined the ranks of DC-9 customers with an order for a single Series 50 in June. SAS also announced a further order for four Series 40s on June 29. Eastern's first Series 50s, wearing the new polished bare-metal scheme, began arriving in mid-July at a rate of two per month.

Designation Change

As a marketing ploy, John Brizendine on August 26, announced that henceforth, the DC-9-55 would be called the DC-9-80 or Super 80 since it was an aircraft designed for the 1980s. At the same time; Swissair re-affirmed its willingness to purchase 10 of the new model, Austrian Airlines indicated it would follow suite. However, MDC was initially unwilling to launch the program until at least one American customer signed up. Pratt & Whitney also announced that the thrust rating on the JT8D-209 had risen to 18,500 pounds, which allowed the MTOW to increase to 140,000 pounds and the landing weight to 128,000 pounds.

MDC officially launched the DC-9-80 program on October 14, 1977, after deciding to drop the American customer requirement. Virtually all the major U.S. carriers had large inventories of comparatively young Boeing 727-200s and could not afford yet another new type.

Swissair announced the purchase of 15 aircraft plus five options, while Austrian ordered eight plus four options. Southern Airways also indicated it would order four Series 80s, however this was to become the subject of much wrangling when the three-pilot cockpit issue arose again. LAV signed an LOI for three Series 80s and placed a further order for two additional Series 50s , bringing the total for this model to 76. Overall orders and options for DC-9s had reached 914 of which 861 had been delivered.

Re-sales Surge

By now, the airlines had weathered the doldrums and traffic was again surging. New aircraft delivery lead times stretched out to 18 months, and prices increased; a new DC-9-30 cost around $8 million. Used aircraft prices jumped as well, with a Series 30 typically fetching $4 million plus an additional $500,000 for refurbishing and repainting.

For many years, Ghana Airways Series 50, 9G-ACM (ln 878/msn 47755) was the only DC-9 in West Africa. It crashed at Abidjan, Ivory Coast in early 1997.

New DC-9 sales continued to be sluggish as airline managers evaluated the Super 80's potential, but some orders continued to accrue, including one for six Series 30s from Texas International in March 1978. SAS exercised four of its five outstanding options for Series 40s, and Garuda added seven Series 30s for 1979 delivery.

Southern Airways bowed to the pressure of its pilots on June 2, 1978, and canceled its Super 80 order, choosing four new DC-9-30s instead, plus eight used Series 10s from Eastern. Southern's order, plus a previous North Central order, were replaced by a single contract for eight Series 50s after the merger of Southern and North Central formed Republic Airlines on July 1, 1979. All were acquired via leasing companies.

Allegheny also purchased four new DC-9-30s on June 14 as part of a package in which all eight of its Series 50s went to Eastern in exchange for cash plus DC-9-30s. Aviaco ordered four DC-9-34s on July 18, and Ozark continued expansion of its 32-strong DC-9 fleet on October 18 with an order for two new DC-9-34s and six used Series 30s from Delta. Allegheny ordered another four new DC-9-30s on November 15. Year end deliveries totaled 893 with orders for 99 aircraft outstanding; just 22 DC-9s were delivered during the year.

By the end of 1978, used DC-9-30 prices had soared to between $5.5 million and $6 million while new aircraft, with an 18-month lead time, were fetching around $9 million. U.S. domestic traffic growth had increased by 17 percent over the previous year compared with an annual rate of 7 percent over the last decade. Part of the shortage was due to Deregulation which led to an influx of start-up carriers such as Midway Airlines. KLM launched 1979 sales with an order for two long-range DC-9-34s on January 29, followed by AeroMexico which added six DC-9-30s on February 12. The 900th DC-9 was delivered to Texas International on March 16.

Delta, in conjunction with MDC and Pratt & Whitney, embarked on a program in April to reduce DC-9 engine noise by adding a new nose cowl plus internal engine sound-absorbent materials. The 44-aircraft contract called for the first installation in spring 1981.

On June 8, Allegheny announced an order for 10 DC-9-32s, the largest single order for some time. A few days later, Finnair ordered three more Series 50s. Deliveries were slowed by two lengthy strikes although production at a reduced rate was maintained by transferring salaried employees to production jobs.

MDC used a new Series 40 on a delivery flight to TDA for a series of flight demonstrations in China between June 19 and 26. Although there was no immediate result from this effort, it eventually led to Chinese co-production of the MD-80. In a combined order,

AeroMexico purchased three more DC-9-32s plus three Super 80s and two DC-10-15s on September 10.

Start-up carrier Midway Airlines agreed on September 25 to lease five used DC-9-10s from MDFC as part of a package which included the purchase of five new Series 21s for 1982 delivery. Though Midway received all five leased aircraft, the Series 21 order was canceled and further used aircraft were acquired instead. In 1979, there were 39 DC-9s delivered, compared with just 22 the previous year.

Turboprop Studies

For some time, NASA had been exploring the use of advanced turbo-props as part of an Aircraft Energy Efficiency (ACEE) program, allocating contracts to the industry to assist in this development. A 1979 feasibility study was conducted to evaluate replacing the DC-9's engines with multi-bladed advanced turboprops. It was expected that such an installation would reduce fuel burn by 17 percent.

By September 1981, the project had been renamed as the Advanced Turboprop Program (ATP). Studies proposed mounting either one or two engines on the wing while retaining the existing engines for safety. This would have required moving the wings forward 90 inches on a Series 10 test aircraft to maintain the center of gravity. Lengthy development of suitable engines delayed flight testing, so it wasn't until May 18, 1987, that the rear-engined installation was flown on the MD-80 prototype. A similar program was carried out using a Boeing 727-100 at about the same time.

End of Production

On February 7, 1980, Ozark set a new distance record for the DC-9 when one of its new DC-9-34s (unofficially designated DC-9-30LR) flew from Minneapolis to Zihuantenejo, Mexico, a distance of 2,054 miles in 4 hours 28 minutes.

The last commercial order for Series 30s came from USAir (its name had changed from Allegheny Airlines) for six aircraft. This contract was announced on February 27, followed shortly afterwards by an order for two additional C-9Bs from the U.S. Navy.

As production of the DC-9 Series 80 accelerated, deliveries of the earlier DC-9 models were completed. The last commercial Series 31 built was Fuselage Number 1058, which was handed over to USAir on April 6, 1982. The last DC-9 to leave the line was Fuselage Number 1084, a C-9B for the U.S. Navy, which was delivered on October 28, 1982, closing out 17 years of DC-9 production.

MDC's proposed twin-engine testbed DC-9 to develop multi-blade prop-fans.

In anticipation of a new identity following the name change to Republic Airlines, North Central applied test liveries to DC-9-31s N961N (above; ln 487/msn 47405) and N963N (below; ln 511/msn 47415). (Jon Proctor)

DC-9-51 N768NC (ln 854/msn 47729) still wears North Central's famous "Herman" mallard duck logo. (Author)

Republic's first standard scheme retained Herman; DC-9-51 N780NC (ln 932/msn 48102) was one of a batch ordered by North Central prior to the merger.

Southern's final livery, is seen on ex-Eastern DC-9-15 N8903E (ln 31/msn 45744). (Author's Collection)

Ex-Southern DC-9-31 N908H (ln 583/msn 47517) poses at Chicago-O'Hare. (Author)

The final Republic scheme, in the early 1980s, also appears on N780NC. (Jeff Burch)

Originally with Southern, Republic DC-9-15 N91S (ln 111/msn 47063) flew for Northwest under the same registration. (Jon Proctor)

Purchased from Continental by Hughes Airwest, DC-9-15RC N9359 (ln 242/msn 45828) flew for Republic before moving into a freighter role with Purolator Courier in 1984. (John Wegg)

DC-9-15RC N9354 (ln 203/msn 47018) also migrated from Continental and served both Hughes Airwest and successor Republic, then Northwest. It later operated in Mexico for Aerocaribe as XA-SMI. (Author's Collection)

Top: Standard Northwest colors were applied to DC-9-51 N785NC (ln 945/msn 48110). (Frank Hines)
Center: Experimental schemes were tried on two DC-9-51s, including N787NC (ln 990/msn 48149). (Author's Collection)
Bottom: DC-9-31 N8979E (ln 392/msn 47328) in the current markings with unusual honoree artwork. (via Eddy Gual)

Chapter XVI
INCIDENTS AND ACCIDENTS

After long stints with Kenya Airways, Alisarda and BMA, this former East African DC-9-32 (5N-MOI; In 609/msn 47430) served in South Africa with Sun Air as ZS-NRA.

The Stolen DC-9

Probably the most unusual incident involving a DC-9 took place in the early morning hours of September 16, 1972 at Dar-es-Salaam Airport in Tanzania. Several individuals dressed in police uniforms entered the control tower and held the staff at gun-point. Shortly afterwards, an East African Airways DC-9 took off from a runway barely 3,000 feet long and headed north.

The following morning, the aircraft was found abandoned at a new airport located at the foot of Mount Kilimanjaro. Although normally closed at night, locks on the unmanned control tower doors had been broken and the runway lights turned on. (The automatic navigation aids were always left on.)

The aircraft had burst all four tires, and the brakes were burned out, suggesting that it landed far down the runway and the crew had braked heavily to avoid running off the end. There were still 8,000 pounds of fuel aboard, enough to return to Dar-es-Salaam.

Just who flew the aircraft remains a mystery, but logic narrows the culprits to a few possibilities. At the time, all of the East African command pilots were either British or Australian. The African co-pilots consisted of 25 cadets and 25 qualified pilots, but only five, of which two were Ugandans, had any DC-9 experience.

The Tanzanian government investigated the incident but failed to solve the mystery. Local conjecture was that a group of guerrillas, intent on overthrowing Uganda's president Idi Amin, had stolen the aircraft with the intention of ferrying 100 men from a camp near Kilimanjaro to Entebbe, Uganda's main airport, and seizing it. They would then airlift in a further 3,000 guerrillas to liberate the capital city of Kampala from Amin. Other rumors suggested that the Tanzanian government was involved in the affair, but nothing was ever proven. The DC-9 was repaired on-site and later returned to service.

Airborne Robbery

An unusual DC-9 hijacking took place on December 7, 1980, when an Aeropostal aircraft was seized in flight. Part of its cargo was $1 million in cash plus $600,000 in negotiable paper belonging to an insurance company. Four hijackers boarded the flight from Porlamar to Caracas, Venezuela, with 104 other passengers including several bank security guards. Twenty minutes after takeoff, the hijackers commandeered the aircraft, threatening the crew and passengers with pistols. The pilot was forced to divert and land at Huiguerote, a small airfield some 70 miles from Caracas. The runway was only 3,600 feet long, but the crew managed to stop without damaging the aircraft. The thieves were met on the ground by accomplices who had taken over the control tower and cut the phone lines. A truck was brought to the aircraft and the loot removed. The perpetrators identified themselves as members of a guerrilla group but were never captured. After the remaining cargo had been removed to lighten the aircraft, it was flown out.

A Political Hijacking

A Garuda DC-9-32 on a domestic flight was taken over by five Indonesian Muslim extremists on March 28, 1981, and forced to fly to Bangkok. The hijackers were demanding the release of 84 prisoners held in Indonesian jails. Indonesia agreed to the swap, but the Thai government insisted on "brutal treatment of the hijackers." After considerable negotiation between the Indonesian and Thai governments, Indonesian commandos stormed the aircraft through the aft service and front door on March 31. In the interim, one British subject had escaped unharmed by jumping from an emergency window and was able to brief the commandos. An American citizen tried to follow and was shot in the back. During the rescue operation, the captain was shot and severely

In 1981, Ship Three was bought back and subjected to accelerated pressure cycles to establish an extended fatigue life. The steel mesh curtains guard against fuselage failure. An MD-80 wing is seen on the rail car in the background, shipped from Toronto, Canada.

DC-9 and a BEA Trident came together over Yugoslavia after the air traffic controller allowed the DC-9 to climb through the Trident's assigned air space.

Three other collisions involved light aircraft which had penetrated air lanes; a TWA DC-9-10 near Dayton, Ohio; an AeroMexico DC-9-30 over Cerritos, California; and an Allegheny DC-9-30 near Indianapolis, Indiana.

At least two losses are attributable to in-flight explosions caused by bombs, and an Itavia DC-9 is believed to have been inadvertently downed by an air-to-air missile over the Mediterranean Sea in 1980. Just who fired the missile was never established, but NATO exercises were taking place in the area.

Two DC-9s have been lost due to fuel starvation. Hangar fires have claimed three aircraft. One was destroyed on the ground in Venezuela during a coup attempt and another during the Iraqi invasion of Kuwait in 1991.

The accidents commanding the highest media hype have been those involving in-flight fires, such as the 1996 ValuJet disaster caused by the improper carriage of oxygen canisters in the cargo hold. Other examples include the Air Canada incident near Cincinnati, where many survived.

A Southern Airways DC-9-30 suffered a singular in-flight incident in heavy turbulence when both engines flamed out due to hail ingestion at 15,000 feet. During an attempted landing on a rural highway, the aircraft struck a tree and crashed into a gas station with dire consequences; there were few survivors.

On rare occasions, crew inattention was blamed for accidents, such as that of a Continental DC-9-10 taking off from Denver with snow-covered wings, and a Delta DC-9-30 at Boston which drifted below the glide path and hit the threshold sea wall. Recently, the crew made a wrong turn at Arrecife, Spain, and taxied over an embankment.

Structural Integrity

No hull losses have been blamed on structural problems with the DC-9, either from corrosion or metal fatigue. However, some preventative fixes were needed in early 1976 when cracks were discovered in the aft bulkhead emergency exit doorjambs on two DC-9s not fitted with rear airstairs. Douglas issued repair instructions and a modification kit that was installed in all other DC-9s of the same design.

While flying between Boston and Halifax on September 17, 1979, the tail cone blew off an Air Canada DC-9-30 following an explosion. The aircraft returned safely to Boston. The rear emergency escape door had blown out, taking the cone with it. Following an FAA alert bulletin, rear bulkhead cracks were found in 33 of 119 aircraft inspected; the largest crack was 5 inches long, but most were very small. In each case, the cracks were in aircraft that had not been modified in accordance with the Douglas bulletin issued two years earlier to strengthen the bulkhead. The cause was a metal fatigue fracture induced by frequent pressure cycling.

In May 1981, Douglas bought Ship Three from Republic Airlines after the airframe had amassed 66,504 landings during 42,900 flying hours. Since the DC-9 was originally certificated for 40,000 landings, this was an

wounded, but the rest of the 55 passengers and crew were unharmed. One commando and two of the hijackers were killed in the fire fight and another later died of his wounds.

Accidents

The DC-9 has suffered a total of 85 hull losses during 32 years of service. Even one loss is tragic, but examined in context of accidents versus high-frequency operations – often involving small airfields and difficult environments – this number is at about the same level as any other jetliner in its class. At of the end of June 1997, DC-9s had logged 52.25 million flight hours and completed 55.8 million cycles.

The largest percentage of accidents occurred in close proximity to or on the airfield. Most resulted from heavy landings, landing short or departing from the runway during roll-out in adverse weather conditions. Wind shear caused several crashes when the aircraft was near the ground in marginal weather conditions. For instance, an Allegheny DC-9 was attempting a go-around at Philadelphia in stormy weather when the tail hit the ground and broke off. Fortunately, all 104 people on board survived.

Two DC-9 hull losses involved other jetliners on the runway. At Madrid, an Aviaco DC-9 crossing an active runway was struck by an Iberia Boeing 727 that had just lifted its nose for takeoff. The DC-9 pilots were unsure of their location in poor visibility. At Chicago-O'Hare a Delta Convair 880 crossed the active runway in front of a North Central DC-9-31 on its takeoff roll. The DC-9 was rotated prematurely in an attempt to avoid the collision but struck the Convair's tail.

Other DC-9 accidents were due to engine failure or aborted takeoffs. Collisions with high ground caused several hull losses, including a West Coast Airlines DC-9-10 near Portland, Oregon. All the high-ground incidents occurred on approach to or leaving airfields located near mountainous terrain.

Six midair collisions have taken place, all in controlled air space; three occurred while en route. A Hughes Airwest DC-9 was hit by an F-4 Phantom east of Los Angeles. The F-4 was operating under Visual Flight Rules (VFR) at the time and not in contact with ATC. An Iberia DC-9 and a Spantax Convair 990 collided over France while under the guidance of military controllers due to a strike by civilian controllers. An Inex-Adria

DC-9-15 0003 (ln 83/msn 47000), shown while leased to the Venezuelan Air Force (FAV). It crashed in 1993, after returning to LAV. (Author's Collection)

Dominicana's DC-9-32, HI-177 (ln 546/msn 47500) crashed on February 15, 1970, just three months after delivery.

Shown at Dusseldorf in 1979, Itavia's DC-9-14 I-TIGE (ln 105/msn 47002) was later destroyed in 1985 while with Airborne Express as N926AX. (Author's Collection)

DC-9-14 YV-C-AVM (ln 89/msn 47056) crashed into a Venezuelan hillside in 1974 while in service with Avensa. (Author's Collection)

ideal candidate for an accelerated test program. Installed in a test rig, the fuselage was subjected to pressurization cycles that compressed a year's equivalent flying into one week, with the intent of raising the total cycles to 200,000. The airframe exceeded this number with only minor repairs, and the tests were terminated after some 204,000 cycles with little evidence that the structure would fail significantly in the near future.

In 1996, a 38-inch crack was discovered emanating from a rivet in the upper skin of a USAir DC-9-30 which had accumulated 82,325 cycles and 70,000 hours flight time. A check of active DC-9s failed to produce similar cracks, but a bulletin was issued requiring inspection by all carriers when the airframe reaches 60,000 flight hours. Corrosion has had minimal effect on the structural life of any DC-9.

Centenarians

At the time of writing, three DC-9s have exceeded the 100,000-landing benchmark, the highest being a DC-9-15 N3310L (ln 53/msn 45738), currently operated by Northwest Airlines, with 103,642 cycles in 76,689 hours. Northwest also operates the other two centenarians,

N3312L (ln 70/ msn 45707) with 100,430 cycles and N91S (ln 111/ msn 47063) with 100,362 cycles. Aero California's DC-9-15, XA-RKT, (ln 224/ msn 47122), is the fleet leader in flight time with 85,964 hours and 89,819 cycles.

It now has been 15 years since the last DC-9 was delivered. Of the 976 aircraft built, more that 850 remain active to date. Inevitably, these numbers will decline more rapidly in the coming years as the type is replaced by aircraft equipped with quieter, more fuel-efficient engines and state-of-the-art systems. However, as can be seen by a recent increase in new operators in Latin America and Africa, the DC-9s will continue to ply the air lanes for many years to come. Even Northwest Airlines, in spite of its recent large order from Airbus Industrie, plans to keep DC-9s into the next century, following completion of its DC-9-2000 program, a total revamping of the interiors and addition of the new sound suppressers to the engine mounts of the younger airframes. Once again, technology advancement rather than structural old age will bring about the eventual demise of the airplane that was designed to take everyone and everything from every place to everywhere.

DC-9-15 N3310L, high-cycle champ, in current Northwest colors. (Greg Drawbaugh)

123

Appendix I
WRITE-OFFS
(Listed By Date)

Airline	Model	Registration	Line No/MSN	Date	Comments
West Coast	14	N9101	052/45794	01-10-66	Hit mountain; near Portland, OR.
TWA	15	N1063T	080/45777	03-09-67	Midair collision with light aircraft; near Dayton, OH.
Ozark	15	N974Z	162/47034	12-27-68	Aborted takeoff; Sioux City, IA.
VIASA	32	YV-C-AVD	448/47243	03-16-69	Hit power line on takeoff; Maracaibo, Venezuela.
Allegheny	31	N988VJ	357/47211	09-09-69	Mid-air collision with light aircraft; Shelbyville, IN.
Dominicana	32	HI-177	546/47500	02-15-70	Lost power after takeoff; Santo Domingo, D.R.
ALM	33F	N935F	457/47407	05-02-70	Fuel starvation; ditched near St. Croix, USVI.
Southern	31	N97S	510/47245	11-14-70	Hit trees on approach; Huntington, WV.
Hughes Airwest	31	N9345	503/47441	06-06-71	Midair collision with F-4; near Los Angeles, CA.
THY	32	TC-JAC	358/47213	01-21-72	On approach in snowstorm; Adana, Turkey.
JAT	32	YU-AHT	592/47482	01-26-72	In-flight bomb explosion; near Mt. Krussne, Czechoslovakia.
Egyptair/Inex-Adria	32	YU-AHR	587/47503	03-19-72	Hit mountain on approach; Khomaksar, Yemen.
Eastern	31	N8961E	332/45870	05-18-72	Heavy landing in poor visibility; Fort Lauderdale, FL.
Delta	14	N3305L	011/45700	05-30-72	Crew training flight; Ft. Worth, TX.
North Central	31	N954N	231/47159	12-20-72	Collision with CV-880 on takeoff run; Chicago, IL.
SAS	21	LN-RLM	440/47304	01-31-73	Aborted takeoff after stall warning; Oslo, Norway.
Iberia	32	EC-BII	148/47077	03-05-73	Midair collision with CV-990; Nantes, France.
AeroMexico	15	XA-SOC	153/47100	06-21-73	In-flight explosion; near Puerta Vallarta, Mexico.
Delta	31	N975NE	166/47075	07-31-73	Hit seawall on approach in fog; Boston, MA.
Eastern	31	N8967E	361/47267	11-27-73	Overran runway; Akron, OH.
Delta	32	N3323L	204/47032	11-27-73	Hit lights on approach; Chattanooga, TN.
Eastern	31	N8984E	443/47400	09-11-74	Hit trees on approach; Charlotte, NC.
Inex-Adria	32	YU-AJN	693/47579	11-23-74	Landed short; Belgrade, Yugoslavia.
Avensa	14	YV-C-AVM	089/47056	12-22-74	Hit cables after takeoff; Maturin, Venezuela.
Inex-Adria	32	YU-AJO	620/47457	10-30-75	Hit hill on approach; Prague, Czechoslovakia.
Allegheny	31	N994VJ	481/47333	06-23-76	Wind shear, aborted landing. Philadelphia, PA.
AeroMexico	15	XA-SOF	254/47124	09-02-76	Overran runway; Leon, Mexico.
Inex-Adria	32	YU-AJR	741/47649	09-19-76	Midair collsion with BEA Trident; Zagreb, Yugoslavia.
Texas Int'l	14	N9104	155/47081	11-16-76	Aborted takeoff after stall warning; Denver, CO.
Southern	31	N1335U	608/47393	04-04-77	Double engine flameout; New Hope, GA.
Air Canada	32	C-FTLV	289/47197	06-26-78	Aborted takeoff after tire burst; Toronto, Ontario.
Alitalia	32	I-DIKQ	334/47227	12-23-78	Crashed into sea on approach; Palermo, Sicily.
Eastern	14	N8910E	056/45771	02-09-79	Wing hit ground on training flight; Dade-Collier, FL.
ATI	32	I-ATJC	776/47667	09-14-79	Hit mountain; near Cagliari, Sicily.
Alitalia	32	I-DIKB	196/47118	01-07-80	Hangar fire; Rome, Italy.
Garuda	32	PK-GND	649/47463	01-13-80	Hard landing; Banjarmarsin, Indonesia.
Texas Int'l	14	N9103	074/45796	03-17-80	Ran off runway in storm; Baton Rouge, LA.
Itavia	15	I-TIGI	022/45724	06-27-80	Hit by missile; near Palermo, Sicily.
AeroMexico	32	XA-DEN	729/47621	07-27-81	Missed approach in storm; Chihuahua, Mexico.
AeroMexico	32	XA-DEO	753/47622	11-09-81	Hit mountain; near Altamirano, Mexico.
Air Canada	32	C-FTLY	338/47200	06-02-82	Fuel explosion (in hangar); Montreal, Quebec.
Avensa	32	YV-67C	106/47025	03-11-83	Hard landing in fog; Barquisimeto, Venezuela.
Air Canada	32	C-FTLU	278/47196	06-02-83	In-flight electrical fire; Covington, KY.
Aviaco	32	EC-CGS	770/47645	12-07-83	Hit 727 on takeoff roll; Barajas, Madrid, Spain.
Garuda	32	PK-GNE	674/47561	06-11-84	Skidded off runway; Kemayoran, Indonesia.
Garuda	32	PK-GNI	758/47636	12-30-84	Overran runway; Bali, Indonesia.
Airborne Express	15	N926AX	105/47002	02-06-85	Aborted takeoff due to wing ice; Philadelphia, PA.
Midwest Express	14	N100ME	393/47307	09-06-85	Engine exploded on takeoff; Milwaukee, WI.
USAir	31	N961VJ	588/47506	02-21-86	Slid off snow-covered runway; Erie, PA.
AeroMexico	32	XA-JED	470/47356	08-31-86	Midair collision with light aircraft; Cerritos, CA.
SAS	41	SE-DAT	727/47625	02-23-87	Heavy landing; Trondheim, Norway.
Garuda	32	PK-GNQ	836/47741	04-04-87	Hit television antenna tower; Polonia, Indonesia.
Continental	14	N626TX	036/45726	11-15-87	Attempted takeoff with snow on wings; Denver, CO.
Eastern	31	N8948E	274/47184	12-28-87	Heavy landing; Pensacola, FL.
Evergreen Int'l	33F	N931F	287/47192	03-18-89	Cargo door opened on takeoff; Carswell AFB, TX.
Aviaco	32	EC-BIQ	222/47092	02-18-90	Heavy landing; Mallorca, Spain.
Alitalia	32	I-ATJA	746/47641	11-14-90	Hit mountain on approach; Zurich, Switzerland.
Northwest	14	N3313L	077/45708	12-03-90	Ground collision with 727; Detroit, MI.
Ryan Int'l	15F	N565PC	346/47240	02-17-91	Stalled on takeoff due to wing icing; Cleveland, OH.
Kuwaiti Air Force	32CF	KAF320	840/47691	02-26-91	Destroyed by Iraqi troops; Kuwait Airport.
Aeropostal	32	YV-23C	846/47720	03-05-91	Hit mountain in fog; near Truillo, Venezuela.
Alitalia	32	I-RIBN	437/47339	12-17-91	Landing gear collapse; Warsaw, Poland.

USAir	31	N964VJ	522/47373	01-18-92	Heavy landing; Elmira, NY.
Intercontinental	15	HK-2864X	044/45721	03-26-92	Heavy landing; Tumaco, Colombia.
Aviaco	32	EC-BYH	657/47556	03-30-92	Heavy landing; Granada, Spain.
Aeropostal	34F	YV-37C	872/47752	11-27-92	On ground during coup; Baraquisimeto, Venezuela.
Aeropostal	15	YV-03C	083/47000	04-02-93	Crashed into water; near Margarita Isle, Venezuela.
Japan Air System	41	JA-8448	885/47767	04-18-93	Wing touched ground on landing; Hanamaki, Japan.
Garuda	32	PK-GNT	907/47790	06-21-93	Heavy landing; Denpasar, Indonesia.
Sevivensa	32	YV-613C	220/47104	07-19-93	Aquaplaned on landing; Cuidad Bolivar, Bolivia.
Aviaco	32	EC-CLE	789/47678	03-21-94	Undershot on landing; Vigo, Spain.
USAir	31	N954VJ	703/47590	07-03-94	Wind shear; attempted missed approach; Charlotte, NC.
ADC	31	5N-BBE	345/45872	08-18-94	Overshot in rain; Monrovia, Liberia.
Intercontinental	14	HK-3839X	026/45742	01-11-95	Faulty altimeter; Cartagena, Colombia.
Intercontinental	15	HK-3564X	417/47127	03-17-95	On-ground electrical fire; Barranquilla, Colombia.
ValuJet	32	N908VJ	455/47321	06-09-95	Engine fire on takeoff roll; Atlanta, GA.
ADC	31	5N-BBA	360/47217	07-26-95	Undershot in rain; Monrovia, Liberia.
Binter Canarias	32	EC-BIR	237/47093	10-16-95	Taxied over embankment; Arrecife, Spain.
Continental	32	N10556	581/47423	02-19-96	Gear-up landing; Houston, TX.
ValuJet	32	N904VJ	496/47377	05-11-96	In-flight fire; Everglades, FL.
Allegro	14	XA-SNR	008/45699	05-14-96	Fuel starvation; Tampico, Mexico.
Ghana	51	9G-ACM	878/47755	04-12-97	Overshot in heavy rain; Abidjan, Ivory Coast.
Austral	32	LV-WEG	561/47446	10-10-97	Control loss in turbulence; near Nuevo Berlin, Uruguay.
AeroMexico	32	XA-DEJ	717/47594	10-18-97	Tail strike on landing; Mexico City.
Cebu Pacific	32	RP-C1507	175/47069	02-02-98	On approach; Cagayan de Oro, Philippines.

Above: Kuwaiti Air Force DC-9-32CFs being prepared for delivery. KAF 320 (ln 840/msn 47691) was destroyed in Kuwait by the Iraqis in 1990. (Harry Gann)

Below: Both aircraft were equipped with this simple VIP interior.

MODEL STRUCTURAL COMPARISON

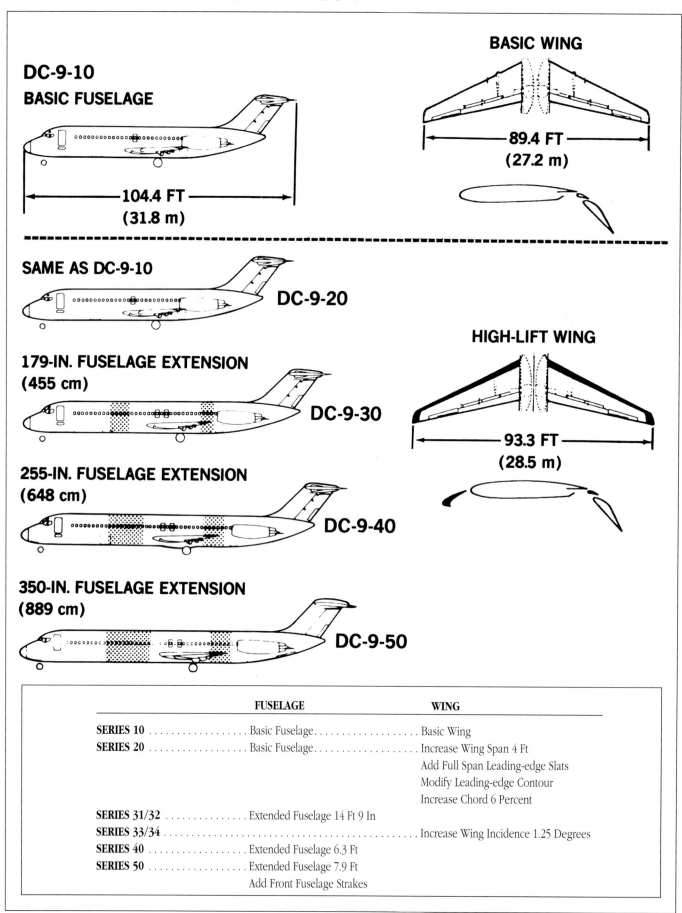

BASIC WING

DC-9-10

BASIC FUSELAGE

89.4 FT
(27.2 m)

104.4 FT
(31.8 m)

SAME AS DC-9-10 — DC-9-20

179-IN. FUSELAGE EXTENSION
(455 cm) — DC-9-30

HIGH-LIFT WING

93.3 FT
(28.5 m)

255-IN. FUSELAGE EXTENSION
(648 cm) — DC-9-40

350-IN. FUSELAGE EXTENSION
(889 cm) — DC-9-50

	FUSELAGE	WING
SERIES 10	Basic Fuselage	Basic Wing
SERIES 20	Basic Fuselage	Increase Wing Span 4 Ft
		Add Full Span Leading-edge Slats
		Modify Leading-edge Contour
		Increase Chord 6 Percent
SERIES 31/32	Extended Fuselage 14 Ft 9 In	
SERIES 33/34		Increase Wing Incidence 1.25 Degrees
SERIES 40	Extended Fuselage 6.3 Ft	
SERIES 50	Extended Fuselage 7.9 Ft	
	Add Front Fuselage Strakes	

WEIGHT UPGRADES
PASSENGER CAPACITY & EXIT REQUIREMENTS

DC-9 Weight Upgrades
(Pounds)

| MODEL | MTOW | | MLW | | ZFW | | ENGINE | |
	INITIAL	TO	INITIAL	TO	INITIAL	TO	INITIAL	TO
-11	77,700	85,700	74,000	81,000	66,400	71,400	JT8D-1	JT8D-1 or -7
-12	79,500	85,700	79,050	81,700	66,400	71,400	JT8D-5	JT8D-1 or -7
-13	83,700	85,700	79,050	81,700	66,400	71,400	JT8D-5	JT8D-1 or -7
-14	87,500	90,700	81,700	N/C	71,400	74,000	JT8D-5	JT8D-1 or -7
-15	90,700	N/C	81,700	N/C	74,000	N/C	JT8D-1	JT8D-7
-15RC	90,700	N/C	81,700	N/C	74,000	N/C	JT8D-7	N/C
-20	94,500	98,000	93,400	N/C	84,000	N/C	JT8D-9	JT8D-11
-31	98,000	108,000	95,300	99,100	84,000	87,000	JT8D-1	JT8D-7,-9,-17.
-32	108,000	110,000	95,000	102,000	87,000	92,000	JT8D-1/7	JT8D-9,-15,-17
-33	114,000	N/C	102,000	N/C	95,500	N/C	JT8D-9	JT8D-11
-34	121,000	N/C	110,000	N/C	98,500	N/C	JT8D-9	JT8D-15 or -17
-40	114,000	N/C	102,000	N/C	93,000	N/C	JT8D-9	JT8D-11 or -15
-50	115,000	121,000	104,000	110,000	98,500	100,500	JT8D-15	JT8D-17

Passenger Capacity & Exit Requirements

SERIES	PASSENGER CAPACITY	TYPE I* PER SIDE	TYPE III** PER SIDE	TAIL***
DC-9-10/-20	79	1	1	1
DC-9-30	94	1	1	1
	109	1	2	1
DC-9-30	114	1	2	1
	127	1	2	1
DC-9-40	128	1	2	1
DC-9-50	139	1	2	1

*forward boarding and galley doors
**overwing positions.
***Via aft bulkhead after the fiberglass tail cone has been jettisoned. For aircraft without ventral stairs, the rear bulkhead is physically similar in size to the overwing exits

ENGINE PERFORMANCE
FUEL CAPACITY

JT8D Engine Performance

	JT8D-1/ -1A	JT8D-7/ -7A	JT8D-9/ -9A	JT8D-11	JT8D-15	JT8D-17
Rating *	14,000 lb	14,000 lb	14,500 lb	15,000 lb	15,500 lb	16,000 lb
EGT (0°F)	1058/1076	1058/1076	1076/1094	1102	1148	1202
TIT *** (0°F)	1852	1852	1860	1930	2005	2087
Rotor Speeds (RPM)	8,600-12,250	8,600-12,250	8,600-12,250	8,600-12,250	8,800-12,250	8,800-12,250
Airflow (lb/sec)	315	315	318	321	324	324
Bypass Ratio	1.10	1.10	1.03	1.01	0.99	1.01
Weight (lb)	3155	3205	3252	3309	3309	3330

* All at 84 degrees F except JT8D-1 which was at 59 degrees F
** Exhaust Gas Temperature
*** Turbine Inlet Temperature

DC-9 Fuel Capacity By Model

SERIES	TANKS	CAPACITY (U.S. gal.)	WEIGHT (Pounds)
-10	2*	2,786	18,666
-10	3	3,693	24,743
-20	3	3,679	24,649
-30	3	3,679	24,649
-40	3	3,679	24,649
-50	3**	4,259	28,535

* Center tank not activated.
** A 580-U.S. gallon supplemental fuel tank is standard on the Series 50 forward of the wing box.

Supplemental Fuel Tank Options***

TANKAGE		LOCATION	
CAPACITY (U.S. gal.)	WEIGHT (Pounds)	FWD	AFT
580	3,886	580	
780	5,226	780	
1,000	6,700	1,000	
1,360	9,112	580	780
1,560	10,452	780	780
1,780	11,926	780	1,000
2,250	15,075	1,250	1,000

*** Located immediately forward or aft of the wing box. Tanks are in four sizes, 580, 780, 1000 and 1,250 U.S. gallons. The latter two are available on Series 30, 40 and 50 aircraft only.

FACTORY DELIVERIES

MODEL	-10	-15MC	-15RC	-20	-30	-30CF	-30F	-40	-50	C-9
AEROMEXICO	9				15					
AIR CANADA	6				44					
AIR JAMAICA					3					
AIR WEST					15					
ALLEGHENY/US AIR	*1				61				8	
ALITALIA					36		2			
ALM					3					
ANSETT / ANA					12					
ATI					14					
ATLANTIS					3					
AUSTRIAN					9				5	
AVENSA	2				1					
AVIACO					12	4 (34CF)				
BALAIR					1	1 (33CF)				
BONANZA	3									
BWIA						1 (34CF)			4	
CARIBAIR					3					
CONTINENTAL	*4		19							
DELTA	14				63					
DOMINICANA					1					
EASTERN	*15				72				9	
EAST AFRICAN					3					
FINNAIR									12	
GARUDA					25					
GHANA A/W									1	
HAWAIIAN	2				8				10	
IBERIA					31	4 (32RC)				
INEX ADRIA					5				2	
ITALIAN AIR FORCE					2					
JAT					14					
KLM	6				12	6 (33RC)				
KOREAN					1					
KUWAITI AIR FORCE						2 (32CF)				
LAV	1				3				5	
MARTINAIR					2	2 (33RC)				
NCA/REPUBLIC					20				28	
NORTHEAST	1				14					
OVERSEAS NAT'L						7 (32CF)				
OZARK	6				13					
PAN ADRIA					1					
PACIFIC SOUTHWEST					2					
PLAYBOY ENTERPRISES					1					
PURDUE					2					
SAS				10			2	49		
SAUDI ARABIAN	3									
SOUTHERN	6				5					
STANDARD	2									
SUDFLUG					2					
SWISSAIR	*5				20		1		12	
TOA DOMESTIC								22		
TRACINDA	1									
TRANS AUSTRALIA					12					
TRANS-TEXAS / TXI	2	5			13					
TWA	20									
TURKISH A/L					10					
US AIR FORCE (C-9A)										21
US AIR FORCE (VC-9C)										3
US NAVY (C-9B)										17
WEST COAST	4									
TOTAL: (976)	113	5	19	10	589	27	5	71	96	41

* Leased

Appendix VI
PRODUCTION LIST

Introduction

This table contains data reported to McDonnell Douglas Corporation through June 1997. Where Flight Hours only are indicated, the aircraft was still reporting monthly activity.

The individual aircraft information that follows is sequenced in the order of actual production by the Line Number (LN). The Manufacturer's Serial Number (MSN) identifies the airframe for legal purposes and remains constant throughout its life. A small steel plate, engraved with this number and other data, is permanently affixed to the forward passenger doorjamb on the left side.

The Registration (REGN), Airline (A/L), MODEL, and Engine (ENG) columns show the status at delivery. Many DC-9s received upgraded engines after delivery, but this did not change the aircraft model number. Model numbers are explained in the main text. (VS) denotes aft Ventral Stairs fitted.

Delivery Dates (DEL) indicate when the aircraft title was transferred to either the airline or financial institution. Title transfer takes place at the precise moment that final payment is transferred to the manufacturer's account, allowing insurance liability to transfer at the same time.

The Status (STAT) column indicates whether the aircraft is Stored (STO), Retired (RET) or Written Off (W/O). For aircraft still active, the Status and DATE columns are left blank. Retired aircraft dates reflect when MDC was officially informed of the status change. In many cases, aircraft may not have flown for several years prior to this date. Flight HOURS and Landings (LDGS) include final figures for aircraft no longer active. An asterisk in the Flight Hours/Landings column indicates last reported figures, but not current to September 1997. The missing Line Numbers, commencing at Fuselage 909, are allocated to MD-80s that were built on a separate production line.

AIRLINE ABBREVIATIONS (A/L) - ORIGINAL DELIVERY CUSTOMERS

AC	.Air Canada		NE	.Northeast Airlines
AL	.Allegheny		OS	.Austrian Airlines
AM	.Aeronaves de Mexico		OV	.Overseas National Airways (ONA)
AN	.Ansett ANA		OZ	.Ozark Air Lines
AO	.Aviaco		PB	.H.H.Heffner
AT	.Aero Transporti Italiani		PD	.Purdue Airlines
AU	.Austral		PS	.Pacific Southwest Airlines
AY	.Finnair		RC	.Republic Airlines
BA	.Balair		RW	.Air West
BW	.British West Indian Airways (BWIA)		SF	.Sudflug GmBH
BZ	.Bonanza Air Lines		SK	.Scandinavian Airlines System (SAS)
CB	.Caribbean International Airways (Caribair)		SO	.Southern Airways
CO	.Continental Airlines		SR	.Swissair
DL	.Delta Air Lines / Delta		ST	.Standard Airways
DO	.Dominicana		SV	.Saudi Arabian Airlines (Saudia)
EA	.Eastern Air Lines		TI	.Trans-Texas Airways / Texas International
EC	.East African Airways		TK	.Turkish Airlines
GA	.Garuda Indonesian Airlines		TN	.Trans Australian Airways
GH	.Ghana Airways		TR	.Tracy Investment Corp.
HA	.Hawaiian Airlines		TW	.Trans World Airlines
IB	.Iberia		VE	.Avensa
JD	.Toa Domestic Airlines		WC	.West Coast Airlines
JM	.Air Jamaica		YJ	.Inex Adria Airways
JU	.Jugoslav Airlines		YX	.Pan Adria Airways
KE	.Korean Air Lines		YY	.Atlantis Airways GmBH
KL	.KLM Royal Dutch Airlines		ZA	.United States Air Force
LM	.ALM-Antillean Airlines		ZI	.Italian Air Force
LV	.Lineas Aeras Venezolanas		ZM	.United States Marine Corps
MP	.Martin's Air Charter (Martinair)		ZN	.United States Navy
NC	.North Central Airlines			

LN	MSN	REGN	A/L	MODEL	VS	ENG	DEL	STAT	HOURS	LDGS	DATE
1	45965	N1301T	TI	14		JT8D-1	09-30-66	RET	58,420	71,064	07-24-91
2	45696	N3301L	DL	14		JT8D-5	07-19-66		71,308	68,708	
3	45697	N3302L	DL	14		JT8D-5	06-09-66	RET	42,900	66,504	05-29-81
4	45711	CF-TLB	AC	14		JT8D-5	04-12-66		64,465	74,994	
5	45698	N3303L	DL	14		JT8D-5	12-04-65		61,334	79,911	
6	45712	CF-TLC	AC	14		JT8D-5	01-06-66		60,504	84,955	
7	45714	N1051T	TW	14		JT8D-1	03-25-66		74,053	75,002	
8	45699	N3304L	DL	14		JT8D-5	09-18-65	W/O	53,563	58,661	05-14-96
9	45713	CF-TLD	AC	14		JT8D-5	02-09-66		63,066	88,293	
10	45715	N1052T	TW	14		JT8D-1	02-05-66		64,683	70,983	
11	45700	N3305L	DL	14		JT8D-5	11-26-65	W/O	18,998	29,018	05-30-72
12	45701	N3306L	DL	14		JT8D-5	11-30-65	RET	66,797	94.057	09-01-91
13	45716	N1053T	TW	14		JT8D-1	02-19-66		61,968	69,769	
14	45728	N945L	BZ	11		JT8D-5	12-19-65		37,909	47,704	
15	45702	N3307L	DL	14		JT8D-5	01-11-66		43,761	57,064	
16	45729	N946L	BZ	14		JT8D-5	01-17-66		62,349	90,018	
17	45718	PH-DNA	KL	15		JT8D-5	03-25-66		61,780	53,174	
18	45719	PH-DNB	KL	15		JT8D-5	04-03-66		60,506	64,850	
19	45725	CF-TLE	AC	14		JT8D-5	02-24-66		67,637	81,367	
20	45717	N901H	HA	15	Y	JT8D-1	03-12-66		38,231	57,495	
21	45703	N3308L	DL	14		JT8D-5	03-16-66	RET	68,399	95,396	04-14-93
22	45724	N902H	HA	15	Y	JT8D-1	03-19-66	W/O	29,543	45,932	06-27-80
23	45842	N8961	CO	14		JT8D-1	03-04-66		79,256	84,410	
24	45704	N3309L	DL	14		JT8D-5	04-28-66	RET	66,117	93,228	10-31-91
25	45735	N1054T	TW	14		JT8D-1	04-21-66		62,922	71,207	
26	45742	N8801E	EA	14		JT8D-1	04-26-66	W/O	65,084	69,716	01-11-95
27	45720	PH-DNC	KL	15		JT8D-5	04-30-66	RET	42,946	44,468	09-20-96
28	45843	N8962	CO	14		JT8D-1	05-01-66		65,086	77,796	
29	45743	N8902E	EA	14		JT8D-1	05-13-66		82,909	86,746	
30	45772	N970Z	OZ	15	Y	JT8D-1	05-27-66		68,221	87,283	
31	45744	N8903E	EA	14		JT8D-1	05-19-66		72,682	97,627	
32	45745	N8904E	EA	14		JT8D-1	05-31-66		66,564	91,852	
33	45844	N8963	CO	14		JT8D-1	06-02-66		56,381	64,319	
34	45731	HB-IFA	SR	15	Y	JT8D-1	07-15-66		14,622	14,730	
35	47048	N8964	CO	14		JT8D-1	07-03-66		66,505	81,448	
36	45726	CF-TLF	AC	14		JT8D-5	06-24-66	W/O	52,424	61,888	11-15-87
37	45730	N947L	BZ	11		JT8D-5	07-01-66		48,878	76,458	
38	45746	N8905E	EA	14		JT8D-1	07-01-66		72,626	96,162	
39	45773	N971Z	OZ	15	Y	JT8D-1	07-08-66		66,692	85,916	
40	45747	N8906E	EA	14		JT8D-1	07-19-66		72,469	95,666	
41	45732	HB-IFB	SR	15	Y	JT8D-1	07-31-66		25,561	66,135	
42	47049	N6140A	AL	14		JT8D-1	07-29-66		73,501	90,686	
43	45727	CF-TLG	AC	14		JT8D-5	07-31-66		77,263	77,047	
44	45721	PH-DND	KL	15		JT8D-1	08-13-66	W/O	54,223	66,352	05-31-92
45	45736	N1055T	TW	14		JT8D-1	08-25-66		78,066	76,514	
46	45841	N972Z	OZ	15	Y	JT8D-1	08-23-66		65,002	82,825	
47	45848	N8907E	EA	14		JT8D-1	08-29-66		73,467	97,308	
48	45733	N8916E	EA	31		JT8D-1	10-20-67	RET	60,583	57,757	12-31-94
49	45737	N1056T	TW	14		JT8D-1	09-12-66	RET	55,148	54,893	10-01-95
50	45749	N8908E	EA	14		JT8D-1	09-11-66		75,072	82,785	
51	45797	N8953U	NE	15	Y	JT8D-1	12-29-66		17,732	23,972	
52	45974	N9101	WC	14		JT8D-1	09-16-66	W/O	168	221	10-01-66
53	45705	N3310L	DL	14		JT8D-1	09-24-66		76,689	103,642	
54	45738	N1057T	TW	14		JT8D-1	10-11-66		60,501	73,585	
55	45722	PH-DNE	KL	15		JT8D-1	10-10-66		60,136	76,346	
56	45739	N1058T	TW	14		JT8D-1	10-28-66		61,051	71,331	
57	45770	N8909E	EA	14		JT8D-1	11-07-66		71,922	78,489	
58	45771	N8910E	EA	14		JT8D-1	10-27-66	W/O	34,513	36,890	02-09-79
59	45798	N490SA	ST	15	Y	JT8D-1	11-03-66		65,751	79,653	
60	45734	N8917E	EA	31		JT8D-1	03-27-67	RET	61,668	60,520	12-31-94
61	45706	N3311L	DL	14		JT8D-1	10-27-66		32,667	46,798	
62	45740	N1059T	TW	14		JT8D-1	11-16-66		33,401	35,203	
63	45723	PH-DNF	KL	15		JT8D-1	11-14-66	RET	59,069	72,526	05-01-93
64	45785	HB-IFC	SR	15		JT8D-1	11-29-66		81,251	83,328	
65	45795	N9102	WC	14		JT8D-1	11-03-66		74,972	87,351	
66	45741	N1060T	TW	14		JT8D-1	11-29-66	RET	53,452	53,082	10-01-95
67	45825	N8911E	EA	14		JT8D-1	11-24-66		74,146	80,927	
68	45829	N8912E	EA	14		JT8D-1	11-30-66		73,527	79,241	
69	45799	N491SA	ST	15	Y	JT8D-1	11-30-66		64,521	78,188	
70	45707	N3312L	DL	14		JT8D-1	11-22-66		74,638	100,430	
71	45775	N1061T	TW	14		JT8D-1	12-20-66		*30,000	*34,000	
72	45776	N1062T	TW	14		JT8D-1	12-22-66		60,473	62,232	

LN	MSN	REGN	A/L	MODEL	VS	ENG	DEL	STAT	HOURS	LDGS	DATE
73	45833	N8918E	EA	31		JT8D-1	01-27-67	RET	50,581	57,253	12-31-94
74	45796	N9103	WC	14		JT8D-1	12-15-66	W/O	36,466	52,493	03-17-80
75	45830	N8913E	EA	14		JT8D-1	12-22-66		73,707	80,920	
76	45831	N8914E	EA	14		JT8D-1	12-29-66		74,436	80,238	
77	45708	N3313L	DL	14		JT8D-5	12-30-66	W/O	62,253	88,255	12-03-90
78	45709	N3314L	DL	14		JT8D-5	01-05-67	RET	64,310	90,888	01-02-92
79	45826	N8901	CO	15RC	Y	JT8D-7	03-06-67		42,235	53,396	
80	45777	N1063T	TW	14		JT8D-1	01-19-67	W/O	309	354	03-09-67
81	47004	VH-CZB	AN	31	Y	JT8D-7	03-31-67		55,542	55,955	
82	45778	N1064T	TW	14		JT8D-1	02-02-67		58,351	57,742	
83	47000	HZ-AEA	SV	15	Y	JT8D-1	02-08-67	W/O	34,415	48,925	04-03-93
84	45832	N8915E	EA	14		JT8D-1	02-08-67		74,507	82,223	
85	45834	N8919E	EA	31		JT8D-1	02-22-67	RET	52,910	57,457	08-01-94
86	47003	VH-CZA	AN	31	Y	JT8D-7	03-17-67		56,460	57,890	
87	47007	VH-TJJ	TN	31	Y	JT8D-7	03-18-67		68,228	72,362	
88	47043	N1302T	TI	14		JT8D-1	02-02-67		77,041	87,090	
89	47056	YVC-AVM	VE	14		JT8D-7	02-28-67	W/O	15,376	26,637	12-22-74
90	45786	HB-IFD	SR	15	Y	JT8D-1	03-09-67		77,110	73,703	
91	45845	CF-TLH	AC	32		JT8D-7	03-07-67		71,203	64,546	
92	45779	N1065T	TW	14		JT8D-1	03-11-67	RET	53,195	52,664	10-01-95
93	45780	N1066T	TW	14		JT8D-1	04-01-67		63,724	64,572	
94	47001	HZ-AEB	SV	15	Y	JT8D-1	03-30-67		65,436	78,286	
95	45835	N8920E	EA	31		JT8D-1	03-29-67		57,681	61,355	
96	45836	N8921E	EA	31		JT8D-1	03-22-67		58,489	62,166	
97	47010	N8902	CO	15RC	Y	JT8D-7	04-11-67		44,244	57,737	
98	47008	VH-TJK	TN	31	Y	JT8D-7	04-15-67		53,524	55,235	
99	47006	N981PS	PS	31	Y	JT8D-7	03-23-67		63,777	74,455	
100	45710	N3315L	DL	32	Y	JT8D-7	04-08-67		60,321	78,350	
101	45781	N1067T	TW	14		JT8D-1	04-11-67		61,843	65,240	
102	47011	N8903	CO	15RC	Y	JT8D-7	04-25-67		42,020	53,073	
103	45837	N8922E	EA	31		JT8D-1	04-13-67		55,009	64,945	
104	45838	N8923E	EA	31		JT8D-1	04-18-67		52,975	59,939	
105	47002	HZ-AEC	SV	15	Y	JT8D-1	04-29-67	W/O	32,435	39,031	02-06-85
106	47025	N3316L	DL	32	Y	JT8D-7	04-30-67	W/O	41,804	58,839	03-11-83
107	47053	N970NE	NE	31		JT8D-7	05-05-67	RET	69,973	80,729	10-31-96
108	47098	N938PR	CA	31	Y	JT8D-7	06-01-67		61,535	70,819	
109	47060	YVC-AVR	VE	14		JT8D-7	05-09-67		42,471	63,737	
110	47054	N971E	NE	31		JT8D-7	05-08-67		73,979	85,668	
111	47063	N91S	SO	15	Y	JT8D-1	05-08-67		72,351	100,362	
112	45846	CF-TLI	AC	32		JT8D-7	05-13-67		68,724	68,664	
113	47019	CF-TLJ	AC	32		JT8D-7	05-21-67		70.904	63,991	
114	45782	N1068T	TW	14		JT8D-1	05-30-67		47,426	49,411	
115	47012	N8904	CO	15RC	Y	JT8D-7	05-23-67		46,688	60.576	
116	45839	N8924E	EA	31		JT8D-1	05-29-67		54,228	59,002	
117	45840	N8925E	EA	31		JT8D-1	04-28-67		55,458	61,245	
118	47050	N970VJ	AL	31	Y	JT8D-7	06-03-67		77,524	91,487	
119	47026	N3317L	DL	32	Y	JT8D-7	06-14-67		75,808	90,054	
120	47064	N92S	SO	15	Y	JT8D-1	06-18-67		72,149	99,271	
121	47037	EC-BIG	IB	32	Y	JT8D-7	06-29-67		53,788	52,799	
122	47057	N972NE	NE	31		JT8D-7	06-14-67		73,351	85,650	
123	47058	N973NE	NE	31		JT8D-7	06-16-67		74,154	85,986	
124	45863	N8926E	EA	31		JT8D-1	06-21-67		52,861	59,472	
125	47059	XA-SOA	AM	15		JT8D-7	05-26-67		82,957	85,781	
126	47020	CF-TLK	AC	32		JT8D-7	05-30-67		70,435	70,303	
127	45787	HB-IFE	SR	15	Y	JT8D-1	06-25-67		64,502	76,775	
128	45783	N1069T	TW	14		JT8D-1	07-01-67		57,195	59,309	
129	47013	N8905	CO	15RC	Y	JT8D-7	06-25-67		46,869	69,531	
130	45864	N8927E	EA	31		JT8D-1	07-01-67		50,495	57,054	
131	47051	N971VJ	AL	31	Y	JT8D-7	06-26-67		77,231	91,279	
132	47027	N3318L	DL	31		JT8D-7	07-10-67		75,255	82,662	
133	47021	CF-TLL	AC	32		JT8D-7	07-07-67		72,140	64,720	
134	47076	EC-BIH	IB	32	Y	JT8D-7	07-19-67		58,094	67,192	
135	45827	HL7201	KE	32	Y	JT8D-7	07-19-67		76,022	66,509	
136	47038	I-DIKA	AZ	32	Y	JT8D-7	08-08-67		60,815	58,227	
137	45865	N8928E	EA	31		JT8D-1	07-27-67		53,298	59,539	
138	45866	N8929E	EA	31		JT8D-1	07-29-67		67,453	63,441	
139	47085	XA-SOB	AM	15		JT8D-7	07-19-67		82,566	85,677	
140	45784	N1070T	TW	14		JT8D-1	08-19-67		55,973	54,836	
141	47014	N8906	CO	15RC	Y	JT8D-7	07-23-67		45,738	60,573	
142	47052	N972VJ	AL	31	Y	JT8D-7	07-28-67		69,329	83,611	
143	47067	N951N	NC	31		JT8D-7	07-27-67		69,173	83,452	
144	47022	CF-TLM	AC	32		JT8D-7	07-27-67		72,615	65,313	
145	47028	N3319L	DL	31	Y	JT8D-7	08-02-67		76,128	83,361	

LN	MSN	REGN	A/L	MODEL	VS	ENG	DEL	STAT	HOURS	LDGS	DATE
146	47078	N93S	SO	15	Y	JT8D-1	07-28-67		71,458	99,355	
147	47033	N973Z	OZ	15	Y	JT8D-1	07-31-67		65,198	82,518	
148	47077	EC-BII	IB	32	Y	JT8D-1	08-14-67	W/O	10,853	9,452	03-05-73
149	47094	SE-DBZ	SK	32	Y	JT8D-7	08-12-67		71,009	72,588	
150	47066	N974NE	NE	31		JT8D-7	08-14-67		74,098	85,258	
151	47005	VH-CZC	AN	31	Y	JT8D-7	08-24-67		64,110	61,875	
152	47009	VH-TJL	TN	31	Y	JT8D-7	08-20-67		57,931	61,525	
153	47100	XA-SOC	AM	15		JT8D-7	08-25-67	W/O	16,450	20,498	06-20-73
154	47039	I-DIKE	AZ	32	Y	JT8D-7	09-01-67		58,174	56,422	
155	47081	N9104	WC	14		JT8D-1	08-23-67	W/O	24,332	36,581	11-16-76
156	47015	N8907	CO	15RC	Y	JT8D-7	08-29-67		42,656	53,614	
157	47029	N3320L	DL	32	Y	JT8D-7	08-31-67		75,443	82,451	
158	47023	CF-TLN	AC	32		JT8D-7	08-30-67		70,210	69,956	
159	47024	CF-TLO	AC	32		JT8D-7	08-31-67		72,666	65,252	
160	47068	CF-TLP	AC	32		JT8D-7	08-31-67		69,623	69,545	
161	47073	N952N	NC	31	Y	JT8D-7	09-01-67		72,664	91,318	
162	47034	N974Z	OZ	15	Y	JT8D-1	09-01-67	W/O	3,458	5,549	12-27-68
163	47079	EC-BIJ	IB	32		JT8D-7	09-15-67		58,055	60,210	
164	47080	EC-BIK	IB	32		JT8D-7	09-14-67		59,060	66,585	
165	47044	N1303T	TI	15MC	Y	JT8D-7	09-28-67		50,257	65,444	
166	47075	N975E	NE	31		JT8D-7	09-25-67	W/O	14,639	15,600	07-31-73
167	47110	OY-KGU	SK	32	Y	JT8D-7	10-08-67		73,884	69,394	
168	47046	I-DIKI	AZ	32		JT8D-7	09-25-67		59,719	55,758	
169	47139	N8930E	EA	21		JT8D-1	19-04-67		82,025	69,056	
170	47152	N8908	CO	15RC	Y	JT8D-7	09-22-67		43,123	57,679	
171	45788	HB-IFF	SR	32	Y	JT8D-7	10-21-67		73,972	69,817	
172	47040	N931F	OV	32CF		JT8D-7	10-06-67		51,832	41,038	
173	47016	N8909	CO	15RC	Y	JT8D-7	10-04-67		65,188	78,275	
174	47030	N3321L	DL	32	Y	JT8D-7	10-03-67		75,502	82,736	
175	47069	CF-TLQ	AC	32		JT8D-7	09-30-67		72,192	64,745	
176	47070	CF-TLR	AC	32		JT8D-7	09-30-67		70,520	63,004	
177	47083	N953N	NC	31	Y	JT8D-7	10-05-67		71,932	91,024	
178	47035	N975Z	OZ	15	Y	JT8D-1	10-10-67		65,159	82,217	
179	47084	EC-BIL	IB	32	Y	JT8D-7	10-11-67		52,348	53,547	
180	47088	EC-BIM	IB	32	Y	JT8D-7	10-28-67		54,780	59,993	
181	47082	N976NE	NE	31		JT8D-7	10-19-67		72,383	77,438	
182	47111	LN-RLS	SK	32	Y	JT8D-7	11-07-67		72,570	69,705	
183	47047	I-DIKO	AZ	32		JT8D-7	10-31-67		56,561	54,784	
184	47045	N1304T	TI	15MC	Y	JT8D-7	11-08-67		44,604	79,600	
185	47153	N8910	CO	15RC	Y	JT8D-7	10-18-67		55,014	69,811	
186	47017	N8911	CO	15RC	Y	JT8D-7	10-28-67		66,538	79,681	
187	47031	N3322L	DL	32	Y	JT8D-7	10-31-67		76,765	82,103	
188	47071	CF-TLS	AC	32		JT8D-7	11-02-67		71,909	64,801	
189	47089	EC-BIN	IB	32	Y	JT8D-7	11-06-67		52,786	52,669	
190	47090	EC-BIO	IB	32	Y	JT8D-7	11-08-67		56,311	56,448	
191	47095	N977NE	NE	31		JT8D-7	11-03-67		72,224	78,169	
192	47096	N978NE	NE	31		JT8D-7	11-03-67		71,696	77,709	
193	47097	N979NE	NE	31		JT8D-7	11-06-67		69,236	74,123	
194	47055	N1305T	TI	15MC	Y	JT8D-7	11-22-67		49,452	64,967	
195	47101	I-DIKU	AZ	32	Y	JT8D-7	11-16-67		60,141	57,214	
196	47188	I-DIKB	AZ	32	Y	JT8D-7	11-22-67	W/O	24,221	25,705	01-07-80
197	47099	N973VJ	AL	31	Y	JT8D-7	11-13-67		76,735	90,035	
198	47102	PH-DNG	KL	32	Y	JT8D-7	11-18-67		62,219	55,476	
199	47112	SE-DBY	SK	32	Y	JT8D-7	12-04-67		71,278	69,954	
200	47041	N932F	OV	32CF		JT8D-7	11-08-67		57,663	51,603	
201	47154	N8912	CO	15RC	Y	JT8D-7	11-28-67		41,799	47,954	
202	47149	N903H	HA	31	Y	JT8D-7	11-22-67		70,268	96,677	
203	47018	N8913	CO	15RC	Y	JT8D-7	11-22-67	RET	64,773	80,003	03-20-97
204	47032	N3323L	DL	32	Y	JT8D-7	11-30-67	W/O	18,233	23,764	11-27-73
205	47103	N3324L	DL	32	Y	JT8D-7	11-29-67		77,829	82,245	
206	47091	EC-BIP	IB	32	Y	JT8D-7	12-04-67		57,020	66,931	
207	47061	N1306T	TI	15MC	Y	JT8D-7	12-22-67		52,307	67,109	
208	47147	N933F	OV	32CF		JT8D-7	12-14-67		47,633	38,633	
209	47120	N939PR	CB	31	Y	JT8D-7	12-11-67	RET	56,521	64,630	06-30-92
210	47128	I-DIKC	AZ	32	Y	JT8D-7	12-11-67		55,553	58,469	
211	47130	N974VJ	AL	31	Y	JT8D-7	12-08-67		76,508	89,630	
212	47140	N8931E	EA	31		JT8D-1	12-07-67		67,176	61,944	
213	47113	OY-KGW	SK	32	Y	JT8D-7	12-19-67		69,227	66,669	
214	47131	PH-DNH	KL	32	Y	JT8D-7	12-11-67		55,027	49,198	
215	47134	N980NE	NE	31		JT8D-7	12-15-67		71,659	77,696	
216	49155	N8914	CO	15RC	Y	JT8D-7	12-11-67		64,866	78,621	
217	45789	HB-IFG	SR	32	Y	JT8D-7	12-22-67		69,880	72,279	
218	47114	SE-DBX	SK	41	Y	JT8D-9	05-23-68		65,056	60,791	

LN	MSN	REGN	A/L	MODEL	VS	ENG	DEL	STAT	HOURS	LDGS	DATE
219	47086	N8915	CO	15RC	Y	JT8D-7	12-16-67		53,101	67,876	
220	47104	N3325L	DL	32	Y	JT8D-7	12-18-67		61,726	77,050	
221	45105	N3326L	DL	32	Y	JT8D-7	12-20-67		68,501	88,190	
222	47092	EC-BIQ	IB	32	Y	JT8D-7	12-20-67	W/O	44,692	49,546	07-31-90
223	47062	N1307T	TI	15MC	Y	JT8D-7	01-26-68		51,811	66,378	
224	47122	XA-SOD	AM	15		JT8D-7	12-19-67		85,964	89,819	
225	47129	I-DIKO	AZ	32	Y	JT8D-9	12-26-67		57,772	53,838	
226	47146	N975VJ	AL	31	Y	JT8D-7	12-28-67	RET	71,505	84,800	10-31-96
227	47141	N8932E	EA	31		JT8D-1	12-23-67		77,828	71,283	
228	47156	N8916	CO	15RC	Y	JT8D-7	12-29-68		62,374	78,835	
229	47132	PH-DNI	KL	32	Y	JT8D-7	01-03-68		59,914	53,420	
230	47133	PH-DNK	KL	32	Y	JT8D-7	01-10-68		62,168	55,417	
231	47159	N954N	NC	31	Y	JT8D-7	12-29-67	W/O	11,912	18,952	12-20-72
232	47142	N8933E	EA	31		JT8D-1	12-30-67		71,106	69,434	
233	47135	N981E	NE	31		JT8D-7	12-28-67		71,472	78,403	
234	47087	N8917	CO	15RC	Y	JT8D-7	01-09-68		33,607	42,870	
235	47106	N3327L	DL	32	Y	JT8D-7	01-12-68		77,328	86,725	
236	47107	N3328L	DL	32	Y	JT8D-7	01-11-68		74,549	82,061	
237	47093	EC-BIR	IB	32	Y	JT8D-7	01-13-68		54,767	58,942	
238	47143	N8934E	EA	31		JT8D-1	01-16-68		71,529	69,875	
239	47144	N8935E	EA	31		JT8D-1	01-15-68		81,815	69,554	
240	47190	PH-DNL	DL	32	Y	JT8D-7	01-24-68		62,423	54,047	
241	47160	N955N	NC	31	Y	JT8D-7	01-16-68		71,523	89,722	
242	45828	N8918	CO	15RC	Y	JT8D-7	01-19-68		52,494	66,697	
243	47136	N982NE	NE	31		JT8D-7	01-24-68		70,738	77,269	
244	47251	N982PS	PS	31	Y	JT8D-7	01-24-68		69,337	82,200	
245	47204	N94S	SO	15	Y	JT8D-1	01-20-68		70,944	98,470	
246	47148	N934F	OV	32CF		JT8D-7	01-25-68		43,137	59,920	
247	47145	N8936E	EA	31		JT8D-1	01-30-68		77,585	72,643	
248	47158	N8937E	EA	31		JT8D-1	01-31-68		81,225	69,478	
249	47161	N8938E	EA	31		JT8D-1	02-02-68		67,471	63,319	
250	47205	N95S	SO	15	Y	JT8D-1	02-09-68		71,203	98,739	
251	47108	N3329L	DL	32	Y	JT8D-7	02-01-68		73,095	79,388	
252	47109	N3330L	DL	32	Y	JT8D-7	02-06-68		74,200	81,569	
253	47123	XA-SOE	AM	15		JT8D-7	02-08-68	RET	61,393	69,840	01-31-91
254	47124	XA-SOF	AM	15		JT8D-7	02-07-68	W/O	25,591	30,228	09-02-76
255	47162	N8939E	EA	31		JT8D-1	02-10-68		78,108	72,743	
256	47163	N8940E	EA	31		JT8D-1	02-15-68		78,230	73,357	
257	47248	N976Z	OZ	31	Y	JT8D-7	02-26-68		71,202	85,258	
258	47137	N983NE	NE	31		JT8D-7	02-23-68		70,662	77,582	
259	47164	N8941E	EA	31		JT8D-1	02-18-68		83,080	67,785	
260	47165	N8942E	EA	31		JT8D-1	02-22-68		65,262	62,234	
261	47115	OY-KGA	SK	41	Y	JT8D-9	02-29-68		66,351	61,031	
262	47312	EC-BIS	IB	32	Y	JT8D-7	02-23-68		58,450	58,765	
263	47172	N3331L	DL	32	Y	JT8D-7	02-29-68		73,514	78,803	
264	45790	HB-IFH	SR	32	Y	JT8D-7	02-27-68		67,609	70,175	
265	47166	N8943E	EA	31		JT8D-1	02-25-68		64,037	61,522	
266	47167	N8944E	EA	31		JT8D-1	02-27-68		67,443	63,635	
267	47181	N8945E	EA	31		JT8D-1	02-29-68		65,999	62,635	
268	47313	EC-BIT	IB	32	Y	JT8D-7	03-08-68		56,081	62,009	
269	47065	VH-CZD	AN	31	Y	JT8D-7	03-08-68		53,859	53,919	
270	47072	VH-TJM	TN	31	Y	JT8D-7	03-07-68		51,454	52,245	
271	47182	N8946E	EA	31		JT8D-1	03-08-68		81,194	67,467	
272	47183	N8947E	EA	31		JT8D-1	03-14-68		82,043	67,847	
273	47173	N3332L	DL	32	Y	JT8D-7	03-18-68		75,212	81,730	
274	47184	N8948E	EA	31		JT8D-1	03-22-68	RET	55,645	52,938	04-30-88
275	47185	N8949E	EA	31		JT8D-1	03-16-68		78,661	72,072	
276	47186	N8950E	EA	31		JT8D-1	03-20-68		67,680	63,566	
277	47121	N967PR	CB	31	Y	JT8D-7	03-22-68		63,754	76,650	
278	47195	CF-TLI	AC	32		JT8D-7	03-21-68		69,674	63,022	
279	47314	EC-BIU	IB	32	Y	JT8D-7	03-27-68		50,206	51,347	
280	47191	PH-DNM	KL	33RC	Y	JT8D-9	04-27-68		50,594	47,853	
281	47241	67-22583	ZA	C-9A	Y	JT8D-9	09-13-68		38,842	41,141	
282	47187	N8951E	EA	31		JT8D-1	03-26-68		67,900	69,055	
283	45867	N8952E	EA	31		JT8D-1	03-28-68		67,231	67,744	
284	47150	N905H	HA	31	Y	JT8D-7	04-05-68		70,150	95,573	
285	47151	N228Z	TR	15		JT8D-7	04-21-68		15,246	8,433	
286	47174	N3333L	DL	32	Y	JT8D-7	04-07-68		73,524	80,003	
287	47192	PH-DNN	KL	33RC	Y	JT8D-9	04-16-68	W/O	41,935	40,811	03-18-89
288	47196	CF-TLU	AC	32		JT8D-7	04-07-67	W/O	36,824	34,987	06-02-83
289	47197	CF-TLV	AC	32		JT8D-7	04-09-68	W/O	25,476	24,140	06-26-78
290	45868	N8953E	EA	31		JT8D-1	04-11-68		75,981	80,072	
291	47188	N8954E	EA	31		JT8D-1	04-16-68		75,837	80,016	

LN	MSN	REGN	A/L	MODEL	VS	ENG	DEL	STAT	HOURS	LDGS	DATE
292	47246	N9333	AW	31	Y	JT8D-7	06-24-68		72,710	79,226	
293	47207	N984VJ	AL	31	Y	JT8D-7	04-17-68		75,074	88,565	
294	47252	N956N	NC	31	Y	JT8D-7	04-15-68		72,059	89,201	
295	47253	N957N	NC	31	Y	JT8D-7	04-19-68		71,810	88,623	
296	47220	I-DIKF	AZ	32F		JT9D-9	05-03-68		49,195	48,379	
297	47249	N977Z	OZ	31	Y	JT8D-7	04-19-68		70,019	84,058	
298	47175	N3334L	DL	32	Y	JT8D-7	04-28-68		71,774	75,625	
299	47222	I-DIKJ	AZ	32	Y	JT8D-9	05-03-68		58,525	54,305	
300	47223	I-DIKL	AZ	32	Y	JT8D-9	04-30-68		58,994	55,539	
301	47254	N958N	NC	31	Y	JT8D-7	04-26-68		71,261	88,474	
302	47198	CF-TLW	AC	32		JT8D-7	04-30-68		69,969	63,168	
303	47189	N8955E	EA	31		JT8D-1	05-04-68		72,591	76,949	
304	47242	67-22584	ZA	C-9A	Y	JT8D-9	08-08-68		37,615	40,622	
305	47221	I-DIKG	AZ	32F		JT8D-9	05-09-68		44,548	39,997	
306	47214	N8956E	EA	31		JT8D-1	05-10-68		65,320	62,510	
307	47208	N985VJ	AL	31	Y	JT8D-7	05-14-68		74,794	88,201	
308	47116	LN-RLK	SK	41	Y	JT8D-9	05-14-68		65,466	60,742	
309	47250	N978Z	OZ	31	Y	JT8D-7	05-10-68		69,148	82,873	
310	47255	N959N	NC	31	Y	JT8D-7	05-13-68		71,183	87,778	
311	47193	PH-DNO	KL	33RC	Y	JT8D-9	05-21-68		48,764	48,240	
312	48218	D-ACEB	SF	32	Y	JT8D-9	05-21-68		70,210	65,852	
313	47215	N8957E	EA	31		JT8D-1	05-23-68		65,505	61,690	
314	47176	N3335L	DL	32	Y	JT8D-7	05-25-68		65,674	78,574	
315	47216	N8958E	EA	31		JT8D-1	05-25-68		75,570	80,287	
316	47224	I-DIKM	AZ	32	Y	JT8D-9	05-25-68		55,926	59,062	
317	47225	I-IKN	AZ	32	Y	JT8D-9	05-27-68		57,999	59,890	
318	47138	N9330	RW	31		JT8D-7	05-29-68		75,759	84,236	
319	47117	SE-DBW	SK	41	Y	JT8D-9	05-27-68		65,878	60,216	
320	47263	N9331	RW	31	Y	JT8D-7	06-05-68		75,639	84,411	
321	47199	CF-TLX	AC	32		JT8D-7	05-31-68		69,218	62,096	
322	47157	N8959E	EA	31		JT8D-1	06-08-68		67,778	67,284	
323	47178	OY-KGB	SK	41	Y	JT8D-9	06-10-68		66,060	62,860	
324	47194	PH-DNP	KL	33RC	Y	JT8D-9	06-12-68		47,840	45,315	
325	47219	D-ACEC	SF	32	Y	JT8D-9	06-13-68		70,885	67,397	
326	47256	N960NC	NC	31	Y	JT8D-7	06-17-68		71,127	86,572	
327	47209	N986VJ	AL	31	Y	JT8D-7	06-14-68		75,326	88,439	
328	47206	N96S	SO	15	Y	JT8D-1	06-17-68		70,180	95,363	
329	47264	N9332	RW	31	Y	JT8D-7	06-20-68		75,339	84,003	
330	47177	N3336L	DL	32	Y	JT8D-7	06-21-68		71,401	84,929	
331	45869	N8960E	EA	31		JT8D-1	06-25-68		67,489	62,775	
332	45870	N8961E	EA	31		JT8D-1	06-22-68	W/O	10,928	11,480	05-18-72
333	47226	I-DIKP	AZ	32	Y	JT8D-9	06-28-68		58,219	60,835	
334	47227	I-DIKQ	AZ	32	Y	JT8D-9	06-29-68	W/O	21,971	21,907	12-23-78
335	47179	LN-RLC	SK	41	Y	JT8D-9	06-25-68		65,050	61,858	
336	45774	TC-JAB	TK	32	Y	JT8D-7	07-09-68		61,036	54,167	
337	47279	PH-DNR	KL	33RC	Y	JT8D-9	07-05-68		46172	43,387	
338	47200	CF-TLY	AC	32		JT8D-7	07-11-68	W/O	34,482	32,937	06-02-82
339	47265	CF-TLZ	AC	32		JT8D-7	07-10-68		70,232	63,348	
340	47295	67-22585	ZA	C-9A	Y	JT8D-9	08-21-68		37,973	40,571	
341	47210	N987VJ	AL	31	Y	JT8D-7	07-12-68		75,258	88,725	
342	47247	N9334	RW	31	Y	JT8D-7	07-17-68		73,410	79,473	
343	47291	PH-MAN	MP	33RC	Y	JT8D-9	07-21-68		42,045	47,299	
344	45871	N8962E	EA	31		JT8D-1	07-19-68	RET	64,560	60,842	03-18-96
345	45872	N8963E	EA	31		JT8D-1	07-26-68	W/O	62,478	58,618	08-18-94
346	47240	N8919	CO	15RC	Y	JT8D-7	07-20-68	W/O	47,573	61,327	02-17-91
347	47273	N3337L	DL	32	Y	JT8D-7	07-25-68		66,710	80,088	
348	47274	N3338L	DL	32	Y	JT8D-7	07-27-68		68,391	81,305	
349	45791	HB-IFI	SR	32	Y	JT8D-9	07-27-68		71,170	67,021	
350	45873	N8964E	EA	31		JT8D-1	08-02-68	RET	62,601	58,596	07-31-95
351	45874	N8965E	EA	31		JT8D-1	08-01-68		65,832	61,326	
352	47266	CF-TMA	AC	32		JT8D-7	07-27-68		69,760	62,874	
353	47289	CF-TMB	AC	32		JT8D-7	07-29-68		70,010	63,225	
354	47180	SE-DBU	SK	41	Y	JT8D-9	07-27-68		64,002	61,371	
355	47228	I-DIKR	AZ	32	Y	JT8D-9	08-09-68		56,634	59,259	
356	47229	I-DIKS	AZ	32	Y	JT8D-9	08-08-68		55,909	57,095	
357	47211	N988VJ	AL	31	Y	JT8D-7	08-09-68	W/O	3,170	3,533	09-09-69
358	47213	TC-JAC	TK	32	Y	JT8D-7	08-13-68	W/O	8,531	7,624	01-21-72
359	47286	OY-KGC	SK	41	Y	JT8D-9	08-16-68		63,654	72,177	
360	47217	N8966E	EA	31		JT8D-1	08-16-68	W/O	66,438	62,709	07-26-95
361	47267	N8967E	EA	31		JT8D-1	08-17-68	W/O	15,612	16,152	11-28-73
362	47296	67-22586	ZA	C-9A	Y	JT8D-9	09-24-76	W/O	5,058	6,119	09-16-71
363	47275	N3339L	DL	32	Y	JT8D-7	08-22-68		72,253	85,318	
364	47287	LN-RLJ	SK	41	Y	JT8D-9	08-24-66		65,782	60,197	

LN	MSN	REGN	A/L	MODEL	VS	ENG	DEL	STAT	HOURS	LDGS	DATE
365	45875	N8968E	EA	31		JT8D-1	08-25-66		70,349	71,929	
366	45876	N8969E	EA	31		JT8D-1	08-29-68	RET	62,824	58,838	12-31-92
367	47290	CF-TMV	AC	32		JT8D-7	08-29-68		69,470	63,047	
368	47212	N989VJ	AL	31	Y	JT8D-7	08-29-68	RET	70,507	83,338	10-31-96
369	47288	SE-DBT	SK	41	Y	JT8D-9	08-28-68		63,276	72,288	
370	47268	N8970E	EA	31		JT8D-1	09-04-68		70,581	63,111	
371	47269	N8971E	EA	31		JT8D-1	09-06-68		63,210	58,888	
372	45792	HB-IFK	SR	32	Y	JT8D-9	09-11-68		68,657	66,716	
373	47276	N3340L	DL	32	Y	JT8D-7	09-14-68		65,056	79,058	
374	47270	N8972E	EA	31		JT8D-1	09-01-68	RET	62,410	58,255	01-31-94
375	47036	N8973E	EA	31		JT8D-1	09-13-68		63,966	60,415	
376	47074	N8974E	EA	31		JT8D-1	09-14-68		62,965	58,610	
377	47297	68-8932	ZA	C-9A	Y	JT8D-9	10-14-68		43,067	48.103	
378	47119	N8975E	EA	31		JT8D-1	09-19-68	RET	61,928	57,473	01-31-94
379	47277	N5341L	DL	32	Y	JT8D-7	09-25-68		70,548	83,364	
380	47278	N5342L	DL	32	Y	JT8D-7	09-26-68		68,723	80,401	
381	45793	HB-IFL	SR	32	Y	JT8D-9	09-28-68		69,339	69,353	
382	47301	LN-RLL	SK	21	Y	JT8D-11	03-22-69		55,986	66,959	
383	47292	CF-TMD	AC	32		JT8D-7	09-28-68		69,791	63,606	
384	47293	CF-TME	AC	32		JT8D-7	09-26-68		69,016	62,133	
385	47317	N1261L	DL	32	Y	JT8D-7	10-09-68		65,949	78,165	
386	47257	N1262L	DL	32	Y	JT8D-7	10-04-68		65,643	78,162	
387	47258	N1263L	DL	32	Y	JT8D-7	10-10-68		65,587	78,916	
388	47125	XA-SOG	AM	15		JT8D-7	10-07-68		74,275	88,183	
389	47271	N8976E	EA	31		JT8D-1	10-09-68		70,109	64,995	
390	47272	N8977E	EA	31		JT8D-1	10-09-68		69,379	71,239	
391	47327	N8978E	EA	31		JT8D-1	10-15-68		65,092	60,340	
392	47328	N8979E	EA	31		JT8D-1	10-17-68		64,968	60,749	
393	47309	YVC-AAA	LV	14		JT8D-7	10-23-68	W/O	31,892	48,903	09-06-85
394	45847	HB-IFM	SR	32	Y	JT8D-9	10-17-67		70,202	65,552	
395	47230	I-DIKT	AZ	32	Y	JT8D-9	10-18-68		57,895	59,549	
396	47231	I-DIKT	AZ	32	Y	JT8D-9	10-19-68		56,545	53,311	
397	47283	I-DIKW	AZ	32	Y	JT8D-9	10-24-68		57,665	54,353	
398	47311	I-DIKZ	AZ	32	Y	JT8D-9	10-23-68		57,186	53,834	
399	47298	68-8933	ZA	C-9A	Y	JT8D-9	11-27-68		42,272	47,332	
400	47202	VH-CZE	AN	31	Y	JT8D-7	11-01-68		63,281	60,131	
401	47203	VH-TJN	TN	31	Y	JT8D-7	10-31-68		51,095	52,778	
402	47294	CF-TMF	AC	32		JT8D-7	11-04-68		68,874	62,358	
403	47340	CF-TMG	AC	32		JT8D-7	11-07-68		69,729	63,469	
404	47341	CF-TMH	AC	32		JT8D-7	11-07-68		69,685	63,592	
405	47126	XA-SOH	AM	15		JT8D-7	11-08-68		81,602	84,343	
406	47329	N8980E	EA	31		JT8D-1	11-09-68		65,971	60,833	
407	47330	N8981E	EA	31		JT8D-1	11-10-68		65,910	65,693	
408	47331	N8982E	EA	31		JT8D-1	11-15-68		64,732	64,197	
409	47259	N1264L	DL	32	Y	JT8D-7	11-15-68		67,140	81,545	
410	47260	N1265L	DL	32	Y	JT8D-7	11-21-68		69,589	82,061	
411	47261	N1266L	DL	32	Y	JT8D-7	11-19-68		69,003	82,300	
412	47262	N1267L	DL	32	Y	JT8D-7	11-23-68		69,773	82,067	
413·	47284	N1268L	DL	32	Y	JT8D-7	11-26-68		67,376	79,474	
414	47285	N1269L	DL	32	Y	JT8D-7	12-07-68		69,425	81,837	
415	47377	N9335	RW	31	Y	JT8D-7	11-27-68		74,459	81,121	
416	47338	N9336	RW	31	Y	JT8D-7	11-26-68		73,840	81,792	
417	47127	XA-SOI	AM	15		JT8D-7	11-27-68	W/O	68,352	78.459	03-17-95
418	47342	CF-TMI	AC	32		JT8D-7	11-27-68		70,008	63,116	
419	47348	CF-TMJ	AC	32		JT8D-7	12-18-68		69,153	63.065	
420	47349	CF-TMK	AC	32		JT8D-7	12-07068		69,917	63,474	
421	47299	68-8934	ZA	C-9A	Y	JT8D-9	12-18-68		43,195	49,789	
422	47302	OY-KGD	SK	21	Y	JT8D-9	12-11-68		54,865	65,673	
423	47168	PH-DNS	KL	32	Y	JT8D-9	12-14-68		57,172	43,388	
424	47169	PH-DNT	KL	32	Y	JT8D-9	12-16-68		50,261	37,779	
425	47170	PH-DNV	KL	32	Y	JT8D-9	12-19-68		55,498	41,141	
426	47318	N1270L	DL	32	Y	JT8D-7	12-14-68		69,404	81,850	
427	47281	HB-IFT	SR	32	Y	JT8D-9	12-19-68		70,727	66,578	
428	47232	I-DIKY	AZ	32	Y	JT8D-9	12-18-68		56,564	59,448	
429	47233	I-DIBC	AZ	32	Y	JT8D-9	12-19-68		56,788	52,774	
430	47399	N8983E	EA	31		JT8D-1	01-24-69		68,309	66,041	
431	47350	CF-TML	AC	32		JT8D-7	12-29-68		69,998	63,489	
432	47303	SE-DBS	SK	21	Y	JT8D-9	01-06-69	RET	54,178	65,371	03-31-97
433	47315	N1308T	TI	31	Y	JT8D-9	01-10-69		70,446	75,952	
434	47319	N1271L	DL	32	Y	JT8D-7	02-06-69		67,349	79,305	
435	47234	I-DIBD	AZ	32	Y	JT8D-9	01-04-69		58,050	52,789	
436	47235	I-DIBJ	AZ	32	Y	JT8D-9	01-09-69		56,836	53,374	
437	47339	I-DIBN	AZ	32	Y	JT8D-9	01-11-69	W/O	48,063	44,737	1-17-92

LN	MSN	REGN	A/L	MODEL	VS	ENG	DEL	STAT	HOURS	LDGS	DATE
438	47300	68-8935	ZA	C-9A	Y	JT8D-9	02-06-69		44,819	51,498	
439	47316	1309T	TI	31	Y	JT8D-9	01-23-69		70,470	76,215	
440	47304	N-RLM	SK	21	Y	JT8D-11	01-30-69	W/O	8,996	13,185	01-30-73
441	47305	OY-KGE	SK	21	Y	JT8D-11	01-22-69		54,045	65,148	
442	47351	6Y-JGA	JM	32		JT8D-7	01-23-69		61,443	62,595	
443	47400	N8984E	EA	31		JT8D-1	01-03-69	W/O	16,861	17,088	09-11-74
444	47401	N8985E	EA	31		JT8D-1	03-21-69		65,771	62,845	
445	47363	PH-MAO	MP	33RC	Y	JT8D-9	02-07-69		53,745	32,410	
446	47282	HB-IFU	SR	32	Y	JT8D-9	01-31-69		66,825	65,396	
447	47392	N393PA	PD	32		JT8D-9	02-03-69		40,996	33,495	
448	47243	YVC-AVD	VE	32	Y	JT8D-7	02-26-69	W/O	75	130	03-16-69
449	47310	N991VJ	AL	31	Y	JT8D-7	02-05-69		72,390	85,160	
450	47236	I-DIBQ	AZ	32	Y	JT8D-9	02-04-69		57,795	54,371	
451	47237	I-DIBO	AZ	32	Y	JT8D-9	02-06-69		53,733	52,513	
452	47355	I-DIBK	AZ	32	Y	JT8D-9	02-12-69		53,733	52,513	
453	47352	6Y-JGB	JM	32		JT8D-7	02-18-69		60,730	62,166	
454	47320	N1272L	DL	32	Y	JT8D-7	02-19-69		69,400	83,516	
455	47321	N1273L	DL	32	Y	JT8D-7	02-28-69	W/O	66,166	79,285	06-08-95
456	47322	N1274L	DL	32	Y	JT8D-7	02-28-69		70,104	82,622	
457	47407	N935F	OV	33CF		JT8D-9	03-07-69	W/O	2,478	1,329	05-02-70
458	47394	N950PB	PB	32	Y	JT8D-9	02-24-69		55,186	56,535	
459	47201	PH-DNW	KL	32	Y	JT8D-9	02-22-69		48,308	39,084	
460	47343	N979Z	OZ	31	Y	JT8D-7	02-25-69		68,266	80,797	
461	47332	N993VJ	AL	31	Y	JT8D-7	02-27-69		74,020	86,445	
462	47306	SE-DBR	SK	21	Y	JT8D-11	02-27-69		54,382	66,440	
463	47307	LN-RLO	SK	21	Y	JT8D-11	03-06-69	RET	53,221	64,182	03-31-97
464	47346	N9337	RW	32	Y	JT8D-7	03-06-69		73,496	81,354	
465	47238	I-DIZA	AZ	32	Y	JT8D-9	03-14-69		57,210	52,193	
466	47239	YU-AHJ	YJ	32	Y	JT8D-9	04-25-69		57,280	46,996	
467	47408	N936F	OV	33CF		JT8D-9	03-14-69		49,000	45,832	
468	47323	N1275L	DL	32	Y	JT8D-7	04-03-69		68,502	82,195	
469	47324	N1276L	DL	32	Y	JT8D-7	04-16-69		70,980	76,440	
470	47356	N1277L	DL	32	Y	JT8D-7	04-18-69	W/O	50,122	58,281	08-31-86
471	47353	CF-TMO	AC	32		JT8D-7	03-26-69		68,780	62,622	
472	47344	N980Z	OZ	31	Y	JT8D-7	03-27-69		67,521	79,366	
473	47171	N906H	HA	31	Y	JT8D-7	03-28-69		68,469	89,946	
474	47308	OY-KGF	SK	21	Y	JT8D-11	03-31-69		56,158	67,168	
475	47360	SE-DBP	SK	21	Y	JT8D-11	04-12-69		55,425	67,345	
476	47357	N1278L	DL	32	Y	JT8D-7	05-02-69		70,560	76,103	
477	47358	N1279L	DL	32	Y	JT8D-7	05-08-69		66,116	81,617	
478	47347	N9338	RW	31	Y	JT8D-7	04-10-69		72,669	81,785	
479	47382	N9339	RW	31	Y	JT8D-7	04-11-69		69,920	75,998	
480	47410	PH-MAR	MP	33RC	Y	JT8D-9	04-19-69		54,092	32,609	
481	47333	N994VJ	AL	31	Y	JT8D-7	04-11-69	W/O	21,320	27,193	06-23-76
482	47402	N8986E	EA	31		JT8D-1	05-08-69		64,468	60,110	
483	47354	CF-TMP	AC	32		JT8D-7	04-17-69		68,178	62,302	
484	47364	EC-BPF	IB	32	Y	JT8D-7	04-17-69		49,716	50,908	
485	47345	N981Z	OZ	31	Y	JT8D-7	04-21-69		68,317	79,186	
486	47042	N89S	SO	31	Y	JT8D-7	04-29-69		70,676	83,777	
487	47405	N961N	NC	31	Y	JT8D-7	05-09-69		69,912	83,109	
488	47361	SE-DBO	SK	21	Y	JT8D-11	05-01-69		51,914	64,169	
489	47389	N9340	RW	31	Y	JT8D-7	04-25-69		72,659	81,797	
490	47390	N9341	RW	31	Y	JT8D-7	04-13-69		73,050	81,559	
491	47391	N9342	RW	31	Y	JT8D-7	05-13-69		72,637	81,791	
492	47362	N907H	HA	31	Y	JT8D-7	05-09-69		68,787	87,456	
493	47334	N995VJ	AL	31	Y	JT8D-7	05-12-69		69,470	82,119	
494	47335	N996VJ	AL	31	Y	JT8D-7	05-14-69		68,914	81,742	
495	47359	N1280L	DL	32	Y	JT8D-7	05-23-69		69,032	81,266	
496	49377	N1281L	DL	32	Y	JT8D-7	05-27-69	W/O	68,401	80,636	05-11-96
497	47409	N937F	OV	33CF		JT8D-9	05-22-69		68,405	64,705	
498	47244	N90S	SO	31	Y	JT8D-7	05-23-69		70,738	83,827	
499	47406	N962N	NC	31	Y	JT8D-7	05-23-69		69,576	83,602	
500	47336	N997VJ	AL	31	Y	JT8D-7	05-27-69		72,348	85,102	
501	47439	N9343	RW	31	Y	JT8D-7	06-04-69		72,186	81,640	
502	47440	N9344	RW	31	Y	JT8D-7	06-04-69		72,129	81,236	
503	47441	N9345	RW	31	Y	JT8D-7	06-04-69	W/O	5,499	8,096	06-06-71
504	47365	EC-BPG	IB	32	Y	JT8D-7	06-06-69		54,677	53,732	
505	47368	EC-BPH	IB	32	Y	JT8D-7	06-06-69		57,891	58,134	
506	47371	N978VJ	AL	31	Y	JT8D-7	06-12-69		72,752	85,252	
507	47403	N8987E	EA	31		JT8D-1	07-11-69		62,731	59,610	
508	47378	N1282L	DL	32	Y	JT8D-7	07-02-69		68,097	80,339	
509	47379	N1283L	DL	32	Y	JT8D-7	07-10-69		68,237	80,251	
510	47245	N97S	SO	31	Y	JT8D-7	06-20-69	W/O	3,665	5,912	11-14-70

LN	MSN	REGN	A/L	MODEL	VS	ENG	DEL	STAT	HOURS	LDGS	DATE
511	47415	N963N	NC	31	Y	JT8D-7	09-15-69		69,213	81,054	
512	47416	N964N	NC	31	Y	JT8D-7	07-31-70		66,660	77,873	
513	47372	N979VJ	AL	31	Y	JT8D-7	07-01-69	RET	68,763	81,277	10-31-96
514	47380	N1284L	DL	32	Y	JT8D-7	08-08-69		51,407	56,678	
515	47325	VH-CZF	AN	31	Y	JT8D-9	07-10-69		50,322	50,987	
516	47326	VH-TJO	TN	31	Y	JT8D-7	07-11-69		62,259	62,261	
517	47376	N394PA	PD	32		JT8D-9	07-16-69		74,451	67,592	
518	47417	N965N	NC	31	Y	JT8D-7	07-31-69		67,004	78,309	
519	47381	N1285L	DL	32	Y	JT8D-7	09-03-69		50,973	56,351	
520	47431	I-ATIA	AT	32	Y	JT8D-9	07-24-69		49,675	62,892	
521	47413	SE-DBN	SK	33F		JT8D-11	07-31-69		39,454	43,802	
522	47373	N964VJ	AL	31	Y	JT8D-7	09-09-69	W/O	59,215	71,240	01-31-92
523	47374	N965VJ	AL	31	Y	JT8D-7	09-09-69		69,893	82,395	
524	47442	TC-JAG	TK	32	Y	JT8D-9	08-24-69		54,684	48,736	
525	47432	I-DIZI	AZ	32	Y	JT8D-9	08-28-69		55,781	58,564	
526	47433	I-DIZU	AZ	32	Y	JT8D-9	08-15-69		53,819	59,853	
527	47488	TC-JAD	TK	32	Y	JT8D-9	08-27-69		58,394	52,358	
528	47489	TC-JAE	TK	32	Y	JT8D-9	08-27-69		57,305	51,971	
529	47369	N1798U	HA	31	Y	JT8D-7	10-31-69		65,643	83,374	
530	47366	68-10958	ZA	C-9A	Y	JT8D-9	09-30-69		42,070	48,251	
531	47375	N967VJ	AL	31	Y	JT8D-7	09-16-69		72,129	84,591	
532	47429	N968VJ	AL	31	Y	JT8D-7	09-16-69		71,745	84,030	
533	47411	N983Z	OZ	31	Y	JT8D-7	12-08-69		65,810	76,588	
534	47412	N984Z	OZ	31	Y	JT8D-7	12-11-69		66,139	76,678	
535	47450	D-ADIT	YY	32	Y	JT8D-9	02-03-70		72,062	66,060	
536	47414	LN-RLW	SK	33F		JT8D-11	10-03-69		43,543	45,816	
537	47434	I-DIZB	AZ	32	Y	JT8D-9	09-29-69		52,607	67,078	
538	47383	HB-IFV	SR	32	Y	JT8D-9	10-03-69		65,479	63,759	
539	47367	68-10959	ZA	C-9A	Y	JT8D-9	11-07-69		41,648	47,598	
540	47435	I-DIZC	AZ	32	Y	JT8D-9	10-15-69		54,906	70,090	
541	47436	I-ATIE	AT	32	Y	JT8D-9	10-08-69		54,756	68,761	
542	47385	PK-GJE	GA	32	Y	JT8D-9	10-15-69		45,859	37,241	
543	47384	HB-IFW	SR	33F		JT8D-9	10-22-69		48,456	44,484	
544	47437	I-ATIO	AT	32	Y	JT8D-9	10-27-69		54,042	68,237	
545	47438	I-ATIU	AT	32	Y	JT8D-9	11-07-69		54,884	68,065	
546	47500	HI-177	DO	32	Y	JT8D-7	12-16-69	W/O	245	350	02-15-70
547	47451	TC-JAF	TK	32	Y	JT8D-9	08-07-70		56,349	49,348	
548	47448	68-10960	ZA	C-9A	Y	JT8D-9	12-01-69		42,553	47,979	
549	47459	D-ADIS	YY	32	Y	JT8D-9	01-15-70		71,912	66,484	
550	47386	PK-GJF	GA	32	Y	JT8D-9	11-13-69		47,188	38,044	
551	47370	N1799U	HA	31	Y	JT8D-7	09-30-71		63,098	77,302	
552	47449	68-10961	ZA	C-9A	Y	JTRD-9	12-31-69		42,730	49,134	
553	47487	N1310T	TI	31	Y	JT8D-9	11-19-69		71,527	74,639	
554	47404	N1332U	HA	31	Y	JT8D-7	11-05-71		63,249	74,072	
555	47395	OY-KGG	SK	41	Y	JT8D-11	11-25-69		62,428	56,111	
556	47420	N966VJ	AL	31	Y	JT8D-7	12-05-69		71,561	83,808	
557	47296	LN-RLR	SK	41	Y	JT8D-11	12-21-69		62,224	55,821	
558	47421	N969VJ	AL	31	Y	JT8D-7	03-30-70		70,465	82,892	
559	47492	SE-DAK	SK	41	Y	JT8D-11	01-09-70		55,730	67,975	
560	49490	N1311T	TI	31	Y	JT8D-9	12-17-69		70,225	72,713	
561	47446	EC-BQT	IB	32	Y	JT8D-7	12-24-69		56,094	54,088	
562	47493	OY-KGH	SK	41	Y	JT8D-11	01-16-70		56,373	53,478	
563	47447	EC-BQU	IB	32	Y	JT8D-7	01-08-70		55,284	53,729	
564	47462	PH-DNY	KL	33RC	Y	JT8D-9	01-17-70		45,450	41,761	
565	47453	EC-BQV	IB	32	Y	JT8D-7	01-09-70		54,330	51,098	
566	47498	SE-DAL	SK	41	Y	JT8D-11	01-29-70		52,785	51,525	
567	47454	EC-BQX	IB	32	Y	JT8D-7	01-24-70		56,197	55,802	
568	47499	SE-DAM	SK	41	Y	JT8D-11	02-18-70		53,618	50,788	
569	47476	PH-DNZ	KL	33RC	Y	JT8D-9	02-06-70		46,086	39,404	
570	47418	VH-TJP	TN	31	Y	JT8D-7	02-05-70		*54,436	*56,189	
571	47501	VH-CZG	AN	31	Y	JT8D-7	02-13-70		66,021	63,001	
572	47426	N1286L	DL	32	Y	JT8D-7	02-19-70		49,655	54,344	
573	47427	N1287L	DL	32	Y	JT8D-7	02-25-70		48,973	54,204	
574	47502	I-DIZE	AZ	32	Y	JT8D-9	02-20-70		53,028	57,830	
575	47464	SE-DAN	SK	41	Y	JT8D-11	09-03-70		52,803	50.017	
576	47422	CF-TMQ	AC	32		JT8D-7	02-28-70		67,045	60,862	
577	47443	N1288L	DL	32	Y	JT8D-7	04-10-70		65,482	77,256	
578	47444	N1289L	DL	32	Y	JT8D-7	04-09-70		66,677	78,070	
579	47455	EC-BQY	IB	32	Y	JT8D-7	03-18-70		54,212	64,491	
580	47456	EC-BQZ	IB	32	Y	JT8D-7	03-26-70		51,104	56,969	
581	47423	CF-TMR	AC	32		JT8D-7	04-09-70	RET	63,163	58,913	04-23-96
582	47424	CF-TMS	AC	32		JT8D-7	04-08-70		66,315	61,273	
583	47517	N908H	HA	31	Y	JT8D-7	04-28-70		64,609	87,276	

LN	MSN	REGN	A/L	MODEL	VS	ENG	DEL	STAT	HOURS	LDGS	DATE
584	47465	HB-IDN	BA	33CF	Y	JT8D-11	04-17-70		40,675	31,860	
585	47445	N1290L	DL	32	Y	JT8D-7	05-06-70		65,295	77,250	
586	47505	N960VJ	AL	31	Y	JT8D-7	06-11-71		66,869	77,825	
587	47503	YU-AHR	YJ	32	Y	JT8D-9	04-27-70	W/O	3,465	2,768	03-19-72
588	47506	N961VJ	AL	31	Y	JT8D-7	11-18-70	W/O	42,104	52,025	04-02-86
589	47425	YU-AHL	JU	32	Y	JT8D-9	05-08-70		60,035	64,984	
590	47469	YU-AHM	JU	32	Y	JT8D-9	05-13-70		60,971	64,086	
591	47470	YU-AHN	JU	32	Y	JT8D-9	05-15-70		46,571	56,593	
592	47482	YU-AHT	JU	32	Y	JT8D-9	02-02-71	W/O	2,092	2,564	01-26-72
593	47523	HB-IDP	SR	32	Y	JT8D-9	11-18-70		56,808	62,709	
594	47507	N962VJ	AL	31	Y	JT8D-7	11-18-70		68,533	80,044	
595	47508	N963VJ	AL	31	Y	JT8D-7	06-14-71		66,701	77,740	
596	47472	YU-AHO	JU	32	Y	JT9D-9	06-08-70		60,688	64,910	
597	47280	N1334U	SO	31	Y	JT8D-7	06-29-71		65,203	75,061	
598	47473	YU-AHP	JU	32	Y	JT8D-9	06-18-70		60,016	63,543	
599	47491	N985Z	OZ	31	Y	JT8D-7	06-25-70		65,377	74,951	
600	47474	I-ATIX	AT	32	Y	JT8D-9	12-04-70		46,048	57,423	
601	47494	OY-KGI	SK	41	Y	JT8D-11	09-15-70		53,026	50,327	
602	47419	VH-TJQ	TN	31	Y	JT8D-7	08-17-70		53,698	57,715	
603	47526	VH-CZH	AN	31	Y	JT8D-7	08-28-70		61,184	56,287	
604	47497	LN-RLB	SK	41	Y	JT8D-11	10-01-70		53,363	50,672	
605	47479	HB-IFZ	SR	32	Y	JT8D-9	09-18-70		60,094	54,452	
606	47522	EC-BYD	IB	32	Y	JT8D-7	06-11-71		44,926	47,843	
607	47480	HB-IDO	SR	32	Y	JT8D-9	10-08-70		62,698	59,819	
608	47393	N1335U	SO	31	Y	JT8D-7	06-29-71	W/O	15,410	23,607	04-04-77
609	47430	5H-MOI	EC	32	Y	JT8D-11	12-22-70		51,255	58,280	
610	47535	HB-IDR	SR	32	Y	JT8D-9	12-03-30		66,018	61,132	
611	47468	5Y-ALR	EC	32	Y	JT8D-11	02-19-71		50,774	57,719	
612	47478	5X-UVY	EC	32	Y	JT8D-11	02-24-71		44,041	46,956	
613	47477	I-ATIK	AT	32	Y	JT8D-9	02-26-71		40,020	51,196	
614	47518	I-DIZO	AZ	32	Y	JT8D-9	02-16-71		51,825	53,196	
615	47519	I-DIZF	AZ	32	Y	JT8D-9	02-18-71		50,303	49,624	
616	47481	PK-GJG	GA	32	Y	JT8D-9	02-04-71		47,583	38,605	
617	47528	VH-TJR	TN	31	Y	JT8D-7	02-05-71		52,446	56,374	
618	47527	VH-CZI	AN	31	Y	JT8D-7	02-17-71		56,703	56,585	
619	47514	PH-MAX	MP	32	Y	JT8D-9	02-24-71		54,839	35,070	
620	47457	D-ADIU	YY	32	Y	JT8D-9	04-01-71	W/O	9,605	7,036	10-30-75
621	47466	N1291L	DL	32	Y	JT8D-7	04-14-71		55,667	66,552	
622	47547	VH-CZJ	AN	31	Y	JT8D-7	03-29-71		58,289	53,566	
623	47550	VH-TJS	TN	31	Y	JT8D-7	04-01-71		53,020	56,904	
624	47530	YU-AHW	YJ	33CF	Y	JT8D-9	04-22-71		49,130	39,485	
625	47529	N1292L	DL	32	Y	JT8D-7	05-12-71		58,252	69,009	
626	47532	YU-AHU	JU	32	Y	JT8D-9	05-07-71		44,743	53,958	
627	47460	YU-AHV	JU	32	Y	JT8D-7	05-14-71		44,528	53,494	
628	47486	N1293L	DL	32	Y	JT8D-7	06-11-71		60,439	70,553	
629	47521	OE-LDA	OS	32	Y	JT8D-9	06-10-71		75,460	56,469	
630	47516	N1294L	DL	32	Y	JT8D-7	06-24-71		60,687	70,074	
631	47525	N1295L	DL	32	Y	JT8D-7	07-08-71	RET	53,795	65,151	05-01-93
632	47524	OE-LDB	OS	32	Y	JT8D-7	07-09-71		70,597	56,051	
633	47548	VH-CZK	31	AN	Y	JT8D-7	07-19-71		55,993	53,481	
634	47551	VH-TJT	TN	31	Y	JT8D-7	07-27-71		52,268	54,977	
635	47520	OE-LDC	OS	32	Y	JT8D-9	08-10-71		68,041	57,950	
636	47397	TC-JAK	TK	32	Y	JT8D-9	08-18-71		54,923	48,234	
637	47539	OE-LDD	OS	32	Y	JT8D-9	08-26-71		68,321	57,188	
638	47531	OE-LDE	OS	32	Y	JT8D-9	09-09-71		66,646	56,680	
639	47549	VH-CZL	AN	31	Y	JT8D-7	11-17-71		60,703	57,706	
640	47552	VH-TJU	TN	31	Y	JT8D-7	10-14-71		50,602	54,180	
641	47533	I-ATIW	AT	32	Y	JT8D-9	12-02-71		*46,079	*59,977	
642	47553	I-ATIH	AT	32	Y	JT8D-9	12-09-71		47,491	57,723	
643	47509	SE-DAO	SK	41	Y	JT8D-11	12-02-71		48,999	47,439	
644	47534	TC-JAL	TK	32	Y	JT8D-9	11-09-71		53,295	47,375	
645	47510	OY-KGK	SK	41	Y	JT8D-11	12-09-71		48,980	47,446	
646	47458	OE-LDF	OS	32	Y	JT8D-9	12-02-71		66,686	52,719	
647	47467	71-874	ZA	C-9A	Y	JT8D-9	12-17-71		32,911	35,874	
648	47484	OE-LDG	OS	32	Y	JT8D-9	12-20-71		60,872	56,532	
649	47463	PK-GJH	GA	32	Y	JT8D-9	01-05-72	W/O	19,549	14,364	01-13-80
650	47471	71-875	ZA	C-9A	Y	JT8D-8	02-10-72		34,098	35,730	
651	47504	EC-BYE	IB	32	Y	JT8D-9	02-04-72		54,489	54,062	
652	45542	EC-BYF	IB	32	Y	JT8D-9	02-21-72		52,892	50,442	
653	47475	71-876	ZA	C-9A	Y	JT8D-9	03-03-72		14,536	11,675	
654	47543	EC-BYG	IB	32	Y	JT8D-9	02-29-72		47,136	44,004	
655	47546	CF-TMT	AC	32	Y	JT8D-7	03-21-72		61,878	55,899	
656	47495	71-877	ZA	C-9A	Y	JT8D-9	03-31-72		32,773	34,529	

LN	MSN	REGN	A/L	MODEL	VS	ENG	DEL	STAT	HOURS	LDGS	DATE
657	47556	EC-BYH	IB	32	Y	JT8D-9	04-10-72	W/O	40,898	45,186	03-30-92
658	47554	CF-TMU	AC	32		JT8D-7	04-20-72		61,203	56,102	
659	47536	71-878	ZA	C-9A	Y	JT8D-9	05-05-72		30,431	30,212	
660	47452	EC-BYI	UB	32	Y	JT8D-9	05-10-72		53,639	51,375	
661	47557	CF-TMV	AC	32		JT8D-7	05-17-72		60,835	55,374	
662	47537	71-789	ZA	C-9A	Y	JT8D-9	05-24-72		31,156	28,271	
663	47641	EC-BYJ	IB	32	Y	JT8D-9	06-09-72		53,804	51,441	
664	47560	CF-TMW	AC	32		JT8D-7	06-14-72		60,775	55,269	
665	47538	71-880	ZA	C-9A	Y	JT8D-9	06-30-72		34,148	33,950	
666	47485	CF-TMX	AC	32		JT8D-7	07-06-72		59,028	53,456	
667	47555	OE-LDH	OS	32	Y	JT8D-9	07-17-72		60,758	56,025	
668	47540	71-881	ZA	C-9A	Y	JT8D-9	07-27-72		31,747	29,162	
669	47428	EC-BYK	IB	33RC	Y	JT8D-9	08-08-72		51,010	42,454	
670	47541	71-882	ZA	C-9A	Y	JT8D-9	08-18-72		26,821	24,327	
671	47545	EC-BYL	IB	33RC	Y	JT8D-9	08-29-72		49,836	44,089	
672	47559	OE-LDI	OS	32	Y	JT8D-9	08-30-72		59,913	55,003	
673	47496	EC-BYM	IB	33RC	Y	JT8D-9	09-19-72		49,418	43,855	
674	47561	PH-GJI	GA	32	Y	JT8D-9	09-21-72	W/O	26,407	19,344	06-13-84
675	47565	EC-BYN	IB	33RC	Y	JT8D-9	10-07-72		49,108	43,769	
676	47544	I-ATIJ	AT	32	Y	JT8D-9	10-18-72		47,626	60,874	
677	47511	LN-RLU	SK	41	Y	JT8D-11	12-01-72		47,887	46,255	
678	47512	SE-DAP	SK	41	Y	JT8D-11	12-05-72		47,911	45,770	
679	47513	LN-RLX	SK	41	Y	JT8D-11	12-15-72		50,319	47,992	
680	47575	I-ATIY	AT	32	Y	JT8D-9	12-13-72		47,141	59,446	
681	47564	N950VJ	AL	31	Y	JT8D-7	02-06-73		62,261	72,337	
682	47576	N951VJ	AL	31	Y	JT8D-7	01-22-73		61,799	71,502	
683	47569	PK-GJJ	GA	32	Y	JT8D-8	01-16-73		41,418	33,352	
684	47570	YU-AJF	YX	32	Y	JT8D-9	05-16-73		49,607	41,600	
685	47562	YU-AJH	JU	32	Y	JT8D-9	02-09-73		43,956	51,320	
686	47577	159113	ZN	C-9B	Y	JT8D-9	05-08-73		38,010	27,474	
687	47563	YU-AJI	JU	32	Y	JT8D-9	02-28-73		38,475	44,457	
688	47567	YU-AJJ	JU	32	Y	JT8D-9	03-19-73		41,174	48,827	
689	47568	YU-AJK	JU	32	Y	JT8D-9	04-06-73		43,641	50,821	
690	47574	N952VJ	AL	31	Y	JT8D-7	04-17-73		61,834	71,591	
691	47566	N949N	NC	31	Y	JT8D-7	04-10-73		60,868	67,507	
692	47581	159117	ZN	C-9B	Y	JT8D-9	05-08-73		36,209	26,637	
693	47579	YU-AJN	YJ	32	Y	JT8D-9	05-10-73	W/O	2,872	2,806	11-23-74
694	47573	N967N	NC	31	Y	JT8D-7	05-15-73		64,162	63,447	
695	47571	YU-AJL	JU	32	Y	JT8D-9	05-21-73		44,150	51,503	
696	47584	159114	ZN	C-9B	Y	JT8D-9	06-13-73		38,910	26,868	
697	47583	N953VJ	AL	31	Y	JT8D-7	06-20-73		61,297	71,598	
698	47585	159118	ZN	C-9B	Y	JT8D-9	07-03-73		41,229	26,530	
699	47588	N956VJ	AL	31	Y	JT8D-7	02-07-74		59,019	68,268	
700	47587	159115	ZN	C-9B	Y	JT8D-9	07-26-73		38,981	27,839	
701	47582	YU-AJM	JU	32	Y	JT8D-9	07-31-73		42,204	48,602	
702	47578	159119	ZN	C-9B	Y	JT8D-9	08-17-73		36,472	27,990	
703	47590	N954VJ	AL	31	Y	JT8D-7	08-24-73	W/O	53,917	63,147	07-02-94
704	47580	159116	ZN	C-9B	Y	JT8D-9	09-14-73		39,154	27,240	
705	47593	N955VJ	AL	31	Y	JT8D-7	09-25-73		59,847	69,235	
706	47591	I-ATIQ	AT	32	Y	JT8D-9	09-27-73		45,332	53,690	
707	47586	159120	ZN	C-9B	Y	JT8D-9	10-30-73		39,597	27,694	
708	47572	N940N	NC	31	Y	JT8D-7	10-25-73		61,577	62,848	
709	47595	MM62012	ZI	32	Y	JT8D-9	01-09-74		26,181	27,800	
710	47600	MM62013	ZI	32	Y	JT8D-9	03-18-74		25,965	24,551	
711	47589	N986Z	OZ	31	Y	JT8D-7	12-04-73		57,613	62,516	
712	47592	CF-TMY	AC	32		JT8D-7	12-19-73		54,637	49,200	
713	47597	OY-KGL	SK	41	Y	JT8D-11	02-27-94		49,400	53,015	
714	47596	SE-DAR	SK	41	Y	JT8D-11	01-14-74		50,362	47,585	
715	47601	PK-GJK	GA	32	Y	JT8D-9	01-23-74		39,390	31,587	
716	47599	LN-RLA	SK	41	Y	JT8D-11	01-29-74		50,103	48,340	
717	47594	XA-DEJ	AM	32	Y	JT8D-15	02-11-74		66,958	69,493	
718	47602	XA-DEK	AM	32	Y	JT8D-15	02-19-74		67,110	69,411	
719	47598	C-FTMZ	AC	32		JT8D-7	02-22-74		54,295	48,339	
720	47603	JA8423	JD	41	Y	JT8D-15	03-12-74		48,663	47,298	
721	47607	XA-DEL	AM	32	Y	JT8D-15	03-21-74		67,277	69,518	
722	47604	JA8424	JD	41	Y	JT8D-15	03-25-74		40,151	55,014	
723	47609	XA-DEM	AM	32	Y	JT8D-15	04-05-74		67,092	69,156	
724	47605	JA8425	JD	41	Y	JT8D-15	04-10-74		39,638	54,061	
725	47610	SE-DAS	SK	41	Y	JT8D-11	04-18-74		48,997	62,263	
726	47611	C-FTMM	AC	32		JT8D-7	04-25-74		54,810	48,919	
727	47606	JA8426	JD	41	Y	JT8D-15	05-07-74	STO	37,478	52,796	11-01-95
728	47623	LN-RLS	SK	41	Y	JT8D-11	05-14-74		48,767	54,398	

LN	MSN	REGN	A/L	MODEL	VS	ENG	DEL	STAT	HOURS	LDGS	DATE
729	47621	XA-DEN	AM	32	Y	JT8D-15	05-21-74	W/O	23,301	27,897	07-21-81
730	47638	N3504T	TI	31	Y	JT8D-9	06-10-74		58,819	56,324	
731	47637	EC-CGN	AO	32	Y	JT8D-9	06-04-74		47,125	50,059	
732	47608	JA8427	JD	41	Y	JT8D-15	06-13-74		34,979	38,390	
733	47624	OY-KGM	SK	41	Y	JT8D-11	06-18-74		48,796	61,769	
734	47640	EC-CGO	AO	32	Y	JT8D-9	07-02-74		45,401	49,053	
735	47639	6Y-JIJ	JM	32		JT8D-7	06-28-74		37,574	34,635	
736	47612	JA8428	JD	41	Y	JT8D-15	07-11-74		34,236	37,389	
737	47625	SE-DAT	SK	41	Y	JT8D-11	07-18-74	RET	28,596	38,460	09-01-87
738	47626	LN-RLI	SK	41	Y	JT8D-11	07-25-74		48,175	51,885	
739	47627	SE-DAU	SK	41	Y	JT8D-11	08-05-74		48,133	61,322	
740	47628	OY-KGN	SK	41	Y	JT8D-11	08-07-74		49,486	61,361	
741	47649	YU-AJR	YJ	32	Y	JT8D-9	02-28-76	W/O	1,136	1,022	09-10-76
742	47613	JA8429	JD	41	Y	JT8D-15	09-13-74	STO	3,7575	52,777	11-05-95
743	47631	SE-DAX	SK	41	Y	JT8D-11	08-28-74		47,702	60,664	
744	47629	SE-DAW	SK	41	Y	JT8D-11	09-05-74		47,976	60,554	
745	47630	LN-RLN	SK	41	Y	JT8D-11	09-12-74		47,642	62,297	
746	47641	I-ATJA	AT	32	Y	JT8D-9	09-19-74	W/O	33,886	43,452	11-14-90
747	47614	JA8430	JD	41	Y	JT8D-15	10-15-74	STO	38,321	53,482	06-30-96
748	47632	OY-KGO	SK	41	Y	JT8D-11	10-03-74		48,010	51,156	
749	47642	EC-CGP	AO	32	Y	JT8D-9	10-10-74		46,525	50,302	
750	47643	EC-CGQ	AO	32	Y	JT8D-9	10-17-74		46,432	50,113	
751	47615	JA8432	JD	41	Y	JT8D-15	11-08-74		38,729	38,366	
752	47633	SE-DBM	SK	41	Y	JT8D-11	11-04-74		47,707	62,313	
753	47622	XA-DEO	AM	32	Y	JT8D-15	11-15-74	W/O	23,627	28,126	11-01-81
754	47635	PK-GNH	GA	32	Y	JT8D-9	11-14-74		35,364	29,679	
755	47646	OY-KGP	SK	41	Y	JT8D-11	11-22-74		47,874	61,615	
756	47634	LN-RLZ	SK	41	Y	JT8D-11	12-18-74		48,284	58,295	
757	47654	HB-ISK	SR	51	Y	JT8D-17	11-19-75		43,280	69,986	
758	47636	PK-GNI	GA	32	Y	JT8D-9	12-19-74	W/O	21,706	15,885	12-30-84
759	47616	JA8433	JD	41	Y	JT8D-15	12-20-74		38,628	36,234	
760	47653	I-ATJB	AT	32	Y	JT8D-9	01-09-75		41,802	50,745	
761	47648	PJ-SNA	LM	32	Y	JT8D-15	01-17-75		46,798	54,686	
762	47617	JA8434	JD	41	Y	JT8D-15	02-14-75		49,170	45,761	
763	47655	HB-ISL	SR	51	Y	JT8D-15	09-12-75		43,777	44,942	
764	47618	JA8435	JD	41	Y	JT8D-15	02-25-75		47,837	44,573	
765	47668	73-1681	ZA	VC-9C	Y	JT8D-9	02-21-74		12,568	14,671	
766	47667	I-ATJC	AT	32	Y	JT8D-9	02-19-75	W/O	10,112	14,167	09-14-79
767	47644	EC-CGR	AO	32	Y	JT8D-9	02-27-75		46,493	49,813	
768	47619	JA8436	JD	41	Y	JT8D-15	03-20-75		32,583	37,533	
769	47670	73-1682	ZA	VC-9C	Y	JT8D-9	03-11-75		11,276	15,486	
770	47645	EC-CGS	AO	32	Y	JT8D-9	03-20-75	W/O	20,079	17,893	12-07-83
771	47650	XA-DEI	AM	32	Y	JT8D-15	05-29-75		62,922	65,320	
772	47666	PJ-SNB	LM	32	Y	JT8D-15	04-11-75		45,322	53,285	
773	47647	N943N	NC	31	Y	JT8D-9	05-13-75		59,757	55,794	
774	47671	73-1683	ZA	VC-9C	Y	JT8D-9	05-02-75		12,227	14,174	
775	47664	N945N	NC	31	Y	JT8D-9	05-20-75		59,857	54,587	
776	47669	PJ-SNC	LM	32	Y	JT8D-15	06-13-75		52,726	53,176	
777	47620	JA8437	JD	41	Y	JT8D-15	07-28-75		32,212	37,411	
778	47672	PK-GNJ	GA	32	Y	JT8D-9	06-26-75		52,604	31,793	
779	47673	PK-GNK	GA	32	Y	JT8D-9	07-07-95		53,843	32,143	
780	47651	OE-LDK	OS	51	Y	JT8D-17	08-25-75		52,178	42,294	
781	47680	PK-GNL	GA	32	Y	JT8D-9	07-22-75		52,041	30,896	
782	47675	EC-CLD	AO	32	Y	JT8D-9	07-25-75		44,546	47,610	
783	47656	HB-ISM	SR	51	Y	JT8D-17	08-14-75		43,756	43,766	
784	47681	160048	ZN	C-9B	Y	JT8D-9	08-18-75		36,763	26,208	
785	47676	N609HA	HA	51	Y	JT8D-17	09-10-75		44,271	52,787	
786	47684	160046	ZM	C-9B	Y	JT8D-9	09-02-75		28,678	19,967	
787	47657	HB-ISN	SR	51	Y	JT8D-17	09-11-75		43,907	45,167	
788	47682	N920VJ	AL	51	Y	JT8D-17	10-10-75		47,357	44,744	
789	47678	EC-CLE	AO	32	Y	JT8D-9	09-26-75	W/O	38,223	41,156	03-21-94
790	47658	HB-ISO	SR	51	Y	JT8D-17	09-25-75		42,192	58,198	
791	47677	N619HA	SR	51	Y	JT8D-17	10-07-75		41,498	52,698	
792	47683	N921VJ	AL	51	Y	JT8D-17	10-21-75		50,140	54,433	
793	47674	TC-JBK	TK	32	Y	JT8D-9	10-22-75		48,865	35,664	
794	47685	N922VJ	AL	51	Y	JT8D-17	11-21-75	RET	49,202	52,701	02-01-97
795	47687	160047	ZM	C-9B	Y	JT8D-9	11-07-95		28,967	20,088	
796	47665	N923VJ	AL	51	Y	JT8D-17	12-16-75		50,437	55,940	
797	47679	N629HA	HA	51	Y	JT8D-17	11-20-75		41,253	57,964	
798	47652	OE-LDL	OS	51	Y	JT8D-17	12-11-75		48,905	40,135	
799	47688	N924VJ	AL	51	Y	JT8D-17	02-27-76		47,117	43,402	
800	47686	N925VJ	AL	51	Y	JT8D-17	02-27-76		47,218	43,935	

LN	MSN	REGN	A/L	MODEL	VS	ENG	DEL	STAT	HOURS	LDGS	DATE
801	47699	160050	ZN	C-9B	Y	JT8D-17	12-19-75		37,370	25,744	
802	47689	N639HA	HA	51	Y	JT8D-17	12-19-75		42,423	69,447	
803	47692	N926VJ	AL	51	Y	JT8D-17	03-12-76		45,134	50,526	
804	47693	N927VJ	AL	51	Y	JT8D-17	02-27-76		47,838	44,376	
805	47694	OY-LYN	AY	51	Y	JT8D-15	01-23-76		47,226	44,659	
806	47695	OY-LYO	AY	51	Y	JT8D-15	01-30-76		47,006	43,787	
807	47659	HB-ISP	SR	51	Y	JT8D-17	02-12-76		43,483	43,695	
808	47696	OH-LYP	AY	51	Y	JT8D-15	02-20-76		46,068	45,038	
809	47698	160049	ZN	C-9B	Y	JT8D-9	02-26-76		36,922	25,913	
810	47660	HB-ISR	SR	51	Y	JT8D-17	02-27-76		44,041	43,939	
811	47700	160051	ZN	C-9B	Y	JT8D-9	03-18-76		34,674	24,901	
812	47661	HB-ISS	SR	51	Y	JT8D-17	03-10-76		44,546	68,286	
813	47708	N760NC	NC	51	Y	JT8D-17	04-06-76		53,585	57,339	
814	47709	N761NC	NC	51	Y	JT8D-17	04-12-76		52,665	56,474	
815	47712	N649HA	HA	51	Y	JT8D-17	04-02-76		39,451	69,823	
816	47697	YU-AJT	YJ	51	Y	JT8D-17	05-12-76		42,440	32,486	
817	47702	EC-CTR	AO	34CF	Y	JT8D-17	04-30-76		43,558	29,070	
818	47710	N762NC	NC	51	Y	JT8D-17	04-23-76		53,371	57,167	
819	47704	EC-CTS	AO	34CF	Y	JT8D-17	05-10-76		44,348	37,786	
820	47713	N659HA	HA	51	Y	JT8D-17	05-03-76		40,995	59,963	
821	47706	EC-CTT	AO	34CF	Y	JT8D-17	05-21-76		43,973	29,683	
822	47701	PK-GNM	GA	32	Y	JT8D-9	05-24-76		3,852	28,154	
823	47707	EC-CTU	AO	34CF	Y	JT8D-17	07-12-76		45,647	37,514	
824	47714	N669HA	HA	51	Y	JT8D-17	06-08-76		40,392	58,254	
825	47715	N679HA	HA	51	Y	JT8D-17	06-16-76		40,225	58,597	
826	47722	PK-GNN	GA	32	Y	JT8D-9	08-02-76		33,802	26,593	
827	47736	OH-LYR	AY	51	Y	JT8D-15	09-15-76		46,838	44,115	
828	47330	PK-GNO	GA	32	Y	JT8D-9	08-12-76		36,321	28,549	
829	47737	OH-LYS	AY	51	Y	JT8D-15	01-24-77		44,588	45,865	
830	47736	OH-LYT	AY	51	Y	JT8D-15	10-04-76		45,744	44,576	
831	47725	OY-KGR	SK	41	Y	JT8D-11	07-29-76		43,763	57,079	
832	47716	N763NC	NC	51	Y	JT8D-17	09-16-76		50,976	52,373	
833	47717	N764NC	NC	51	Y	JT8D-17	12-20-76		51,897	54,442	
834	47718	N765NC	NC	51	Y	JT8D-17	11-29-76		51,806	54,604	
835	47740	PK-GNP	GA	32	Y	JT8D-9	11-02-76		33,687	26,699	
836	47741	PK-GNQ	GA	32	Y	JT8D-9	12-16-76	W/O	20,587	15,480	04-04-87
837	47744	PK-GNR	GA	32	Y	JT8D-9	12-16-76		33,680	26,946	
838	47723	TC-JBL	TK	32	Y	JT8D-9	09-30-76		44,418	36,587	
839	47747	SE-DDP	SK	41	Y	JT8D-11	11-23-76		42,452	55,660	
840	47691	KAF320	ZK	C-9B	Y	JT8D-15	10-15-76	W/O	6,895	3,591	02-26-91
841	47703	YV-22C	LV	51	Y	JT8D-17	10-15-76		36,075	56,688	
842	47705	YV-20C	LV	51	Y	JT8D-17	10-19-76		39,777	62,461	
843	47690	KAF321	ZK	C-9B	Y	JT8D-15	11-01-76		12,121	5,612	
844	47711	HB-IDT	BA	34	Y	JT8D-17	11-03-76		45,540	34,076	
845	47719	YV-21C	LV	51	Y	JT8D-17	11-12-76		37,846	59,765	
846	47720	YV-23C	LV	31	Y	JT8D-17	11-18-76	W/O	32,448	50,294	03-05-91
847	47721	YV-25C	LV	31	Y	JT8D-17	12-10-76		40,617	62,211	
848	47727	YV-24C	LV	31	Y	JT8D-17	12-17-76		37,886	57,697	
849	47726	OE-LDH	OS	51	Y	JT8D-17	12-17-76		45,006	62,100	
850	47662	HB-IST	SR	51	Y	JT8D-17	02-04-77		38,809	65,740	
851	47663	HB-ISU	SR	51	Y	JT8D-17	02-16-77		41,100	54,699	
852	47739	N766NC	NC	51	Y	JT8D-17	03-25-77		51,278	53,434	
853	47724	N767NC	NC	51	Y	JT8D-17	04-15-77		51,501	53,673	
854	47729	N768NC	NC	51	Y	JT8D-17	05-27-77		51,022	52,936	
855	47748	LN-RLH	SK	41	Y	JT8D-11	11-01-77		41,386	39,234	
856	47754	YU-AJU	YJ	51	Y	JT8D-17	05-24-77		39,455	30,259	
857	47742	9Y-TFG	BW	51	Y	JT8D-17	06-27-77		31,331	52,861	
858	47728	N991EA	EA	51	Y	JT8D-17	07-13-77		44,828	40,106	
859	47743	9Y-TFH	BW	51	Y	JT8D-17	07-29-77		30,110	40,656	
860	47731	N992EA	EA	51	Y	JT8D-17	08-16-77		44,937	40,094	
861	47732	N993EA	EA	51	Y	JT8D-17	08-31-77		44,790	39,644	
862	47733	N994EA	EA	51	Y	JT8D-17	09-22-77		43,887	38,963	
863	47745	N995EA	EA	51	Y	JT8D-17	10-05-77		42,339	42,724	
864	47746	N996EA	EA	51	Y	JT8D-17	10-21-77		44,551	39,432	
865	47749	N997EA	EA	51	Y	JT8D-17	11-03-77		44,698	37,672	
866	47751	N998EA	EA	51	Y	JT8D-17	11-14-77		44,636	39,469	
867	47753	N999EA	EA	51	Y	JT8D-17	11-21-77		44,863	39,825	
868	47734	N920L	OZ	32	Y	JT8D-9	11-21-77		47,659	46,919	
869	47735	OE-LDN	OS	51	Y	JT8D-17	12-03-77		42,422	59,045	
870	47750	SE-DDR	SK	41	Y	JT8D-11	12-16-77		41,378	38,816	
871	47759	JA8439	JD	41	Y	JT8D-15	12-16-77		30,006	34,970	
872	47752	9Y-TFI	BW	34CF	Y	JT8D-17	01-13-78		24,006	44,294	
873	47756	OE-LDO	OS	51	Y	JT8D-17	01-31-78		41,423	34,506	

LN	MSN	REGN	A/L	MODEL	VS	ENG	DEL	STAT	HOURS	LDGS	DATE
874	47760	JA8440	JD	41	Y	JT8D-15	02-08-78		32,199	38,586	
875	47761	JA8441	JD	41	Y	JT8D-15	03-06-78		31,397	37,214	
876	47762	JA8442	JD	41	Y	JT8D-15	04-21-78		31,170	36,994	
877	47757	N969NC	NC	51	Y	JT8D-17	05-10-78		48,637	49,247	
878	47755	9G-ACM	GH	51	Y	JT8D-17	07-13-78	W/O	28,004	36,397	04-14-97
879	47763	N699HA	HA	51	Y	JT8D-17	07-11-78		32,080	81,002	
880	47758	N770NC	NC	51	Y	JT8D-17	07-28-78		48,125	48,677	
881	47769	N771NC	NC	51	Y	JT8D-17	08-11-68		47,933	48,383	
882	47764	N709HA	HA	51	Y	JT8D-17	08-25-78		29,915	74,469	
883	47771	OH-LYU	AY	51	Y	JT8D-17	09-08-78		43,756	38,221	
884	47774	N772NC	NC	51	Y	JT8D-17	09-01-78		47,584	47,866	
885	47767	JA8448	JD	41	Y	JT8D-15	09-20-78	W/O	24,168	28,599	04-18-93
886	47766	OY-KGS	SK	41	Y	JT8D-11	10-13-78		38,772	36,341	
887	47768	JA8449	JD	41	Y	JT8D-15	10-07-78		30,424	35,412	
888	47775	N773NC	NC	51	Y	JT8D-17	10-26-78		47,395	47,468	
889	47776	N774NC	NC	51	Y	JT8D-17	11-14-78		47,513	47,311	
890	47772	N8713Q	AU	51	Y	JT8D-17	12-08-78		41,995	39,788	
891	47773	N8714Q	AU	51	Y	JT8D-17	12-14-78		41,863	40,026	
892	47770	YV-32C	LV	51	Y	JT8D-17	11-22-78		36,506	57,144	
893	47782	YV-33C	LV	51	Y	JT8D-17	12-20-68		34,960	54,329	
894	47780	JA8450	JD	41	Y	JT8D-15	01-09-79		29,906	34,775	
895	47781	JA8451	JD	41	Y	JT8D-15	01-31-79		29,798	34,566	
896	47777	SE-DDS	SK	41	Y	JT8D-11	01-30-79		38,868	36,301	
897	47778	LN-RLP	SK	41	Y	JT8D-11	02-07-79		38,611	36,377	
898	47779	SE-DDT	SK	41	Y	JT8D-11	03-07-79		38,452	36,320	
899	47783	HB-ISV	SR	51	Y	JT8D-17	03-07-79		32,648	36,648	
900	47765	N3506T	TI	32		JT8D-15	03-14-79		50,373	39,389	
901	47788	N3507T	TI	32		JT8D-15	03-23-79		50,673	39,491	
902	47784	HB-ISW	SR	51	Y	JT8D-17	05-02-79		35,115	51,788	
903	47796	9Y-TGC	BW	51	Y	JT8D-17	04-19-79		33,036	53,906	
904	47785	N775NC	NC	51	Y	JT8D-17	04-20-79		46,352	45,589	
905	47786	N776NC	NC	51	Y	JT8D-17	04-27-79		46,068	45,335	
906	47789	PK-GNS	GA	32	Y	JT8D-9	05-11-79		26,949	24,149	
907	47790	PK-GNT	GA	32	Y	JT8D-9	05-16-79	RET	22,851	19,479	09-30-93
908	47791	PK-GNU	GA	32	Y	JT8D-9	05-25-79		29,037	24,096	
910	47792	PK-GNV	GA	32	Y	JT8D-9	06-13-79		28,222	25,762	
911	47793	PK-GNW	GA	32	Y	JT8D-9	06-20-79		28,413	25,110	
912	47787	N777NC	RC	51	Y	JT8D-17	06-22-79		45,896	44,482	
913	47797	N3508T	TI	32	Y	JT8D-15	07-03-79		48,948	38,587	
914	47798	N3509T	TI	32	Y	JT8D-15	07-12-79		49,386	38,424	
915	47794	PK-GNX	GA	32	Y	JT8D-9	07-27-79		30,688	25,745	
916	47795	PK-GNY	GA	32	Y	JT8D-9	08-06-79		28,265	24,481	
918	47799	N3510T	TI	32	Y	JT8D-15	08-21-79		48,723	37,980	
919	48114	N934VJ	AL	31	Y	JT8D-9	08-28-79		44,635	48,848	
920	48115	N935VJ	AL	31	Y	JT8D-9	09-11-79		44,288	48,461	
921	48116	N936VJ	AL	31	Y	JT8D-9	09-19-79		43,921	48,827	
922	48117	N937VJ	AL	31	Y	JT8D-9	09-28-79		44,115	48,061	
923	48111	N3512T	TI	32	Y	JT8D-15	10-09-79		48,318	37,909	
925	48103	EC-DGB	AO	34	Y	JT8D-17	10-31-79		38,140	23,732	
926	48112	N3513T	TI	32	Y	JT8D-15	11-02-79		47,995	37,889	
927	48100	N778NC	RC	51	Y	JT8D-17	11-02-79		44,566	42,704	
928	48104	EC-DGC	AO	34	Y	JT8D-17	11-19-79		40,038	31,977	
929	48105	EC-DGD	AO	34	Y	JT8D-17	12-02-79		40,008	32,361	
930	48113	N3514T	TI	32	Y	JT8D-15	12-06-79		47,485	37,160	
931	48101	N779NC	RC	51	Y	JT8D-17	12-07-79		44,329	42,529	
932	48102	N780NC	RC	51	Y	JT8D-17	12-14-79		45,157	42,795	
933	48106	EC-DGE	AO	34	Y	JT8D-17	12-29-79		39,934	31,891	
934	48123	N927L	OZ	34	Y	JT8D-15	12-28-79		44,651	36,153	
935	48121	N781NC	RC	51	Y	JT8D-17	12-28-79		44,375	42,232	
936	48107	N782NC	RC	51	Y	JT8D-17	01-24-80		44,240	41,929	
937	48108	N783NC	RC	51	Y	JT8D-17	01-30-80		44,050	41,805	
939	48109	N784NC	RC	51	Y	JT8D-17	02-20-80		44,745	41,751	
940	48131	N928VJ	AL	31	Y	JT8D-9	02-20-80		43,050	47,004	
942	48118	N929VJ	AL	31	Y	JT9D-9	03-03-80		42,841	46,945	
943	48119	N938VJ	AL	31	Y	JT8D-9	03-12-80		42,654	46,392	
945	48110	N785NC	RC	51	Y	JT8D-17	04-01-80		43,638	41,455	
947	48125	XA-AMA	AM	32	Y	JT8D-17	04-04-80		48,854	47,680	
949	48120	N939VJ	AL	31	Y	JT8D-17	04-25-80		42,614	46,570	
951	48126	XA-AMB	AM	32	Y	JT8D-17	04-30-80		48,662	46,717	
954	48124	N928L	OZ	34	Y	JT8D-15	06-10-80		44,029	35,439	
956	48132	PH-DOA	KL	32	Y	JT8D-9	06-10-80		35,811	24,905	
959	48133	PH-DOB	KL	32	Y	JT8D-9	07-21-80		35,473	25,156	
961	48127	XA-AMC	AM	32	Y	JT8D-17	07-25-80		47,757	45,836	

LN	MSN	REGN	A/L	MODEL	VS	ENG	DEL	STAT	HOURS	LDGS	DATE
964	48128	XA-AMD	AM	32	Y	JT8D-17	08-20-80		47,798	46,465	
968	48129	XA-AME	AM	32	Y	JT8D-17	10-11-80		46,959	45,347	
972	48122	9Y-TGP	BW	51	Y	JT8D-17	01-26-81		28,402	49,432	
976	48130	XA-AMF	AM	32	Y	JT8D-17	12-05-80		45,736	43,931	
980	48134	OH-LYX	AY	51	Y	JT8D-15	01-23-81		37,484	33,734	
982	48137	161266	ZN	C-9B	Y	JT8D-9	03-17-81		28,378	19,070	
984	48148	N786NC	RC	51	Y	JT8D-17	12-31-80		42,207	38,860	
987	48135	OH-LYY	AY	51	Y	JT8D-17	03-23-81		37,082	33,138	
990	48149	N787NC	RC	51	Y	JT8D-17	04-17-81		41,119	37,993	
993	48136	OH-LYZ	AY	51	Y	JT8D-17	04-22-81		35,636	34,851	
1014	48150	N1003P	AM	32	Y	JT8D-17	10-08-81		43,102	41,220	
1017	48151	N1003U	AM	32	Y	JT8D-17	11-24-81		42,212	40,244	
1021	48138	N918VJ	AL	31	Y	JT8D-9	10-14-81		38,674	41,795	
1024	48139	N919VJ	AL	31	Y	JT8D-9	10-21-81		38,597	41,856	
1027	48140	N920VJ	AL	31	Y	JT8D-9	11-17-81		38,686	41,785	
1030	48141	N921VJ	AL	31	Y	JT8D-9	12-01-81		38,474	41,325	
1033	48142	N922VJ	AL	31	Y	JT8D-9	12-06-81		38,288	41,424	
1036	48143	N923VJ	AL	31	Y	JT8D-9	12-14-81		38,546	41,716	
1039	48144	N924VJ	AL	31	Y	JT8D-9	12-18-81		38,221	41,456	
1042	48145	N925VJ	AL	31	Y	JT8D-9	12-22-81		38,265	41,406	
1044	48146	N926VJ	AL	31	Y	JT8D-9	01-14-82		38,156	41,477	
1046	48154	N927VJ	AL	31	Y	JT8D-9	01-25-82		37,917	41,065	
1048	48147	N976VJ	AL	31	Y	JT8D-9	02-19-82		37,773	40,931	
1050	48155	N977VJ	AL	31	Y	JT8D-9	02-16-82		37,747	40,754	
1052	48156	N980VJ	AL	31	Y	JT8D-9	03-11-82		37,642	40,683	
1054	48157	N981VJ	AL	31	Y	JT8D-9	03-18-82		37,702	40,829	
1056	48158	N982VJ	AL	31	Y	JT8D-9	03-25-82		37,710	40,756	
1058	48159	N983VJ	AL	31	Y	JT8D-9	04-06-82		37,606	40,733	
1081	48165	161529	ZN	C-9B	Y	JT8D-9	09-30-82		27,225	18,709	
1084	48166	161530	ZN	C-9B	Y	JT8D-9	10-28-82		27,065	17,436	

Douglas Test Registrations

LN	MSN	MODEL	TEST REG	REGN
1	45695	11	N9DC	N1301T
4	45711	14	N9864Z	CF-TLB
218	47114	41	N8960U	SE-DBX
261	47115	41	N8961U	OY-KGA
287	47192	33RC	N8963U	PH-DNN
382	47301	21	N8965U	LN-RLL
440	47304	21	N1794U	LN-RLM
699	47588	31	N54630	N956VJ
713	47597	41	N54631	OY-KGL
741	47649	31	N54638	YU-AJR
757	47654	51	N54641	HB-ISK
763	47655	51	N54642	HB-ISL
817	47702	34CF	N19B	EC-CTR

Douglas Temporary Registrations

LN	REGN	LN	REGN
505	N1798U	687	N1346U
524	N1797U	688	N1347U
533	N1330U	710	N54635
534	N1331U	768	N54645
535	N1796U	780	N13627
547	N1795U	812	N8706Q
551	N1779U	816	N8709Q
554	N1332U	875	N8910Q
597	N1334U	890	N8713Q
606	N1336U	891	N8714Q
684	N1343U	902	N13627
685	N1345U